Screens That Eat Children

Living, parenting and teaching in an age of digital devices

ROSS PARKER

Copyright © 2022 Ross Parker

All rights reserved. No part of this book may be reproduced or used in any manner without the prior written permission of the copyright owner, except for the use of brief quotations in a book review.

ISBN: 9798362091064

DEDICATION

To Danielle, Matthew & Holly, who suffer so graciously
my unusual relationship with screens.

To the families who have sought and accepted my help,
from whom I have learned so much.

To Simeon. We will always miss you.

CONTENTS

Acknowledgments	7
About The Author	9
Foreword	11
Introduction	15
Chapter 1 – Screens Are Bad	19
Chapter 2 - What Children Need	53
Chapter 3 - Homo Technologicus	70
Chapter 4 – Framing Childhood	97
Chapter 5 - Becoming Whole	107
Chapter 6 - Memeland	133
Chapter 7 - The Environment	152
Chapter 8 - Won't School Save Us?	158
Chapter 9 - Early Computing	169
Chapter 10 - The Computer Explosion	201
Chapter 11 - A Fantastical Tale	225
Chapter 12 - Changing Times	232
Chapter 13 - The Individual	243
Chapter 14 - The Family	251
Chapter 15 - The School	270
Chapter 16 - The Government	282
Chapter 17 - The Corporation	287
Conclusion	290
Epilogue - An Autobiographical Sketch	295
Appendix 1 - ICHK IT Policy Full Text	304
Appendix 2 - ICHK IT Policy Agreement	319
Appendix 3 - ICHK IT Policy Visual Overview	325
Appendix 4 – Example Device Use Contract	326
Working With Ross	328

ACKNOWLEDGMENTS

With thanks to my family
Danielle, Matthew & Holly
Monika, Lee, Nic, Alex & Morgan
Granny, Grandad, Omi, Opa, aunts, uncles & cousins
Sheryl & Dan

To Toby Newton for adding oil to my thinking, and always making time for this project

To my editors Kevin Coniam, Phil Morgan
and Danielle Parker

To Holly Parker for her cover illustration, and Sandra Kuipers for her cover design

To my friends, to my colleagues and to my collaborators

To all of the early readers and critical commenters on this book, including Sing Lee, Marianne Atkins, Sean Moran, Jon Rees, Toby Newton, Geraint Johnes, Felix Olesen, Becky Fox, Cheri Chow, Claire Griffiths, Lee Parker, Monika Parker, Nicolas Arriaga, Momoko Ng, Jacques-Olivier Perche, Jeff Coey, Jen Goldthorpe, Lee Lyons, Lisa Day, Marcus Ko, Queenie Hon, Peter Falvey, Sandra Kuipers, Skye Jeynes & Yumei Tang

ABOUT THE AUTHOR

Ross Parker is the Director of Technology & Assessment at International College Hong Kong, a small, innovative school in the North East of Hong Kong's New Territories. Born in Hong Kong to Austrian and English parents during the final years of Britain's empire, Ross has lived most of his life in a state of identity confusion.

As an educator, Ross is passionate about making learning a positive, anxiety-free process centred around personal transformation. Once an enthusiastic advocate for the role of technology in education, and in life, he has gradually become increasingly sceptical, and now chooses his tools very carefully. In the search of better ways to use technology, Ross founded Gibbon, the open source school platform, through which he has also developed the Free Learning pedagogy. Ross believes that education should focus on learning to learn through choice, rather than simply studying content to pass an exam.

As a parent, Ross is deeply concerned about the impact of screens on himself and his family.

Screens That Eat Children

FOREWORD

"In every field of inquiry, it is true that all things should be made as simple as possible – but no simpler. (And for every problem that is muddled by over-complexity, a dozen are muddled by over-simplifying.)" - Sydney J. Harris[1]

Humankind is faced with an intractable problem: how to understand itself, so as to guide and govern itself, so as to secure its future? That is, taking ourselves as our own topic of inquiry, how to encapsulate the human situation so as to render it subject to constructive comprehension, leading to sustainable courses of long-term action? Which is to say, wanting to avoid muddle through either over-complexity or over-simplifying, with a field of inquiry as nuanced as human being, what passes the test when sketching our project in terms that are "as simple as possible - but no simpler"? This, I take it, is the pre-eminent riddle of and challenge for education, in its formal and informal aspects: how to model, for the benefit of learners (which is all of us), a viable life for viable people on the one planet they call home?

---

[1] Sydney J. Harris , Chicago Daily News, January 2nd, 1964

The question is a pressing one because the evidence suggests that for many years we've been getting the answer wrong. For how many years? Since the birth of a technology called school, perhaps. On the strength of what evidence? Climate collapse; the sixth mass extinction; rogue bioengineering; malignant AI; weapons of mass destruction[2]. The period left us to come up with a new answer? Estimates differ - 100 years? 50? 10?

The first step to a new and better education would be a more accurate point of departure when framing the question, "how to understand being human?" Our current answer - as Homo sapiens, as "wise man" - is dangerously inaccurate and misleading. Dangerous because it breeds complacency: "wise" people make wise decisions, by default. This is by no means a track record to which we can ourselves lay claim, not now nor previously.

A better answer would be, as Homo technologicus, as "technological man", as the primate who, uniquely among animals, is utterly wedded to and dependent on the use of technology, in all its many guises, for bare survival. Such a framing sounds a cautionary note, pointing towards the vital inquiry that humans must make of themselves at a time of great hazard: as technological animals, what technologies are we using, to what ends, and with what effects? And if we are unable to answer these questions satisfactorily - unable, for example, to explain or justify our ends, or to identify or comprehend the effects, intended and unintended, of our chosen technologies - this should give pause for thought.

---

[2] The Precipice, Toby Ord, Bloomsbury (https://bit.ly/3WwyITA)

Ross Parker's Screens That Eat Children is a timely addition to the growing chorus of voices calling for such a pause, for a period of reassessment, for a moratorium on unbridled technological "progress", for a reexamination of what it is we're intending as a species - and why. Focussed on our preoccupation with digital devices, in particular, and on the opportunities we take them to provide, the book's central insight might be extended more generally to the fate of Homo technologicus in the two hundred and fifty years since the advent of the first Industrial Revolution. We recognise it as the fate of Der Zauberlehrling, of the Sorcerer's Apprentice, of the inept meddler, who has, in his callow naivety, unleashed the power of technologies by which he is fascinated, but which he does not properly understand, and which he cannot fully control; technologies that grow in potency, in seduction, in impact, in speed, in ubiquity, as the transfixed apprentice watches on, besotted, addled, entirely consumed, and, yet somehow, vestigially, appalled. In exploring and analysing some factors in this troubled scene, in ways that are as simple as possible, but no simpler, Screens That Eat Children offers its service.

Toby Newton
November 2022

Screens That Eat Children

INTRODUCTION

In 2011, Marc Andreessen, venture capitalist and co-founder of the venerable Netscape web browser, quipped that "software is eating the world"[3]. Writing on his corporate blog, he then noted that "this is a profoundly positive story for the American economy", and what is good for the economy, we are told, must be good for us all.

Andreessen's positive esteem for all things digital aligned perfectly with the spirit of the times, coming, as it did, at the height of early-21st century techno-utopianism. Silicon Valley, home of the digital revolution, had germinated in the fertile soil of post-1960s San Francisco. Deeply influenced by beat and hippie sensibilities, the Valley brought to digital technology strong undertones of mysticism, rebellion, progressivism and self-righteousness. Despite being home to nerds, geeks and other misfits, digital technology was cool, and it was revolutionising the world. It promised to bring us a civilisation that was more democratic, more equal, more efficient and more open. If only we could disrupt enough industries, and sell enough devices, we could build

---

[3] Why Software Is Eating the World, Marc Andreessen, Andreessen Horowitz (https://bit.ly/3zCj3lw)

the perfect world.

Despite this epic narrative, despite the great optimistic promise of liberation from the human condition, fault lines were visible even as Andreessen blogged. To the astute observer the red flags were legion: fractured focus, compulsive overuse, hostility towards "the other", trolls, hackers, bad state actors, growing inequality, a shift to being "always on" and a feeling of living in "anywhen".

Today, in the early 2020s, we seem to live in a world in which it is impossible not to stare at a screen. We work at screens, relax in front of screens and pacify our children with screens. There are screens on buses, screens on trains and screens on planes. There are screens in bus stops, on buildings, and in buildings. We need not worry that we will ever be too far from a screen, for we are now all in the habit of carrying a portable screen in our pockets or hands...at all times. In fact, one now has to make a conscious effort in order to entertain oneself in a non-screen-based manner, for the screens beep and buzz at all hours in order to retain our attention.

Screens, it turns out, are not delivering what we had been promised. Rather than setting us free they have enslaved our minds. Rather than making us knowledgeable they have made us distracted. Perhaps, on reflection, having an insistent, inescapable, 24/7 popularity contest in your pocket is a bad idea.

This book offers a front row seat to the ways in which screens have distorted our culture, rewriting the rules of childhood along the way. Researchers have confirmed it, and the media are rapidly catching up. Screens That Eat Children is not intended to induce a moral panic, but it is an invitation to think, a call to action. Do we want to allow screens to eat childhood, to eat our culture, or ought we choose a different course?

Of course, laying the blame for any complex phenomenon solely at the feet of a single cause would be unwise. For that reason, this book seeks to consider the many interrelated forces at play, in order to tease out the role played by digital technology in shaping the changes we are experiencing. It is via this broader story that I seek to reveal, through a consideration of childhood and culture, the impact that screens have, the road that led us here and, finally, where we might be headed.

Screens That Eat Children

CHAPTER 1
SCREENS ARE BAD

Returning Home

As a child of colonial Hong Kong, it was common for me to spend my summer holidays visiting family in England and Austria. Whilst northern Europeans headed south for some summer sun, we migrated north to escape July's oppressive heat and humidity. When I was younger, this journey was taken with my parents and older sister, and I still retain many amazing, formative memories from those early trips. Despite repeated insistence by my parents, I remained blithely unaware of just how fortunate, and unusual, our lifestyle was.

By the early 1990s, having turned eleven, I was deemed old enough to make the journey on my own. It was always with a sense of impending adventure that I bade my parents farewell at Hong Kong's old Kai Tak Airport and boarded the British Airways midnight flight to London. This was the prelude to the visceral excitement of landing at Heathrow Airport, locating my Uncle Ross in arrivals, and making the final leg of the journey to my father's family home. Immediately before arriving at the house we would drive through a dense patch of woodland, which always appeared as a forested tunnel. This novelty was only just eclipsed by hugging my Granny and Grandad, sliding down their bannister and eating a bowl of crunchy nut cornflakes with proper English milk. This was the immutable order in which such visits to the fatherland began.

It was on one of these trips, some time in the mid-90s, that my eldest cousin introduced me to William Gibson's debut novel, Neuromancer[4]. Nik lived with my grandparents and worked in IT. He rode a motorbike, came and went as he pleased, and occasionally spoke of Unix, a computer system beyond my ken. He met his girlfriend on the Internet, something I'd only just started to use. For a fifteen-year-old, Nik was someone to take seriously, and in lending me that book he paved the way to a lifetime spent working with computers.

Neuromancer, published in 1984, tells the fictional story of down-and-out hacker Henry Case. Fired from his job, and prevented from accessing cyberspace, Case enters into a shady, underground deal, exchanging his hacking skills for restored access to the network. Along the way Case navigates cyberspace, encounters artificial intelligence and hacks various systems. Now seen as hugely prophetic, I remember finding both its setting and its characters almost impossible to imagine. How could cyberspace possibly be as rich as Gibson made it seem? His manner of describing logging onto the Internet as "jacking in" seemed too physiological, too hypodermic, too addict-like, especially when compared to the mundane act of operating a dial-up modem.

What the passage of time has made apparent is not simply that Gibson was right, but just how far ahead of his time he

---

[4] Neuromancer, William Gibson, Ace (https://bit.ly/3DB8OFt)

was. For today, twenty five years later, we are all jacked-in, and thanks to our ubiquitous screens and their high-speed connectivity, we are all addicts. Our device usage is compulsive, repetitive, joyless and damaging. Almost everywhere you might care to look you will find a screen of some kind, and if there is not a screen today, there probably will be tomorrow. These screens are in your pocket, on your desk, in your school, in your hand, on the bus, on the train and on the plane. They are in elevators, waiting rooms, buildings and bedrooms. They are in front of your eyes, and on your mind, all the time. If this list sounds familiar, say from the introduction to this book, that is because it is a point which needs to be made front and centre.

On these screens you will find a non-stop torrent of information, a deluge of text, images, audio and video. There is no authority, no consistent measure of truth. There are no standards, other than profitability, and seemingly no morals either. What is fresh, new and cool today, is passé tomorrow. The moment we think we know what is happening, it has already changed. Culture, politics, families and schools, none of them seem to stand a chance in the face of this onslaught.

Whilst some readers may be on board with the statements above, others might need a little convincing. With this in mind we will spend some time considering the ways screens impact us, before turning our attention to why this is so important to us, and our young.

Are Screens Really That Bad?

Yes.

In short, screens really are that bad.

Specifically, the screens that we have collectively arrived at today, whose services are provided to us for free via advertising and data harvesting, really are that bad. These are, to be clear, screens that are produced by companies whose tools allow them to manipulate our behaviour in ways both dangerous and opaque, and whose profit motive implores them to do so broadly and consistently. These are screens whose content is deliberately manufactured to keep us jacked in for as much of the day as possible, and which exist in a market that rewards only the most compelling platforms. In this chapter, we'll look in depth at these dynamics.

Ask the parent of any screen-owning child, and they will confirm for you the veracity of the statements above. They may not be aware of the mechanisms at play, but they will have seen the massively negative impact that screens have on the behaviour, emotion, motivation and social-orientation of their child.

Ask any teacher who has been in the profession for more than 10 years, and they will be able to confirm for you these same impacts, seen through the lens of classroom teaching and playground behaviour.

Recently I was sitting beside a swimming pool, when I noticed four school-aged children at play. At a guess I would place their ages at between nine and twelve. Regretfully, they were not swimming. Rather, each was staring at their own phone. Their behaviour was robotic, hypnotised and thoroughly distressing. For over an hour they scrolled and looked, scrolled and looked, scrolled and looked. Across their screens flashed image after video after image after video. Funny dances, makeup tutorials, travel, fancy food, silly cartoons. They had it all. And yet, they did not speak, they did not look up and they did not look happy. Captivated? Yes. Entranced? Yes. Stimulated? Yes. Mostly, however, they looked bored, lonely and lost. To me this is not childhood, it is enslavement. It is a classic example of children whom screens have eaten.

Of course, it does not have to be this way. Screens can be massively enabling, and hugely enjoyable. They can liberate, they can inspire, they can connect. As we will see, much hinges on the economic paradigms from within which our screens emerge.

What Are Screens?

In talking about "screens" we are referring to a set of very contemporary technologies with a range of overlapping names: devices, smartphones, computers, the Internet, the Web, cellular data, 4G, 5G, operating systems, CPUs, and touchscreens. In order to avoid initially overcomplicating the situation, we will, as a shorthand, refer to all of these simply as *screens*, with the emphasis being placed upon the most disruptive of these: the smartphone.

In the discourse around technology, it is common practice to refer to tools as being neutral. There are, so the theory goes, no good or bad tools, merely good or bad applications. According to this logic, "guns don't kill people, people kill people". A hammer can be used to build, or to destroy. Almonds can be both food and poison.

There is undoubtedly a certain appeal to such arguments, given our desire for neat answers to complex problems. However, the truth is rather more nuanced. A more useful approach might well be to say that whilst technologies can be used for both good and bad, each technology has, in a given context, a bias towards one or the other. For example, in contemporary Western culture a hammer is a symbol of construction and carpentry. Children see adults using hammers to create things, and are hopefully invited to engage in the same kind of work. Children who misuse hammers are corrected, most often swiftly, by an adult. As far as weapons go, hammers are fairly crude, and very messy: they also require an assailant to get very close to their victim. Given all of this, hammers are, in this context, mostly used for good, and only rarely for bad.

To formalise this point, we can say that each technology has its own set of *affordances*. These are the uses that the design of a device makes available to a user. A chef's knife, far more than a spatula, affords us the opportunity to cut, slice or stab. When we hold a knife, we are keenly aware of these affordances, and they influence our thinking. The balance of the tool in our hands, the inescapable conclusion of the blade in a point, the electric thrum of a sharp blade scraped across the thumb. The designers of such a device do not want us to prise open a tin can, turn a screw or spread butter: they want us to slice, dice and julienne. In this sense, each different technology is, to some degree, suggestive of the intentions of its creators.

But these affordances do not live and operate on their own: they exist within a culture, and the culture also directs users of the technology to some ends more than others. The culture opens up some avenues of use whilst closing down others. In the case of our knife, a culture obsessed with violence, whose members are saturated with images of knife crime, tilts the balance away from cooking and towards violence. Given this, we should certainly pay attention to the findings of a Scottish study from 2014[5], which found that "kitchen knives were used in 32 of 55 homicides" which represents 94% of the sampled crimes that involved "sharp object homicide".

---

[5] Kitchen knives and homicide, Kidd et all, SAGE Journals (https://bit.ly/3zG2P0L)

Is the knife still to be seen as neutral? I don't believe so: it exists within a complex environmental topography, which subconsciously steers its users towards particular means and ends. The affordances of the knife are mediated by the culture in which it is used.

This same logic applies, to a greater or lesser degree to every human invention (or "technology" for short). Toilet paper can be used to wipe and to blow, but can also serve to wrap a Halloween mummy. A wine bottle can deliver a pleasant evening or a Molotov cocktail[6]. Screens can be used to connect and enlighten, but they can also be used to deceive and destroy. The shifting sands of a desert make a good analogy for our relationship with our technologies, which can quickly bury us if we are not careful. This requires of us a shared commitment to constantly and critically revisiting our technologies, how they are used and what they mean.

To some, this kind of thinking may appear to be mere intellectualising, an act that ends in talking, not action. I disagree. Unless we position ourselves to critically deconstruct the meaning of our technologies, we are doomed to thrash wildly in the wake of their misuse.

With this in mind, let's consider how screens are normally positioned, and then consider whether or not this holds water.

---

[6] The orgins of the name of this handheld weapon are worth a read (https://bit.ly/3VXbFkh)

The Conventional Narrative

Derived from Europe's Age of Enlightenment, the philosophy of *progress* has long held us in its sway. This set of beliefs tells us that a knowledge of science, and the technologies that this allows us to produce, will set us free from the human condition. If only we can become rational enough in our thinking, then we can acquire enough knowledge to suspend human suffering. This is heady stuff, allowing us to pick from the unpredictable chaos of our lives a thread of meaning to which we can cling. Our lot in life, it tells us, is slowly getting better. As a species, we are improving, and progressing towards some distant point of perfection. It is no wonder that, deep down, we really want to believe in the idea of progress, particularly as it gives us a greater level of control than the many spiritual doctrines that it has been steadily replacing.

It should not come as a surprise to learn that the people who created the digital technologies that underlie modern screens leaned heavily on this story in order to create their own narrative. Now known as "techno-utopianism"[7], this belief leaves us in no doubt that it is digital technology that will deliver humans to the promised land afforded by progress. By unleashing a wave of digital information, which the market will automatically sort and prune, humans will flourish. By connecting us, at all times, to each other and to all human knowledge, we will escape the earthly ties that bind us. Coming of age in the 1990s, I could not avoid being caught up in this. Reading John Perry Barlow's A Declaration of the Independence of Cyberspace[8] I could

---

[7] The Dark Side of Techno-Utopianism, Andrew Marantz, The New Yorker (https://bit.ly/3FH2HSO)

[8] A Declaration of the Independence of Cyberspace, John Perry Barlow, Electronic Frontier Foundation (https://bit.ly/3FGgXeb)

clearly picture myself as a part of this vanguard, this brave new world:

> "Governments of the Industrial World, you weary giants of flesh and steel, I come from Cyberspace, the new home of Mind. On behalf of the future, I ask you of the past to leave us alone. You are not welcome among us. You have no sovereignty where we gather."

Barlow tapped into a deep-seated need for me to feel involved in a movement of great importance, which would build on the past to deliver a better future. I was, unsurprisingly, hooked.

If only I'd read Aldous Huxley's Brave New World[9] before encountering Barlow, I might not have been so easily seduced: its focus on the ways in which technology promises to make our lives better, whilst actually enslaving us, would have brought some balance to my raw optimism. But, alas, I was young, impressionable and yet to realise that behind every successful new technology lies some very compelling storytelling. This tends to go hand-in-hand with the obfuscation of changes to the balance of power, which such new technologies can bring about.

For this I do not blame myself, as the story is a bloody good one. In fact, it is so good that the vast majority of our political, economic, social and personal beliefs are intimately and firmly wedded to it.

I would learn, in a very personal fashion, the strength of this

---

[9] Brave New World, Aldous Huxley, Harper Perennial Modern Classics (https://bit.ly/3sVTUEY)

story, when circumstances began to challenge it. Initially, a steadily growing tide of evidence proved unable to dislodge me. My own identity was simply too invested: abandoning the story felt like a betrayal of myself. I remember feeling a visceral anger the first time I read about Nicholas Carr's The Shallows[10], one of the earlier pieces of antithetical evidence I encountered. So aroused was I, that I flatly refused to even consider reading it, a position from which it took me a long time to climb down.

When I did eventually allow the light to shine in, I began to witness the unravelling of my own world view. Was it possible that digital technology, far from setting us free, was actually enslaving us? Were my efforts to integrate technology into the learning of my students actually resulting in them learning less?

Tipping Point

I believe I've now come to see things a little more clearly, helped along by Huxley, Carr, Lasn[11] and a string of other writers and thinkers, as well as the weight of my own experience. These stories and ideas, which are explored in the sections and chapters below, are presented in the hope that they will help others to see the techno-utopian story for the myth that it really is.

In retrospect, it is clear that what was missing from my thinking was the power of the market, which has ultimately meant that the great tools that exist to promote meaningful learning are generally not what students encounter online.

---

[10] The Shallows, Nicholas Carr, W. W. Norton & Company (https://bit.ly/3fwMODI)

[11] Culture Jam, Kalle Lasn, Harper Paperbacks (https://bit.ly/3U4sbOf)

Screens That Eat Children

Video games, memes and clickbait dominate, and so learning and personal growth rarely stand a chance.

My own journey from techno-utopian to *digital sceptic* was neither easy nor direct. It occurred in small increments, through a variety of experiences that gradually chipped away at some of my most cherished mental constructs. When the penny finally dropped, it did so in a flash, with a singular event that turned out to be my own personal tipping point[12].

Shortly after their release, my wife was generously gifted an iPad. Despite neither of us being gadget lovers, we were nonetheless intrigued as to whether it would live up to the hype. We set it up, installed some apps, and used it for casual web browsing and watching movies. Mostly underwhelmed by the experience, and still more focused on our laptops, the device was left in the living room, mostly unused. What surprised us was the way our son, then only one and a half, picked up the device and started prodding the screen. He obviously enjoyed the process, and the IT teacher in me was pleased to watch him. Gradually he worked out how to find videos, and with a little help typing he found things he enjoyed watching.

Quite quickly we came to realise that rather than just passively watching videos, he was actively using the recommended list to jump around, finding things that interested him. By the time he was three he could reliably jump from one video to another, using numerous intermediary steps that he had committed to memory.

What started off as innocent fun soon revealed itself to be

---

[12] The Tipping Point, Malcolm Gladwell, Back Bay Books (https://bit.ly/3DqiWAM)

something darker. It became clear that he relished the absolute control granted by the device: he could do whatever he wanted, without anyone to stop him. Taking the device away from him would be met by howls of frustration, leading us to limit his access. In retrospect none of this should surprise me, but touch-based devices were still pretty new at this point, and so our experiences were limited. Certainly he showed no such interest in a laptop, which demonstrates the power of touch as a human-computer interface paradigm.

The seeds of doubt had been sown, but they were easy to compartmentalise: this was an issue for very young children, relating to phones and tablets. It did not impact my students, and we had things under control in our own home.

It was not long thereafter that I started to become aware of the ways in which the Internet's own constantly morphing culture did present problems for my students. As background noise I found myself competing for cultural space at school with jokes based around Internet memes (more to come on this later). Some of these were funny, but many more were cruel and divisive. My young students tended not to see the xenophobia built into these jokes, yet it would subtly cloud their world view. I began to notice the way this content primed young boys to readily consume and ingest some of the more overt misogyny that they encountered online. It definitely got my attention when male students expressed outrage at the evils of "feminazis", despite having no understanding of feminism, nor of the negative impact of thousands of years of patriarchal living. The Internet, one meme at a time, had led them to see women as dominant and evil, rather than having only very recently been entitled to various freedoms long taken for granted by men.

In two extreme cases, I have witnessed these online

influences bloom into alt-right radicalisation. The students in question were highly impassioned, and presented a rather muddled collection of beliefs and assertions, in which facism, death squads, men's rights and white supremacy were all seen as positive, rational ways to organise society. As these views came to light I engineered opportunities to spend time with the boys, and despite many hours spent in conversation with them, I was unable to make any real headway against their indoctrination. The jarring dissonance in both cases was that the children citing white supremacy as their adopted ideology were ethnically Chinese: the irony of this seemed lost on them.

By this point I had become quite alert to what I felt were fringe elements in Internet culture to which some people might fall prey. Over time, these elements seemed to become more and more mainstream, which began to make sense when I discerned cultural roots in video gaming, particularly in MMOs (massively multiplayer online games), where large numbers of strangers interact. Whilst gaming itself can be a fun and healthy pursuit, young children who find themselves in the unmoderated world of MMOs can quickly be drawn into negative ways of understanding competition, language and gender. In such settings it seems that winning is not enough: instead, what is desired is the total humiliation of all opponents.

It was under these conditions that I started to see "get rekt", "noob" and "fail" migrate into classroom conversation, where, as a teacher I felt that they sat uneasily. Without a strong grasp of the importance of context, students can find themselves in difficult territory. Take, for example, a student who once used the gamer slang "tea bagging" to refer to the act of squatting on one's haunches, oblivious to the fact that its origins lie in the sexual act of repeatedly dipping one's testicles into someone's mouth.

A closer study of modern game design revealed the manifold ways in which games are designed to turn the act of play into a compulsive habit. The use of carefully calibrated challenge, unpredictable rewards, streaks, timeouts and real-time team play all combine to make games very hard to walk away from. Today it often feels that leaving young people to use computers without close supervision amounts to inviting them to play video games.

In my work I have always encountered a certain number of students who display distinct signs of addiction to games. This manifests itself in a variety of behaviours, including foregoing sleep and food to play games, mood swings, lying to parents and teachers, and anger when play is interrupted or denied. Lately this background rate has been swollen by swathes of students whose default behaviour is to scroll through social media and play video games on their phones. Almost all of my students now show some signs of addiction.

Meanwhile, on weekends and afternoons I began to notice changes in my own use of technology, which I would not have described as addiction, but definitely represented a shift. Where I had previously been attentive to my own children, I found myself more and more holding a smartphone in my hand. Often I did not really know how it came to be there, or what I was intending to do with it. In the end, I would glance at the time, check my emails and look in on my social media feeds. Hoping no one had noticed, I'd put the phone back in my pocket and get back to family life. I began to also notice the way my phone would jump, unconsciously, into my hand at all sorts of dull moments, including trips to the toilet and whilst waiting at the bus stop.

It was with all of this going on that I encountered that tipping point, leaving me with no choice but to fully recast

Screens That Eat Children

my relationship with, and understanding of, screens. The event took place on a routine ride on one of Hong Kong's ultra-modern MTR[13] trains. I looked up from my own smartphone to note just how many other passengers were using a phone of their own. As my eyes scanned the scene, they came to rest on a couple in an embrace. Young woman, young man, bodies pressed intently together. She was staring deeply into his eyes, signalling a desire to do the thing that we're all here to do: reproduce. However, rather than reciprocating, he was gazing over her shoulder, to the point where his own arm protruded. In his hand he held a smartphone, and into it he poured his attention. I sensed in an instant the way that phones have the power to disrupt aeons of evolution, rendering our most human instincts moot. I glanced at my own phone, put it sheepishly back in my pocket, and vowed to change.

Image 1.1 - Banksy's Mobile Lovers (origin unknown)

When, a few months later, I encountered Banksy's Mobile Lovers[14], it felt entirely familiar, instantly comprehensible

---

[13] Mass Transit Railway, aka Tube, Underground, Subway, etc.

[14] "Mobile Lovers" by Banksy, Kyleigh Dalkin, Medium (https://bit.ly/3UgE5nC)

and very alarming.

In a single moment it had become suddenly impossible to argue against the power of screens to change our behaviour. Faced with evidence that screens were in fact powerful enough to derail our most important drives, I knew I had to act. And so began a journey of discovery, about the tech industry and about myself, that led, through many intermediate steps, to the creation of this book.

Our own experiences can only ever reveal to us a thin slice of human experience, seen through our own distorting lenses. As such, they are not a good basis for serious analysis, and for this reason, most of this book deals with published theory and accounts documented in the media. However, our own experiences, and the stories we draw from them, are too rich to be entirely ignored, and it is in this spirit that I share them here, where they balance some of this book's more theoretical passages.

Our Evolutionary Achilles Heel

Given the stories above, it is worth asking why we find screens so compelling. The answer to this question lies in our biological past. Our evolutionary story is one of gradually diminishing physical strength traded off in return for increased brain mass. As in any system with finite resources, it would have been impossible to pursue all outcomes simultaneously: sacrifices in some areas were required in order to achieve gains in others. Against the odds, the human approach of brains over brawn, coupled with the ability to accrue and transmit culture, enabled us to thrive in a wide range of environments, and thus become our planet's dominant animal.

As a species, our closest relative is the chimpanzee, with

whom we share 98.8%[15] of our DNA. It is believed that the last common ancestor shared by humans and chimps was an animal that lived six to seven million years ago[16]. Thought to be tree dwellers, these medium-sized creatures (about the size of a gibbon[17]) would have foraged for fruit. Over time, this species diverged into a number of lineages, two of which became chimpanzees and bonobos, and another of which became us.

Although the details are impossible to reconstruct, the study of fossils, biomechanics and DNA suggest that at some point we left the relative safety of the trees and began moving bipedally on the ground. During this time, and continuing for much of our history, we would have been relatively exposed to predators, from whom we would have had little defence. Whilst our emerging social structures may have helped to keep us safe, a key element of our survival would have stemmed from our ability to monitor and understand our environment. Research[18] suggests that in terms of visual perception, this happens in a wave-like pattern, in which we rhythmically sample the scene in front of us, alternating between states of narrower and broader focus. Even when we believe we are highly focused, we are in fact scouring the visual field, oscillating between states at a rate of three to eight times per second.

This makes logical sense in terms of our survival and

---

[15] DNA: Comparing Humans and Chimps, American Museum of Natural History (https://bit.ly/3zAgFSD)

[16] Fossil Reveals What Last Common Ancestor of Humans and Apes Looked Like, Scientific American (https://bit.ly/3N4asDF)

[17] New Study Suggests that Last Common Ancestor of Humans and Apes was Smaller than Thought, American Museum of Natural History (https://bit.ly/3sufUXg)

[18] A Dynamic Interplay within the Frontoparietal Network Underlies Rhythmic Spatial Attention, Fiebelkorn et al, Neuron (https://bit.ly/3Uj5vth)

evolution: paying too much attention to any one object or idea might lead us to miss both opportunities and threats, be they food, mates or predators. In a relatively flat and stationary visual field, where greens, browns and blues predominate, it would be highly beneficial to be very sensitive to both bright colour and movement.

Put another way, those of our ancestors who were too focused would have ended up starving, mateless or in some other creature's digestive tract. As a result of these natural selection pressures, we are the progeny of many thousands of generations of individuals who were prone to distraction, to keeping an eye out, to reacting rapidly to visual change. In other words, the human traits that we today label as ADHD are in fact survival mechanisms. In psychological terms, this tendency to scan the environment is known as the "orienting response", and it is a key to understanding the grip that screens have on us.

Sadly, in the context of the 21st century, these traits, once so vital to our survival, have been turned against us. Designers know[19] that colour and motion drive "engagement" with their products, and are keen to profit from this fact. Our fleeting attention has become our Achilles' heel, and it is ruthlessly exploited. Meanwhile, a combination of clever marketing and media reinforcement have led us to believe that we can handle the massive surge in the speed and variety of disrupting inputs that our screens bring us, that we can multitask, that we can get better at living this way. But the truth is that we cannot. Machines like computers can multitask, but humans can't: nonetheless

---

[19] "Animated digital content consistently attracted 4 to 6 times the number of viewers compared to the equivalent static posters." A Report on a Field Trial of Anonymous Video Analytics (AVA) in Digital Signage, Intel (https://intel.ly/3gtvWh4)

we strive to act like machines. As Johann Hari points out, this affects us deeply, not least in the fact that 1 in 5 car accidents are now caused by distracted driving[20]. It is no wonder that dealing with this bombardment results in diminished cognitive capacity, even if our smartphone is merely idling nearby[21]. As the fictional character Ron Swanson puts it "Never half-ass two things, whole-ass one thing."[22]

At ICHK, the school in which I work, we tell our students the story of a strange species, one with weak muscles, no fur, poor eyesight, tiny claws, puny teeth and a giant brain. This creature evolved in the forest and the grassland, in a environment with relatively few colours:

Image 1.2 - Forest (Freepik)

---

[20] Stolen Focus, Johann Hari, Crown (https://bit.ly/3h79D1h)

[21] Brain Drain: The Mere Presence of One's Own Smartphone Reduces Available Cognitive Capacity, Ward et al, The University of Chicago Press (https://www.journals.uchicago.edu/doi/full/10.1086/691462)

[22] Ron Swanson, Parks and Recreation, Good Reads (https://bit.ly/3UkPX8f)

Within this environment it was essential to keep an eye out for bright colours in order to find enough food:

Image 1.3 - Forest & Berry (Freepik + Roundicons). If you are reading this in grayscale, the berries are a bright red colour.

It was also vital to be alive to movement, in order to avoid being eaten:

Image 1.4 - Tiger (Freepik)

Over time the survival of this species became easier and easier, mostly because of the many technologies that they developed. Some of these were relatively simple:

Image 1.5 - Fire (Freepik)

Others were far more complex:

Image 1.6 - Television (Freepik)

Unfortunately for this hapless species, they managed to take all of the things that had helped them survive, and build them into the most complex and compelling technology of all:

Image 1.7 - Smartphone (Freepik & Roundicons)

The result? They built screens at which they could hardly stop staring, which made a small group of them incredibly rich, but which also caused untold distraction and misery.

I find the ICHK approach to smartphones worth sharing here, as it has proven effective in significantly reducing phone use in school. This work compliments a range of other in-school initiatives, which, taken together, have allowed us to create what we refer to as a *therapeutic environment*. The result is a community that feels very different to the criminogenic vibe that schools generally deal in.

Despite this, we still find students magnetically drawn to their devices, which is evident when school ends, and phones immediately reappear in student hands. Whilst this could evoke despair, I take comfort in knowing that for eight hours a day, five days a week, our students are buffered from the worst of screens. I also hope that over time we'll be able to tip the balance further, and help our families do the same. This is a theme that we will return to in considerably more detail later on.

The Attention Economy

Now, I don't for a moment believe that any one individual envisioned or set out to build the kind of device we describe to ICHK students. However, whatever good intentions existed at the outset have undoubtedly been hijacked by the promise of massive financial returns within what we now call the *attention economy*. The promise of untold fortunes has resulted in an all-out battle for our eyeballs, in which the smartphone sits front and centre. In an economic and technological environment that promotes monopolies[23], the company that produces a moderately enticing app will simply not survive. In order to win, an app or game must demand all of our attention, all of the time.

---

[23] Ten Arguments for Deleting Your Social Media Accounts Right Now, Jaron Lanier, Henry Holt and Co. (https://bit.ly/3DTycrf)

Screens That Eat Children

In this race to the bottom, the relatively young science of psychology has been exploited to show exactly where our levers and buttons are located, and modern software design has ruthlessly exploited them. There is, quite literally, an instruction manual[24] for this process: written by Nir Eyal, an alumni of Stanford University's famed Persuasive Technology Lab, the book Hooked outlines a host of ways for engineers to entrance their users. Unsurprisingly, it has proven hugely influential in Silicon Valley.

Should you find all of this hard to believe, the paragraphs below cover a handful of the many ways in which our attention is deliberately captured by software designers.

Notifications are one of the key tools used to keep you staring at your device. These combine colour (the icon is almost always red), movement (notifications slide into view), sound (bing!) and vibration (buzz, buzz). With three of our senses targeted simultaneously, it is very hard for us to ignore the siren song of our screens. In fact, the phenomenon of phantom notifications highlights the ways in which our phones have trained us to interrupt ourselves. Even if we decide not to react to a notification, it still intrudes on our experience, exerting a subtle cognitive load onto whatever we were presently doing. Should the notification be tied to an app or system we care about, our brain will reward us with a little squirt of dopamine, the neurotransmitter linked to motivation and pleasure. Designers know that each reward will contribute to getting and keeping us hooked.

Recently I've noticed a rise in notifications that exploit a company's knowledge of my habits. Just this morning, for

---

[24] Hooked, Nir Eyal, Portfolio (https://bit.ly/3NDZt4o)

example, I got in the car and Spotify, perhaps guessing at the word "Kia" in the name of the Bluetooth speaker, offered to play me some audio suitable for driving:

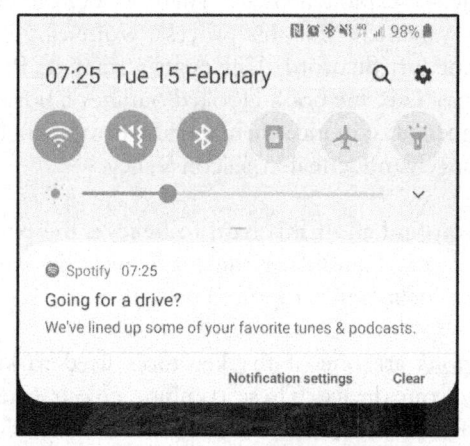

Image 1.8 - Screenshot of Intrusive Spotify Notification (Ross Parker)

On a technical level this is a neat hack, and I suspect that the engineers behind it would argue that it offers me a more personalised experience, for which I ought to be grateful. To me, however, it is an unnecessary intrusion into my time, and represents a large, faceless company using my own data against me in a distinctly paternalistic fashion. Fortunately, it is a feature that can be disabled…something that sadly required a little more time on my device.

However, even rewards can get old, and so many games and apps rely on unpredictable rewards, which affect us in the same way as gambling: we know that if we play for long enough then something good will happen. And it could happen at any moment, which keeps us playing, even if it is just "one last go". These statistically driven events happen, for example, when we stumble upon some loot in a game: we believe this to be related to luck or skill, but in reality the probabilities and intervals involved are precisely calibrated and tested. Generally we will be presented with an easy early win, which acts like a hook, and allows us, subconsciously, to accept subsequently lower odds. Slightly less controlled are those occasions on which we use infinite scroll (the content never ends!) or pull-to-refresh. This last innovation is all too familiar to anyone compelled to play slot machines[25] (aka fruit machines or pokies): pull, wait and win…pull, wait and lose…pull, wait and repeat.

Likes provide similarly unpredictable rewards, but in a more social setting. Rather than having to guess at how popular we are, our screens offer to tell us, repeatedly and numerically. Posting content to social media is often habitually followed by checking for likes, as well as comments and subscriptions, as we search for validation from peers and strangers alike. This suits the needs of platform creators, as it keeps us coming back, whilst also encouraging us to promote our own content. Our fixation on these numbers is such that some users simply delete content that does not get enough positive feedback[26], in order to maintain their status or identity as an important user. Over time, we gain a sense of what content "works" (e.g. gains likes), allowing us to shape ourselves to fit our audience. Some users are known to maintain multiple accounts on a single platform, in order to communicate varying aspects of themselves to different audiences. One result of this is a gradual encouragement to portray a very skewed slice of who we are, another is diminished trust in our own judgement.

Similarly social in nature, streaks are counts of the time span

---

[25] Social media copies gambling methods 'to create psychological cravings', Daniel Kruger, University of Michigan (https://bit.ly/3D71Zv6)

[26] Stop Deleting Your Instagram Photos Because They're Not Getting Any Likes, kidfromthe6ix (https://bit.ly/3st8Zxg)

across which we have managed to maintain app usage. Popularised by SnapChat, in which they count the number of unbroken days on which two users have communicated, streaks encourage us to turn habitual use into ritualised use. Once invested in a streak, users are known to go to extreme lengths to maintain it, including begging friends to streak by proxy[27]. Part of the power of both likes and streaks seems to be their ability to quantify and make visible our social capital, which offers us a means of shoring up our fragile self-esteem against the existential terror of social irrelevance.

In regards to video streaming sites, such as Netflix and YouTube, autoplay is used to reduce our resistance to switching from one site to another, or getting offline altogether. At the end of each video we are given a short amount of time (often three, five or ten seconds) to cancel the playing of the next video. This might be the following episode in a TV series, or an algorithmically generated guess at what you might like. For Netflix, whose CEO Reed Hastings once cited "sleep" as their biggest competitor[28], this is one of many tricks used to keep us tuned in. For other sites, like Facebook, this allows the platform to pad out their video engagement statistics, making for a better sell to advertisers. Facebook has historically counted a video as "watched" when it reaches the three second mark, even if it is autoplayed[29].

In video games, real-time multiplayer environments are

---

[27] Inside the Mind of a Snapchat Streaker, Lizette Chapman, Bloomberg (https://bloom.bg/3h73phQ)

[28] Netflix's biggest competitor? Sleep, Alex Hern, The Guardian (https://bit.ly/3zEGQaO)

[29] Facebook v. Snapchat: What Counts as a Video View?, Kurt Wagner, Vox (https://bit.ly/3DwnfdJ)

used to keep players in their seats. Traditionally it was relatively easy to stop playing a game: your mum called you for dinner, you finished the segment you were in by getting to a save point, and you switched off. Sometimes you made her wait 5 minutes whilst you completed the level. This is now much trickier: mum calls, but you are in the middle of a mission with your clan. Duck out now and you not only let your friends down, but you'll miss out on levelling up. On finishing the current mission, you are enticed by the next, and now you definitely can't leave your friends unsupported. Hours pass and you remain in your chair. It's a comfortable gamer chair, though, with flashing lights and built-in speakers, so your friends and enemies all know you're legit. Who cares if you never leave your room, never shower, pee in a bottle and live in the dark?

In order to ensure that their user engagement strategies are effective, major platforms engage in constant A/B testing. During such tests, users arriving at a site are, unbeknownst to them, split into two groups: A and B. Group A is shown the current version of the site, whilst B is given a slightly modified version. Perhaps an important button has been slightly enlarged, shifted over a few pixels or presented in a different hue. Various data analytics, including mouse movement and timing, are gathered and used to compare the way the change alters user engagement. These data points are then used to decide whether or not the change works, and whether it should become the new default interface. Conducted repeatedly, on massive audiences, these tests allow platforms to be weaponised against their users.

Facebook in particular is so comfortable adjusting these parameters, that they found it ethically acceptable to conduct research to see if they could alter the mood of their users[30]. The 689,003 users involved in the study had no idea that they were being manipulated, through tweaks to their feeds, to feel either happy or sad. For tech giants, the emotional manipulation of their users is a given, which says a lot about how much the industry has changed over the past few decades.

This list is by no means exhaustive, but rather seeks to give a flavour of some of the techniques that are used against us. What they all have in common is that they seek to compel us to engage with platforms and the content they offer. With each turn of the ratchet we encounter more advertisements, from each of which the platforms stand to make money. Whilst we may consider ourselves to be the customers of such platforms, we are not. The customer in this business model is in fact the advertiser, and what they are buying is generally a chance to sell us their wares and exercise control over our thoughts and feelings. This is a level of social control that not even dictators could previously have attained.

To be clear, this is not a side business for tech giants like Google and Facebook: it is their primary revenue stream. According to CNBC, for example, "More than 80% of Alphabet's revenue comes from Google ads, which generated $147 billion in revenue last year."[31]. We like to think of these companies as tech companies, but it might be more realistic to consider them as advertising agencies. Unlike traditional ad firms, however, the tech giants are running the largest data collection and emotional manipulation machine ever constructed.

---

[30] Facebook Manipulated 689,003 Users' Emotions For Science, Kashmir Hill, Forbes (https://bit.ly/3StG7zv)

[31] How Google's $150 billion advertising business works, Megan Graham & Jennifer Elias, CNBC (https://cnb.cx/3TRayRf)

As you might expect from such an agency, major platforms make extreme claims to those purchasing ads, highlighting their ability to position, influence and manipulate us into clicking on ads. Take, for example, the case of Facebook's Australian operation, who showcased to advertisers it's ability to identify when teenagers feel "stressed", "defeated", "overwhelmed", "anxious", "nervous", "stupid", "silly", "useless" and a "failure"[32]. Presumably, these occasions would make the ideal time to present such users with an advert for products and services that might alleviate these feelings.

The galling thing is just how deliberate and calculating this manipulation is. Facebook's first president Sean Parker[33] is on record as saying[34]:

> "The thought process that went into building these applications, Facebook being the first of them...was all about: 'How do we consume as much of your time and conscious attention as possible?'...And that means that we need to sort of give you a little dopamine hit every once in a while, because someone liked or commented on a photo or a post or whatever. And that's going to get you to contribute more content, and that's going to get you...more likes and comments...It's a social-validation feedback loop...exactly the kind of thing that a hacker like myself would come up with, because you're exploiting a vulnerability in human

---

[32] Facebook told advertisers it can identify teens feeling 'insecure' and 'worthless', Sam Levin, The Guardian (https://bit.ly/3T3KDoN)

[33] Best known for founding Napster, the first free music-sharing app

[34] Sean Parker unloads on Facebook: "God only knows what it's doing to our children's brains", Mike Allen, Axios (https://bit.ly/3VSNxzr)

psychology…The inventors, creators — it's me, it's Mark [Zuckerberg], it's Kevin Systrom on Instagram, it's all of these people — understood this consciously. And we did it anyways…*God only knows what it's doing to our children's brains.*"

Take a moment to consider those last three statements: we knew what we were doing, we did it anyway, and we have no idea how it is harming our children. It is statements like these that are leading industry observers to start comparing big tech to the tobacco industry.

Some in Silicon Valley, most notably ex-Google employee Tristan Harris[35], have started to call out their own industry for such unethical practices. Others have gone on record to express their misgivings:

> "I feel tremendous guilt," admitted Chamath Palihapitiya, former Vice President of User Growth at Facebook, to an audience of Stanford students. He was responding to a question about his involvement in exploiting consumer behavior. "The short-term, dopamine-driven feedback loops that we have created are destroying how society works." [36]

Tellingly, many Silicon Valley executives send their own children to schools that do not rely on screens for learning[37], whilst also restricting such use at home. As Alan Eagle, Director of Executive Communications at Google put it, "If

---

[35] Tristan Harris (https://www.tristanharris.com)

[36] Dopamine, Smartphones & You: A battle for your time, Trevor Haynes, Harvard University (https://bit.ly/3Uk84Lr)

[37] Ten Arguments for Deleting Your Social Media Accounts Right Now, Jaron Lanier, Henry Holt and Co. (https://bit.ly/3DTycrf)

I worked at Miramax and made good, artsy, rated R movies, I wouldn't want my kids to see them until they were 17"[38]. His children both attend a screen-free Waldorf School. Those in charge at Silicon Valley evidently know all too well the danger of getting high on their own supply[39].

Proof of the sway held over us by the corporations that run the attention economy can be seen in figures to do with media usage, particularly those relating to young users. What most parents and educators intuit is confirmed by such research. In 2005 the Kaiser Family Foundation reported[40] that the average US eight- to eighteen-year-old spent 6 hours and 21 minutes per day using entertainment media, of which only 43 minutes was print-based. By 2015, when they re-investigated this topic, that number had increased by 20% to 7 hours and 38 minutes, with print media making up only 38 minutes. Add in multi-tasking and the average child was able to consume 10 hours and 45 minutes of media in a single day.

The non-print media included in the study spans TV, music, computer, video games and movies, and although some of these will be viewed through non-digital devices, more and more they are converging onto computer and smartphone screens.

Alarmingly, the report goes on to note that only "about three in ten young people say they have rules about how much time they can spend watching TV (28%) or playing video games (30%), and 36% say the same about using the

---

[38] A Silicon Valley School That Doesn't Compute, Matt Richtel, The New York Times (https://nyti.ms/3gVVtjn)

[39] Slang for not consuming the drugs that you plan on selling to others

[40] Generation M2: Media in the Lives of 8- to 18-Year-Olds, Kaiser Family Foundation (https://bit.ly/3Tv5y58)

computer". However, in cases where those rules exist, they are effective, as they bring average consumption down by 2 hours and 52 minutes. Such rules are a theme we will return to in Chapter 14.

With different organisations using different research methods, it is hard to get a sense for how these patterns are developing over time, but given the rise of smartphones since 2010, it is hard to imagine the numbers decreasing. Of course, between the demands of school and sleep, there is a limit to how much media can be consumed, which begs the interesting questions of just where that limit lies, and what we sacrifice as we approach it.

Smartphones Are The Worst

Of course, not all screens are created equal: if we compare a TV with a laptop with a smartphone, we will see a range of overlapping and distinct affordances, as well as the formation of differing cultural habits. Put plainly, some devices are simply more distracting than others.

In a distinct departure from traditional thinking, I've come to think of TV watching as relatively healthy screen time. In general it promotes monotasking (as long as you don't have a phone in your hand), and the complex narrative structures and characterisation in many modern TV shows are relatively thoughtful. The fact that it is passive has gone from con to pro, as it can be that rare time where we sit still and focus on one thing.

At first blush it might seem that desktops, laptops, tablets and smartphones are all equally distracting. Whilst much rests on how they are used, in my experience desktops and laptops lend themselves less to distraction and more to serious work, at least for adults. This is partly due to the culture that surrounds them, as they are tools of the office, as well as the home. However, it is also to do with their lack of touch input, as well as the fact that many contemporary apps don't run natively on them. Sure, you can use your web browser to access Instagram, but you are much more likely to do so via the app on your phone or tablet. In addition, a laptop, although portable, still requires you to be seated, or very flexible! Finally, these devices tend to deal less in notifications, and although such functionality is available, it is not as pervasively implemented as on our more mobile devices.

It seems to be the combination of extreme portability, touch screen, always-on wireless connectivity, apps and notifications that makes smartphones so very compelling. This is only slightly less true for tablets, which share most of the same features. In fact, it is misleading to even really call these devices "phones": ultra-portable handheld computers would be a far more accurate description, given the amount of processing power they pack, and the relatively low frequency of phone calling that we actually engage in.

To apply a drug analogy, where TV might be compared to alcohol and laptops to pot, smartphones are much more akin to heroin or crystal meth. In working with students, it is possible to encourage them to use laptops in moderation, especially when parents are attentive and supportive. However, smartphones are a very different kettle of fish, and ultimately prove much harder to curtail.

With smart watches and health trackers already on a lot of wrists, virtual reality (VR) and augmented reality (AR) on the horizon as the perpetual "next big thing" and artificial intelligence (AI) making headlines daily, any analysis of the kind offered above is bound to need revisiting.

For now, however, I rate smartphones, and the kind of Internet usage they encourage, as one of the most destructive forces humans have ever produced.

CHAPTER 2
FRAMING CHILDHOOD

Our Children

Should this situation concern you, then the spotlight of your concern might well fall on our children. As the youngest and most impressionable of our fellow humans, and the future of our species, their experiences are of the utmost importance. Of course, it is normal to worry about our children, for that is how we keep them alive. Despite this, our current situation is suggestive of something that goes beyond the normal level of parental worry, something deeply troubling and worthy of further investigation.

Some years ago I entered the teaching profession. I was young, full of hubris, and ready to "change the world". The problem, as I saw it, was that teaching and schools were out of date. They were analogue, but the future was most evidently digital. Equipped with the latest technology, and emboldened by a strong ideological outlook, I knew that education could be changed for the better. I would write software, introduce young minds to the marvels of the machine, and all would be well.

As it turns out, I was 100% wrong: digital technology, far from making things better, seems to have made everything worse. And by "everything", I don't just mean everything at school, but also almost every other facet of human experience. You can imagine my surprise when I discovered just how monumentally I'd misjudged my tools of choice, my world view, and my own profession. Of course, I was not alone in this act of misjudgement, as our latest technologies came bundled with a suite of spectacular promises, which most of us were all too happy to buy into…literally.

In switching sides, as it were, I have found myself in the minority, the holder of new, unorthodox and sometimes unpopular views.

This book is an attempt to explain the path I've travelled, the curtains I've seen behind, and the ways in which my life has been reoriented as a result. Despite being a work of nonfiction, this is, in many ways, a sci-fi horror story, complete with mass psychological manipulation, radicalised children, greedy titans of industry and out-of-control algorithms. The ending of this story remains unwritten, and may yet turn out for the best, especially if we each take responsibility for our role within it.

In moving forward with our analysis of this unfolding situation, we will be well served by coming to grips with the word "child".

Rites of Passage

Human childhood begins with birth and terminates in adulthood, but its exact length varies considerably according to time, place and culture.

Historically, childhood might be expected to end with the

onset of puberty, and the undertaking of a rite of passage[41]. Such a rite would generally involve three elements: the separation of a child from their family and tribe, a trial or ritual experienced with a group of elders and a celebratory return to the fold. A child enters, and an adult emerges.

Joey Lawrence's haunting short film, People of the Delta[42], offers a glimpse into this traditional approach to coming-of-age. It tells the story of Uri, a young boy who lives in Ethiopia's Lower Omo Valley as a member of the Hamar tribe. Reliant on cattle herding, the Hamar find themselves caught in a drought, and thus in conflict with their neighbours. It is against this severe backdrop that Uri will pass into adulthood, undertaking a rite of passage in which he must run over the backs of a group of bulls in front of the whole tribe. This task is accompanied by dancing, singing and ritual head shaving. At the end of the rite he receives a new name and is "reborn a warrior".

Prior to the ceremony, Uri explains that he is not afraid of the rite, but rather of the responsibilities of manhood. His elders coach him in his adult responsibility to protect their ancestral land from trespassers, asking him if he would be prepared to avenge a friend killed in such conflict. Towards the end of the film we hear gunshots, and Uri is called to action against invading neighbours. Ultimately a Hamar tribesman is killed, and an elder notes that "To come of age in a harsh place is to truly become a man".

Despite its dramatised telling, Uri's story offers us a yardstick by which to assess childhood as it is experienced in more economically developed regions. Seen in this light,

---

[41] The Making of Men, Arne Rubinstein, Brio Books (https://bit.ly/3zERNJc)

[42] People of the Delta, Joey Lawrence (https://bit.ly/3T7l2uZ)

we might well note how much less concise we are in such matters: childhood is generally followed by teenagerhood, then young adulthood and finally, some time into the third decade, adulthood. Given the demands of a modern economy, which requires adults to have mastered a substantial body of knowledge in order to enter the workforce, it makes sense to stretch childhood out. Add in the premature birth that all humans endure, slow maturation and a massively extended life expectancy, and there is clearly no need to hurry.

Whilst some of our traditional rites remain, in the form of the débutante ball, the high school prom, and various academic graduation ceremonies, they are reduced from occasions of genuine transformation to mere pageantry. Without the rather pressing need to produce strong, capable and dependable defenders of the tribe, we've somewhat lost a grip on childhood.

This is in no way to glorify the way things used to be, but simply to remark on how much they've changed. Pre-industrial life is, to a post-industrial human, unimaginably, brutally hard. To illustrate this point, consider the description below, offered by Jared Diamond[43] on the topic of infanticide:

> "Infanticide - the intentional acknowledged killing of an infant - is illegal in most state societies today. In many traditional societies, however, infanticide is acceptable under certain circumstances. Whilst this practice horrifies us, it is difficult to see what else the societies could do under some of the

---

[43] The World Until Yesterday, Jared Diamond, Viking Adult (https://bit.ly/3T2ZGiC)

conditions associated with infanticide. One such condition is when an infant is born deformed or weak."

The child described by Diamond might draw on uncertain and inadequate food supplies with no promise of future contribution. Alternatively, they might be unable to walk sufficiently well to participate in nomadic wanderings. In such cases, the survival of an entire tribe may be at stake, requiring difficult decisions to be made. Today we find the idea of killing a newborn unimaginable, but given different life circumstances, this is a task we may well have had to carry out.

In truth, we need not reach quite so far back into our collective history to see how much the life of a child has changed. In 1800, the United Kingdom, the world's richest country at the time, had a child mortality rate of 329 child deaths per 1,000 births[44]. Its 2020 rate of 4 deaths per 1,000 births tells a very clear story. And although these improvements have not been equally distributed, the global median in 2019 was, according to Unicef[45], 37.7 child deaths per 1,000 births. As the late Hans Rosling was keen to help us see[46], in material terms, life today, right across the world, is considerably more comfortable than it has ever been.

Add to these trends the rise of child rights over the past 100 years[47], the growth in universal schooling, and steep

---

[44] Child mortality rate in the United Kingdom from 1800 to 2020, Statista (https://bit.ly/3Dv7KCZ)

[45] Under-five mortality, Unicef (https://data.unicef.org/topic/child-survival/under-five-mortality)

[46] 200 Countries, 200 Years, 4 Minutes, Hans Rosling, BBC (https://bit.ly/3h9qS1R)

[47] History of child rights, Unicef (https://uni.cf/3zG5g3H)

reductions in child labour, and you might feel yourself pushing back against a book, published in 2022, that suggests childhood is in some way imperilled.

Socrates

Of course, every generation worries about the next, and each new technology signifies the beginning of the end of something for someone. I am quite certain that my grandparents believed that radio would harm my parents, in the same way that my parents knew that TV would harm me, in the same way that I fear for my own children's generation. Our nicknames for such devices, be it The One-Eyed Monster or The Boob Tube, reveal our anxieties. And of course, our elders, with all their experience, were not wrong: those new technologies really did harm us, in the sense that they caused us to slough off certain ways and traditions that had genuine value. I strongly believe that TV made me considerably more idiotic as a young man: at times it must have seemed as if I was Beavis and Butthead, combined.

These changes are far from insignificant, and many of them seem to have accelerated rather recently. Take for example, music. As a species, after thousands of years of gradually evolving musical traditions, we have only very recently given up on collective music production, opting to become mere consumers instead. We ceased sitting out on porches and joining clubs, and instead began to stay at home. We traded our instruments for radios, records, tapes, CDs and MP3s. In the process, we have come, as Johann Hari has so aptly put it[48], to lose some of the vital connections that bind us. And what has been observed in relation to music has been

---

[48] Johann Hari, Lost Connections, Bloomsbury (https://bit.ly/3DB4PZh)

repeated in many other areas of our lives.

However, it is worth noting that this habit of generational fretting can be traced back almost two and a half thousand years, to ancient Greece. Socrates, the founder of modern philosophy, lived through a cultural shift as powerful as any other: the transition from oral to written culture. A member of the old world, Socrates was illiterate, and believed unequivocally that handwriting would diminish our mental faculties. Sitting by a stream outside of Athens, Socrates, in discussion with Phaedrus, contends that[49]:

> "You have invented an elixir not of memory, but of reminding; and you offer your pupils the appearance of wisdom, not true wisdom, for they will read many things without instruction and will therefore seem to know many things, when they are for the most part ignorant and hard to get along with, since they are not wise, but only appear wise."

Socrates' accusations against the youth of 370 BC feel as if they could spring from the mouth of any parent of any era. They provide us with an uncanny reminder of how little changes, even when everything seems different. They also remind us, given our educational fixation with reading and writing, how much our collective values can, in the most rational of ways, swing from side to side.

As an aside, we might also wonder what Socrates would make of his ongoing popularity, which was only made possible by the handwriting of one of his own students, Plato.

---

[49] True Stuff: Socrates vs. the Written Word, David Malki (https://bit.ly/3ftBZlR)

Moral Panics

Given the generational tendency described above, one might justly ask whether any concern about the "youf"[50] is merely a reflex action. Is our current concern not simply a reprise of all previous such concerns, both those based on technological change, as well as those with wider causes? This seems to be the spirit in which Stanley Cohen presents the "moral panic"[51], that singular, media-fueled issue that grabs our attention and suggests that the normal order of things is under siege. Whether it is, as Cohen writes, "vandalism, drugs and football hooliganism", or more contemporary embodiments, such as terrorism or vaping, there is always something to be afraid of. And, presumably, somebody who profits by stoking that fear.

The difficulty with moral panics is that the underlying cause of each instance is, in fact, often worthy of careful consideration. Where things tend to go wrong is in the witch hunting and hand-wringing that follows. In such cases, knee-jerk reactions end up masking the subtle complexities of the issue.

For these reasons, we need to tread carefully in addressing any area in which childhood, culture and human progress appear to be impacted. If we fail to give due consideration, then things worsen gradually; however, when we ignite a moral panic, things get worse in a hurry. What is called for is considered thought, careful discussion and incremental action, which the following sections seek to gradually develop.

---

[50] Tongue-in-cheek British slang for "youth", with negative connotations

[51] Folk Devils and Moral Panics, Stanley Cohen, Routledge (https://bit.ly/3TUwB9I)

Culture Shocks

It is an undeniable fact that childhood in 2022 is, in physical terms, far better than it was in 1922, 1822, or at any previous time in human history. Sadly not every child enjoys the standard of living that we might wish them to. Even worse, this unequal distribution often falls along colonial lines drawn long ago, and beyond the control of the families caught up in it. No child living in sub-Saharan Africa is responsible for the rise of 16th century Europe, and its subsequent and calamitous race to control the world. Likewise, no parent living in a town poisoned by heavy industry is personally responsible for the unsanitary water flowing into their homes.

For these children, and their families, it seems wrong to suggest that their physical needs are being met, when they are demonstrably not. Clearly much remains to be done in the quest to live in a fairer and more equal world. Yet, without detracting from these very real concerns, it seems that for a growing number of children, it is their emotional wellbeing that should concern us. It is impossible, living in the current moment, to avoid reading about escalating rates of adolescent depression, anxiety, self-harm and suicide.

These emotional issues, ironically, seem to stem from the very same cause as improved physical conditions: growing wealth. During the post-war boom of the 1950s, countries around the world experienced an unprecedented surge in wealth[52]:

---

[52] Economic Growth, Max Roser, Our World in Data (https://bit.ly/3WpVvQP)

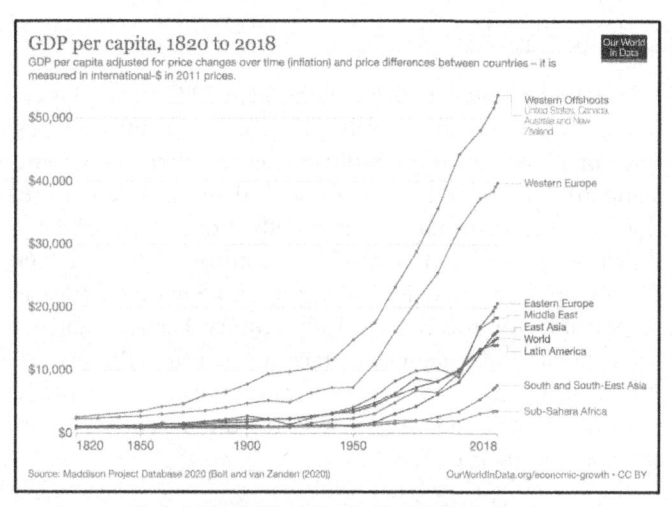

Image 2.1 - GDP per Capita (Our World In Data)

This economic miracle can be explained in many different ways, from the post-war economic liberation of women to the founding of a new global order based around the Bretton Woods Institutions[53]. In the context of this book its roots need not worry us: it is enough to know that today we are, collectively, far richer than we have ever been. Whatever the explanation of its causes happens to be, what is important is that this surge in wealth has come to be associated with a time of rapid cultural change. Initially located in Western European nations and their offshoots, these changes, which are explored below, are now a global phenomenon.

One chain of causality that allows us to explore these changes starts with increased life expectancy and decreasing

---

[53] This name refers to the World Bank and International Monetary Fund, which were set up in 1944 at a conference held in Bretton Woods, New Hampshire (https://bit.ly/3NBTLQk)

child mortality, achieved through surplus wealth, better nutrition and medical breakthroughs. These shifts, in turn, generated decreasing fertility rates, and thus smaller families. Such families, in which both parents are more likely to be working, are also more and more likely to live in cities. Such urbanisation combines with social mobility, increasing rates of divorce and media-induced atomisation, all of which reduces the strength of our collective social bonds. The effect is, like a set of dominoes collapsing, catastrophic.

Fueled by the neo-liberal deregulation of the economy, ever larger companies dealing in ever more esoteric goods and services require a growing army of specialist workers. Whilst out-sourcing of production guts the working class, a shift towards "the knowledge economy" leads to a scramble for ever greater skills and knowledge, resulting in a growing demand for education. Rising education costs, pushed ever higher by heightened academic competition, couple with an elongated period of childhood education to drive up the cost of raising children.

Parents come to attach ever more value to fewer and fewer children, whom they protect more and more closely[54], and whose success is ever more entwined with their own. Children spend less time with their peers, less time in nature, and less time making decision for themselves.

Meanwhile, the economic engine driving us forward requires constant growth: maintenance is not sufficient, only expansion will do. Each of us, adult and child alike, is required to consume in ever increasing quantities, in order to keep the system from stalling. Politicians are incentivised to create conditions amenable to economic growth.

---

[54] The Overprotected Kid, Hanna Rosin, The Atlantic (https://bit.ly/3gDBcyO)

Corporate lobbyists ensure that our leaders always know what to value and who to believe. A ceaseless parade of adverts, covering every available space, keeps us tuned into this new religion.

At every turn we are more dependent upon technology, which saves us from expending our own energy, but demands ever more of our time and money to manage. Things like cars, that we used to fix ourselves, we now pay to have serviced. Our ability to understand has been outstripped by a technology we no longer have the skills to engage with. Smaller devices we simply throw away and replace: it is cheaper and cleaner that way, or so we are told. At each turn our technological appendages grow, enhancing our power and giving us the illusion of independence and self-determination. The twin ideologies of individualism and meritocracy allow us to take credit for our own success, whilst holding others responsible for their failings.

An ever-shortening news cycle presents us with constant affirmation that bad things happen to other people somewhere else, whilst social media echo chambers convince us that everyone else either thinks and acts like us, or is completely insane.

Our institutions are left to crumble, our safety nets recede, and we peer fearfully at a dangerous world, knowing that we have only our own resources to protect us.

The prototypal modern child, the privileged individual, is whisked through this cultural wreckage, coddled by its carers, over-praised, and deeply entitled. Gorged on a diet of processed food, shod in the latest trainers and clad in synthetic fast fashion. Ears wrapped in noise-cancelling wireless headphones, eyes glued to a screen. Cocooned, held safe from danger and thoroughly ensconced in abstractions. Primed to succeed, groomed to compete, yet largely lacking in the non-cognitive skills that life requires. Ever more disconnected, totally fragile, forever fated to search for "authenticity" and "meaning" in a world of chaos.

Of course, this is a caricature, a hyperbolic exaggeration. And yet, it is based on a reality that we each can recognise. None of it is the fault of any one of us. Rather, it is a way of being into which we have gradually drifted. I know it well, for I have lived it, as I suspect have you. It is a situation neatly summed up by the following meme[55]:

Image 2.2 - Did You Know? (origin unknown)

---

[55] Did you know meme, origin unknown, Meme (https://bit.ly/3zFjq4N)

Working With Children

Somehow, in spite of all of these challenges, working with children still has an irresistible draw. No matter the circumstances, children manage to embody the best of our species. Their company never ceases to surprise and enrich. Their energy, honesty and creativity can beguile, their unique perspectives intrigue. I find it completely relatable that in Cantonese, children are generally referred to as "siu pang yao"[56] (小朋友), which, taken literally, means "little friend". It is always used with affection. Children are our best hope, a reminder of what we might be, a constant fresh start.

As these two opposing descriptions of children suggests, we live in times of unprecedented cognitive dissonance, where it is often possible to simultaneously hold two contradictory views, each of which makes sense on its own.

The version of reality sketched out in the previous paragraphs, this embryonic model, can of course never capture the full complexity of our lives. It is not intended to, and is offered in the knowledge that no model ever can. It would be virtually impossible to separate the various intertwined strands that form the fabric of our modern lives. Tomes could be written on this topic alone, without fully explaining the way things are. However, despite its limitations, this brief introduction hopefully serves to set the scene for what is to come.

It is also not intended to be a criticism of any individual in particular: it is simply the way things are, and represents the best effort we've been able to make, as a species, at

---

[56] siu2 pang4 jau5 (https://bit.ly/3h7gHLf)

organising the lives of the almost eight billion people who call Earth home. Whilst some people are certainly more scrupulous than others, and some are undoubtedly bad, there is no evil genius pulling strings, no grand conspiracy. Rather, what we have is simply the result of very many humans, with their very many flaws, attempting to survive on an often inhospitable and over-crowded planet. We could well do worse, but of course, we could also do better.

Hero Systems

In making sense of why this cultural turbulence might have left us feeling lost and devoid of meaning, we might turn to the work of Ernest Becker. In his 1971 book The Birth and Death of Meaning[57], Becker offers us a key insight into our own nature. Each of us, he argues, needs to be the hero of our own story. Without playing this part, we are unable to function as complete human beings. However, in spite of our own individual creativity and the possibility that we might create our own route to heroism, most of us are bound to a small number of heroic stories, provided to us by our culture.

For a European or American child coming of age in the 1950s, heroism could be found in conforming to some clearly defined social norms. For a boy this might look like undertaking an apprenticeship and mastering a trade, joining a company for life, marrying for love or becoming a pillar of the local community. For a girl it might be getting married, raising a family and caring for an extended community[58]. Albeit not the most egalitarian or inspiring

---

[57] The Birth and Death of Meaning, Ernest Becker, Free Press (https://bit.ly/3h7vk18)

[58] Sadly, these options are skewed to favour the male

options, these heroic roles were at least well-trodden and easily located.

Fast forward twenty years and the lines had started to blur. In exchange for a tremendous amount of personal freedom and economic power, we had inherited, thanks in part to the swinging 60s, a life much harder to navigate. No longer were the milestones so clear, nor the punishments for transgression so fierce. Yes, we could have it our way, but on the flip side, uncertainty seemed to lurk at every turn.

And what of today? What hero systems might a ten-year-old begin to tap into in 2022? Becoming a YouTuber, pro gamer or athlete? Notching up 1,000,000 followers on Instagram and becoming an influencer? Studying for eighteen years[59] to compete for a diminishing number of highly sought-after jobs? Or perhaps founding a tech startup, striking it rich via an IPO and then joining the global elite? What is important here is not whether or not you can become a hero: rather, it is the quality of the hero your culture allows you to become, and what this means for the society in which you live.

Of course, some among us might be strong enough to beat their own path to genuinely meaningful and positive heroism, but most of us are not. Joseph Conrad[60] offers us an insight into why this is so: "Few men realize, that their life, the very essence of their character, their capabilities and their audacities, are only the expression of their belief in the safety of their surroundings.". We can mostly become only that which our environment makes available to us, which is why the impact of culture on childhood is so profound.

---

[59] 6 of primary, 7 of secondary, 3 of undergraduate, 1 of postgraduate

[60] Tales of Unrest, Joseph Conrad (https://bit.ly/3sVVqH2)

With this in mind we might ask what it says about our culture, and our hero systems, that have made it so easy for screens to become such a dominant force so quickly? How, in the span of ten years have we gone from no children owning smartphones to so many children owning them? Why is it that taking a trip on public transport reveals to us a world in which adults cannot stop staring at screens? In the same vein, what does it reveal when the best part of a child's day is that portion spent staring at a screen? When a parent's strongest instinct is to fish out their phone, and thus stop paying attention to their child?

Many of today's children seem to exist in an impossible contradiction, in which they have everything that they want, but nothing that they need.

CHAPTER 3
WHAT CHILDREN NEED

In order to continue unpacking the impact of screens on our young, it is important to consider what kinds of experiences children need if they are to grow into healthy, happy, capable adults.

The Telling of Stories

In many ways, the experience of childhood is fated to be both confusing and vexing. Kieran Egan's work[61] on the acquisition of language, and its impact on thought, reveals a lot about this aspect of childhood, especially in its formative years. Egan proposes five stages of linguistic development, each of which define and constrain the kind of thinking of which we are capable. By thinking through these stages we are able to understand why childhood is such a tricky time. In the paragraphs below, each of the five stages (underlined) is described and briefly unpacked.

Initially, lacking spoken language, we have only the ability

---

[61] The Educated Mind, Kieran Egan, University Of Chicago Press (https://bit.ly/3zGvIdm)

to think <u>somatically</u>, through our bodies. In other words, at this age, it is sensations and emotions that form our ability to think. We are unable to use abstraction in order to understand the world, nor to make ourselves understood. Naturally these early years are deeply frustrating for a child, as anyone who has held an upset baby can attest.

As language begins to accrue, we become <u>mythic</u> thinkers, with our concepts of the world based on magic, myth and misunderstanding. The world is chaotic, power is mysterious and we lack control over our lives. Much of our primary education is characterised by such mythic thinking. During this stage it can be hard to engage rationally with a child, and we may from time to time encounter adults who seem to be stuck in the mythic stage, whose thinking can be characterised as magical, or black and white.

Over time we hopefully start to solidify the borders of reality, and, through an interest in extremes, come to think <u>romantically</u>. We ask questions about the scale of things, ponder the boundaries between possible and impossible, and often treat the Guiness Book of World Records as a user manual for our lives. It is in this stage that most of us enter secondary education, full of curiosity and wonder. We've realised that there are rules, but we don't yet understand them: the process of learning these rules thus occupies much of our cognitive capacity.

Given the right conditions, we may gradually move into <u>philosophic</u> thinking, which is based on systems, rules, cause and effect. We become interested in ideology and politics, and seek to explain unfairness through logic. Often this stage is associated with the latter years of our secondary education. Developing further, we might move into the <u>ironic</u>, in which we realise the limits of our systems for knowing. This stage is often associated with university and certain elements of intellectualism.

As we develop, the new types of thinking layer atop the old: the previous stages never disappear, we simply add new tools, and re-prioritise the use of existing ones.

The reason that this model is so useful is that it alerts us to the fact that childhood, the home of mythic and romantic thinking, is a time of prolific storytelling, in which we are most often telling stories about ourselves and our place in the world. We are constantly looking around us, and trying to make sense of the great complexity we observe. As our linguistic and cognitive skills develop, we continually reassess the world and our place within it, and it is by refining the stories that we tell ourselves that we do this. In the process, we come to decide how we might live with meaning in a world of other people. We ask ourselves whether or not the world is a kind and just place? Are we worthy of love? Will others treat us with respect? Will hard work pay off? The answers we arrive at will ultimately shape the person we become: in other words, our identity is inextricably linked to the formative stories that we tell ourselves as we seek to make sense of our own experiences.

Of course, these stories are up for revision, should we be willing to invest the time and energy required to do so. The need for this kind of reframing is highlighted by the sheer number of us that crack under the multiple assaults of adult life, as well as the consistently high demand for self-help books, antidepressants and counselling. Often, it transpires, our stories are simply not robust enough to defend us against the onslaughts of an unpredictable life.

Why is it, we might ask, that our stories are so often not fit for purpose? In answering this question we butt up against one of the greatest ironies of the human condition: the very point at which we tell ourselves the most important stories, the ones that really shape our lives, is the exact same time at which we are capable mostly of mythical thinking. This critical developmental stage is described by a variety of theorists in different ways, and goes by many different names. However, for our purposes, it can be thought of as ages three to seven. It is at this time, where we most need to think clearly, that we are least able to do so. A cruel set of circumstances indeed.

Not only is our own cognitive development stacked against us, but so is the physical world. Trapped in a land of giants, we exist as small, helpless creatures, beholden to rules we don't understand. Our minders are ideally kind and caring, but they may equally be ill-prepared, capricious or downright cruel. Either way, we will struggle to make sense of how life works, and are likely to come to some very misguided understandings about ourselves and the world we inhabit.

In Transactional Analysis[62] (see the Emotional Awareness section below), a field within psychoanalysis, this pattern is spelled out clearly. Each of us, so the theory goes, will at some point make a handful of critical decisions about ourselves. Called "life decisions" these will determine much of how we perceive and interact with the world around us. From these decisions will stem a set of "scripts", which we can think of as groups of repeated behaviours, things we do over and over, never quite sure why, as if merely acting out someone else's plans. Given positive scripts, our life will play out towards the good. Given negative scripts, life will seem a constant struggle.

One of the critical factors in determining the quality of our scripts is how early we make our life decisions: those made

---

[62] Scripts People Live, Claude Steiner, Grove Press (https://bit.ly/3h2sdHH)

when Egan's mythic thinking is the only tool to hand will tend to be irrational and harmful, leading to negative scripts. The odds of this happening seem unfairly high.

Of course, the confusing nature of childhood is not helped by the complexity of the world into which we are born, a situation that has only worsened for our own children. As noted by Richard Florida[63], someone from 1900 arriving in 1950 would be mystified at the scope of the technological changes the world had undergone. And yet, this would be relatively light going compared to the experience of someone from 1950 arriving in 2000, who would be entirely baffled by unthinkable changes in culture. As a concrete example, think for a moment about how many of our traditionally rigid hierarchies and formalities have been dissolved during that latter 50 year span. Even in the 1980s I always called my friends' parents by their title and surname (e.g. Mr. & Mrs. McMath), whereas today my children call their friends' parents by their first names (e.g. Paul and Amanda).

In military theory, the world we inhabit would be described as VUCA[64]: volatile, uncertain, complex and ambiguous. This alarming set of descriptors offers us a great starting point for considering what children require if they are to grow into healthy adults. It reminds us that if adults find the world to be so complex, then children surely need our carefully considered support.

---

[63] The Rise of the Creative Class, Richard Florida, Basic Books (https://bit.ly/3FXMusz)

[64] Managing in a VUCA World, MindTools (https://bit.ly/3DAFH59)

This is not to say that we need to obsess over creating the perfect childhood. For, as Alain de Botton's School of Life[65] is keen to remind us, all childhoods are messy and traumatic in their own way. What we need is a set of guiding constellations, a way to frame childhood development, so that we can start our children on the right foot. What we need are better stories to tell ourselves, and to tell our children. Some of these stories we will consider below, others will emerge in later chapters.

The Good Enough Family

The famed developmental psychologist and psychoanalyst Erik Erikson described[66] eight stages[67] through which humans develop and grow, from cradle to grave. At each stage we experience a dilemma, which we resolve either positively or negatively. Positive resolution of the dilemma leads to the generation of *virtue*.

The first three of these stages are covered in the first three to five years of life, underscoring how vital, and busy, this time is in the development of a well rounded individual. And it is with the first stage that we concern ourselves here. In this stage, we decide whether the world, and those who populate it, are fundamentally trustworthy. Are we fed when we are hungry, changed when we are dirty and soothed when we are upset? Does our crying reliably bring our mother or father to our side? Are pain and frustration temporary blips or sustained experiences? Given sufficiently

---

[65] The Only Subject You Need To Study, Alain de Botton, The School of Life (http://bit.ly/34paoHC)

[66] The Life Cycle Completed, Erik Erikson, W. W. Norton & Company (https://bit.ly/3FBFuRQ)

[67] A ninth stage was added by Erikson late in his own life

positive experiences, we will emerge from this phase trusting, and possessing the virtue of *hope*. Lacking such positive experiences we may well fall into despair. Each of the successive stages will then follow from this one, as we gradually accumulate experiences in the world, and form patterns of our place within it.

D. W. Winnicott, the British psychoanalyst, expresses the parental aspect of these early stages in a slightly different way, through the concept of the "good enough mother". Winnicott's insight was that mothers[68] need not be perfect, but rather need only be reliable enough for their children to develop a sense of trust. Initially this means near constant attention in offering rapid relief from suffering. However, over time, minor lapses and imperfections are vital in order to develop a sense of resilience and autonomy in the child. This frames parenting as a very subtle balancing act, in which care and independence are in constant tension as we try to support children in the development of a robust and independent self.

In many ways Winnicott's idea of diminishing parental attention dovetails nicely with Erikson's second phase, in which the dilemma is between autonomy and shame. It is at this stage, partially through learning to control urination and defecation, that independence begins to emerge.

For parents, this early childhood story can come as both a relief and a cause for concern. It can help us to realise that we don't need to be perfect, but that we do need to be very attentive at the outset, before deliberately allowing lapses in certain ways at certain times. Our children need our love and our care, but they also need the space in which to

---

[68] We can extend this to include fathers, and more broadly to include carers

develop autonomy and agency.

Emotional Awareness

Dealing with emotions, especially strong negative ones, is possibly the hardest part of growing up. The Australian educator and parenting specialist Maggie Dent[69] calls these "big, ugly feelings", and they impact all of us. Each day we observe other people, noting that some are generally emotionally reliable, whilst others struggle in this regard. Adults will (hopefully!) strike us as less volatile, and over time we will infer, for better or worse, that growing up requires us to understand, manage, master or suppress our emotions. If we succeed in this, life is much more pleasant: if we fail, disaster lies in wait.

And yet, despite the central importance of our emotional lives, we expend relatively little educational energy on developing a structured understanding of emotion. Perhaps, collectively, we know too little, or perhaps the adults in our lives are themselves unready to guide us in this area. Maybe we just expect children to work it out, like the many generations who have come before.

It was not until my mid-30s that I was properly introduced to any kind of structured model of emotion. Initially sceptical, I soon grew amazed at the depth of understanding it gave me, and it has subsequently become a cornerstone of my professional and personal self.

That model, known as Transactional Analysis (TA), comes from a school of psychotherapy developed in the late 1950s by the Canadian psychiatrist Eric Berne. It builds on the

---

[69] From Boys to Men, Maggie Dent, Macmillan (https://bit.ly/3gWZN1E)

Freudian tradition, yet is grounded in Berne's observations that traditional psychotherapeutic treatments took too long, and, being one-on-one, were extremely expensive. In addition, Berne was dissatisfied with his profession's habit of producing diagnoses that were too complex for the patient to understand.

In TA we find the practical expression of Berne's observations: an easy-to-use, yet profoundly insightful set of psychoanalytical tools that can be applied quickly and in a group context. The framework uses direct and accessible language, and although the model becomes more complex as you dig deeper, it is accessible to the lay person from the outset.

For families, and in professions where adults work with children, TA offers some genuine insights as to how we can help children navigate the complex business of living with other people. As most adults grew up without these understandings, they are equally useful when grownups self-apply them. It should be noted that whilst I have studied and gainfully applied this model, I am not an expert, nor a therapist: as such, this introduction seeks to set the scene, but is neither definitive nor exhaustive. In addition, it is worth noting that TA is just one of many models that we could apply here.

Transactional Analysis suggests that human beings have within them three quasi-distinct ego states, between which they may shift repeatedly, moment-to-moment throughout the course of a day: parent, child and adult. Each state is associated with different feelings and behaviours, as described below:

- <u>Parent</u> - concerned with rules and morals, seeking to guide and shape the child.
- <u>Child</u> - unconcerned with the needs of others, busy

responding to the environment around it with energy, curiosity and emotion.
- <u>Adult</u> - concerned with getting the best out of any situation for all involved, operates in the here and now.

Diagrammatically, these can be represented as follows, a picture that will be expanded upon gradually as we explore the model:

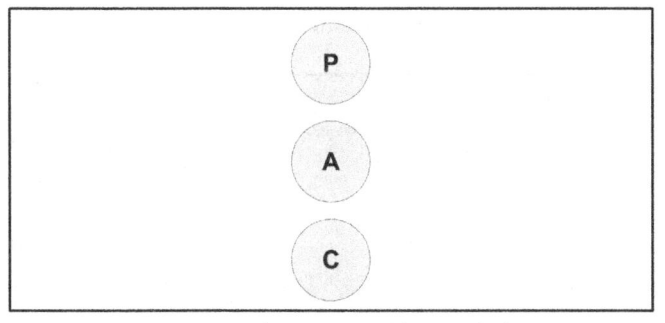

Image 3.1 - Three PAC States (Ross Parker)

Despite their names, these ego states are not directly connected to age. We might see a grownup who has lost their temper and thus shifted into the child state. Alternatively, we could observe one child scolding another, as if they were a parent. Rather, the states represent the different categories by which we exist in, and respond to, the world around us.

From this simple start, we can subdivide the parent and child states to recognise that they each contain two sub-states. The parent state contains critical parent (CP) and nurturing parent (NP). The former uses discipline, firm language and possibly a wagging finger to interact with others, where the latter cares for and protects those around them. At this point it can be useful to start thinking of people you know who tend to spend time in these two different states. Perhaps you had a parent who was very strict (critical parent) or a sibling who was exceptionally caring (nurturing parent). You might also start to identify your own tendencies.

The child state contains adapted child (AC) and free child (FC). The former fits itself to the needs of the parent, listening and paying attention, being neat, tidy and diligent. The latter is unconcerned with others, and full of boisterous energy, which can turn destructive. Again, you may find yourself making connections here to people you know.

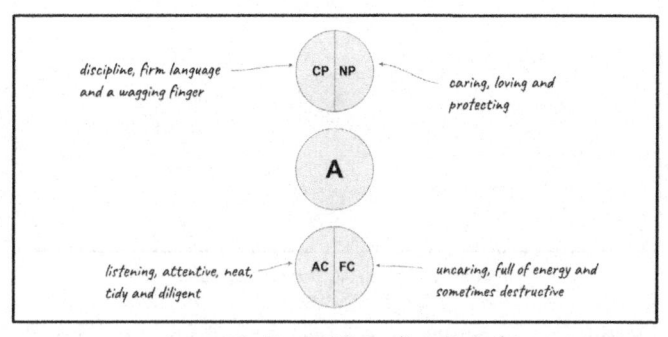

Image 3.2 - Five PAC States (Ross Parker)

The adult state, it should be noted, does not subdivide.

Whilst we might start to identify these new sub-states with the words "good" and "bad", it is important to note that each can be variously positive or negative, leading to a final set of sub-divisions, which delivers us a total of nine possible ego states.

We can come to understand the eight variations of parent and child, and thus sense their importance, by considering those people in our lives who exemplify their behaviours:

- <u>Positive Critical Parent</u> - intervenes quickly and effectively in emergency situations. Shouts "watch out" when a child is in danger, for example. You might bring to mind here a firm but friendly surf instructor or scout leader, a calm first aider, or an older child who firmly keeps a sibling safe from harm.

- <u>Negative Critical Parent</u> - critical and overly demanding of a child, unable to be flexible and spontaneous. Spanks, scolds and berates. Here you might think of an overly controlling father, or a child who constantly scolds their siblings and friends.
- <u>Positive Nurturing Parent</u> - cares for a child who is vulnerable or hurt, using soft, soothing words and a gentle touch. Kind, caring, loving. A classic example is a loving mother, or a child who cares for a fallen friend.
- <u>Negative Nurturing Parent</u> - overprotective and fearful on behalf of a child. Smothers, controls and coddles. Perhaps this is a grandparent who spoils a child, a helicopter parent who constantly intervenes to keep their child out of harm's way, or a child who always tells the teacher about their classmates' misdeeds.

And:

- <u>Positive Adapted Child</u> - understands that there is a time to listen and accommodate oneself to others. Trusts the adults in their lives. In terms of school this is often the quintessential model student. It is also the adult who sits and listens patiently in a boring meeting.
- <u>Negative Adapted Child</u> - gives the impression of listening, but is internally distracted or hostile. May tolerate behaviour that is harmful to them, including sustained abuse. Characterised by repressed negative emotions, including fear, anger

and loathing. This state can be hard to spot, but we often see it in a sullen teenager or the sulking romantic partner.

- Positive Free Child - able to occupy themselves, plays creatively, energetically and with imagination. Resilient to surprises and changes to routine. This is the child who is completely immersed in creative imaginative play, or the musician lost in their instrument.
- Negative Free Child - unable to effectively channel energy, and so engages in destructive or hurtful play. Uses outbursts to convey frustration. This is the child lying on the floor of the supermarket, screaming because they did not get what they wanted. It is also the frustrated boss shouting at their team, or the angry golfer snapping their putter over their knee.

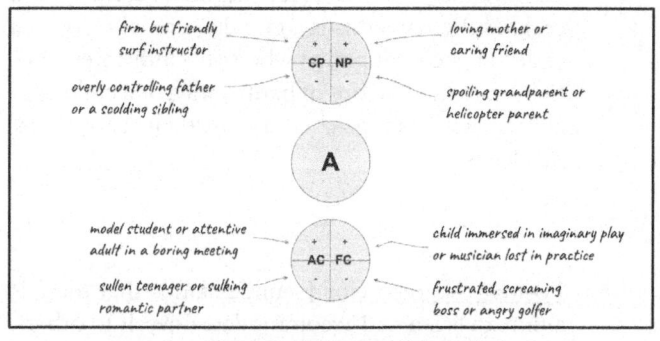

Image 3.3 - Nine PAC States (Ross Parker)

Whilst we all generally know people who fit these states well, it is also likely that, in considering our own behaviours and feelings, we can see aspects of ourselves in each one. Most of us will have filled each role at some point in our lives, whilst also having some dominant roles to which we repeatedly return.

Having applied this model to myself over a number of years, I recognise that my own negative free child tendencies evoked in my mother a negative critical parent response. At the time this filled me with negative emotions, but gradually, with work, I've come to understand that her intention always tended toward nurturing...I was just a pain in the rear end!

Likewise I can see my own son struggling to sustain positive free child and positive adapted child states, and I recognise that sometimes his behaviour "hooks" my own inherited negative critical parent, just like a hook snags a fish. In a very real sense, some of his behaviours snap me into a different ego state, in just the same way that some of my behaviours give him only one way to respond. I may wish to stay in positive free child, playing and having fun, but I'm nonetheless drawn back to negative critical parent when he says or does a particular thing.

In my daily life, as a parent, teacher, husband and son, I use this model to try and reflect upon and deconstruct my own reactions. Despite some failures, the net impact over a number of years has been sustained, positive growth in both my relationships and self-awareness.

In the last few paragraphs we have moved from <u>structural analysis</u>, where we investigate the states of a single person, to <u>transactional analysis</u>, in which two or more people interact, influencing each other along the way. This dual nature is part of what makes TA so powerful: we can use it to understand not only ourselves, but also how we react to others, and how they react to us. It can disarm our natural tendency to blame our feelings on the capriciousness of others, and start to take responsibility for our part in the human drama within which we inescapably exist.

All of this can help us, in our dealings with our children, to stay in those more positive states, which in turn encourages the same from them. The model can also be taught explicitly to children, who can then apply it to themselves. These approaches can allow for a greater level of emotional self-awareness and maturity within a family, classroom or school.

Whilst there is no magic set of ego states to aim for, adult-adult offers a great starting point for many of life's difficult conversations. I am lucky to work with a boss who is capable of sustaining adult for extended periods, and as a result, I come to him already in the adult state. This is so different to the negative free child that other leaders have nudged me towards, and allows us to deal with tricky problems without emotion or rancour. Sometimes we slip into positive free child and share a joke, at others we let off some steam with some negative critical parent. In many ways, our school represents an institutionalised application of TA, which has led to more positive relationships all around.

As a teacher I am now quite consistently able to conduct my lessons in the adult ego state. This increases the chances that students respond with adult, and so requires less adaptive child from them. Sometimes they struggle, and I tend back to the critical parent. More often, however, I can maintain adult, and draw them back. Sometimes I use nurturing parent to counsel and console. On a good day I can channel my positive free child, telling tall stories and rolling around on the floor...all without unleashing a wave of negative free child in my students! It's a constant balancing act, a push and pull in which we all impact each other. In all of this, TA has given me the tools needed to understand the forces at play.

As a parent, I have much yet to learn: my aim is generally adult, but I often get derailed. I'm still trying to puzzle out the difference between my own two children and a class of twenty students. Perhaps, in the safety of our home, my own children's free child is just freer, their adapted child less adapted. Perhaps my critical parent is just that much closer to the surface when I am off duty, tired after a long day's work.

In sharing Transactional Analysis it is not my aim to suggest that it has all the answers, nor that it is the one true way to understand emotion. Rather, it is offered as an example of how we need such models to understand and deal with the complexity of our emotional lives, and to underscore how important it is for children to be coached in such systems. There are plenty of approaches out there, and TA is just one of them. In Chapter 5 we'll look at another useful model of emotion developed by leading neuroscientist Lisa Feldman Barrett.

I often wonder how differently I might have developed had I known about TA and other such models as a teenager.

Positive Scripts

Digging deeper into TA reveals an aspect of life called scripts, which we touched upon earlier in the chapter. A script is what is happening when we feel that our actions are not our own, as if we are playing a part composed by someone else. We often use short-term scripts in order to save time. Someone says "Hi, how are you?" and we say "Fine", whether or not we really are. The script acts as a social lubricant, and allows us to operate in a busy urban setting without becoming overwhelmed. Much of the time these scripts work for us, but at times we might also find ourselves walking away simultaneously furious and mystified that we did not do or say what we really intended.

Sometimes we fall back on old scripts, seemingly

abandoned, but still lingering in the recesses of our minds. A classic example of this is when we run into the parent of a childhood friend and revert to old modes of thinking, speaking and feeling: "Yes, Mrs. Hooley" we might say without conscious thought. Teachers often experience this when they meet former students who, as adults, still cannot refer to the teacher by their first name.

Of great significance are <u>life scripts</u>, which are those long-term patterns to which we habitually return. Think of the man divorced three times and madly in love yet again, the woman who dates the same type of unsuitable partner over and over, the alcoholic, or the child that lies compulsively. Each wants to change, but each finds themselves back in the same position no matter what they do. Some call it fate...others call it scripts.

These scripts stem from the repeated playing out of a set of ego state changes: the addict wakes up hungover one time too many, shifts into critical parent and berates themselves into sobriety. The adult state is then evident in rational and thoughtful decisions that lead to good outcomes. However, some unexpected shock or stimulus pushes them back into negative free child and they relapse. After too many hangovers they awake again to the voice of their own critical parent.

As discussed earlier, our scripts are based on decisions we've made about ourselves, and tragically, we often make these decisions at a very young age, before we have the cognitive resources to know any better.

Most schools, families and workplaces operate on the basis of a set of well-worn scripts, which explains why we can interchange various elements and still end up with the same results. You dislike your boss and are relieved when she is reassigned...only to find that your new boss is a virtual clone.

The people have changed, but the scripts remain.

Given the way that parenting generally seeks to recreate the status quo, and the ways in which our formative years colour the rest of our lives, it is not surprising that many of the scripts we run as adults are, in some way, parent-to-child. It took TA to help me realise, for example, that my own clashes with authority figures reflected not the ills of authority (which can be very real) so much as my own tendency towards negative free child, and the negative critical parent reaction that this brought about in others. Once I changed myself, the world around me changed too.

Within our families and our schools we can seek to replace the traditional parent-child scripts with those founded on adult-adult transactions. Whilst this is not to say that there is not a place for parent-child, it is worth noting how easily positive nurturing parent - positive adapted child can become negative critical parent - negative free child, as shown in the diagrams below:

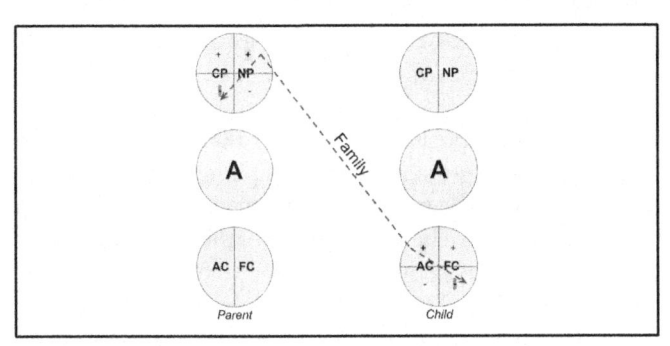

Image 3.4 - Parent & Child PAC States (Ross Parker). Positive is coloured green, negative red.

In this example, the parent (on the left) starts off as positive nurturing parent (+), and the child adapts themselves to the parent in a positive fashion (+). Perhaps dad is reading to daughter, who is listening attentively. Gradually, daughter becomes bored and fidgety, distracts dad, and nudges him towards negative critical parent (-). Daughter feels dad's displeasure and is in turn nudged towards negative free child (-). Daughter gets more fidgety, then talks rudely to dad. Things spiral, and an argument breaks out, seemingly from nowhere.

When we hit this point we are generally deep into conflict, tempers are frayed, emotions run high and the wheels are falling off. The participants have now become combatants, and there may well be shouting, crying or worse. In other words, they are flooded with emotion.

In the hands of a well-versed practitioner, TA can be used to spot these patterns as they are emerging, allowing evasive manoeuvres to be taken before they escalate. By understanding and modelling this ourselves, we can provide our children with significantly more positive scripts to run. For example, rather than turning frustration into negative critical parent, parents can turn it into positive free child, thus hooking a child away from negative adaptive child or negative free child. My wife, I have learned, is particularly good at this switch…myself less so!

Children running positive scripts based on adult-adult and a range of other ego states that compliment those around them are likely to be more content, amenable and settled in their relationships. Their feelings about themselves are likely to be more productive too.

If you are interested in learning more, I can't recommend better introductions than two classic TA texts: Thomas Harris's I'm OK, You're OK[70] and Claude Steiner's Scripts

---

[70] I'm OK, You're OK, Thomas Harris, Harper & Row (https://bit.ly/3UqJ59z)

People Live[71]. The only caveat is that they were written in the 1960s and 70s, and, in terms of gender stereotypes, they have not aged well. If you can overlook some dated views on the roles of men and women, then there is a lot to be gained from reading them.

Free Range Children

As discussed earlier[72], one of the results of lower fertility rates and rising parenting costs is that we have become far more protective of our children. This has been exacerbated by many factors, including the rise of organised, adult-run activities, media-driven concerns for the safety of our children, and the capitalist drive to sell us products to keep our children safe. In many ways, as the comic below suggests, this may be linked to a broader social phenomenon that aims to minimise risk in all endeavours.

Victorian risk assessment

Image 3.5 - Victorian Risk Assessment (origin unknown)

---

[71] Scripts People Live, Claude Steiner, Grove Press (https://bit.ly/3h2sdHH)

[72] See Chapter 2

Of course, the safety of children, and humans more generally, is a genuine and worthwhile concern. Legislation, standards and cultural norms that reduce the chances of a child being electrocuted, trapped in a folding table or exposed to dangerous chemicals are all positive steps. I don't believe that any of these things are symptoms of a "nanny state", as many now suggest. Rather, they are sensible ways to avoid individual and familial tragedy.

However, there are strong arguments to be made that we have, as parents, collectively failed to get the balance of risk and independence correct, and that this is to the detriment of our children. This is an argument that is very convincingly made in a Hanna Rosin article entitled The Overprotected Kid[73]. Writing in The Atlantic, Rosin argues that a decades-long focus on safety, particularly in terms of playgrounds, has failed to protect children, whilst actually depriving them of the opportunities to enjoy independence and learn to assess and take risks. Phil Morgan, a colleague of mine, tells the following tale of a school he used to work at: "a piece of play equipment was removed from my last school. It was said to be too dangerous and there were many falls and broken arms, but only because the students were too weak to use it well. Now there are no accidents but also no means of getting stronger."

Describing the way in which childhood and parenting have changed, Rosin explains that:

> "My mother didn't work all that much when I was younger, but she didn't spend vast amounts of time with me, either. She didn't arrange my playdates or

---

[73] The Overprotected Kid, Hanna Rosin, The Atlantic (https://bit.ly/3gDBcyO)

drive me to swimming lessons or introduce me to cool music she liked. On weekdays after school she just expected me to show up for dinner; on weekends I barely saw her at all. I, on the other hand, might easily spend every waking Saturday hour with one if not all three of my children, taking one to a soccer game, the second to a theater program, the third to a friend's house, or just hanging out with them at home. When my daughter was about 10, my husband suddenly realized that in her whole life, she had probably not spent more than 10 minutes unsupervised by an adult. Not 10 minutes in 10 years."

Rosin's claims are not simply anecdotal. She cites the work of Roger Hart, who spent time studying the geographical habits of children at a New England elementary school in the early 1970s. His ethnographic approach involved spending time moving around the local area with children, being introduced to their network of paths, dens and secret places. He recorded the great extent to which children played without adult supervision, the surprising distances they roamed and the pride they took in knowing their land. In an age of organised play dates, stranger danger, team sports and private tutors, children no longer play in these ways. Much has been lost in this shift.

Tellingly, Hart's attempt to run a follow-up study at the same school in 2004 was rejected by the school's new principal because it was seen not to fit with the curriculum. This is indicative of how much schools have changed, and generally not for the better

Whilst there is a temptation to romanticise our own childhood experiences, there is little doubt that times have changed, and that children today are losing out on vital skills as a result. Consider a child-initiated game of football, with

Screens That Eat Children

jumpers for goal posts, no adult referee or coach, and no parents on the sideline. This is a context rife with opportunities for imagination, creativity, conflict resolution, leadership, and knowing when not to push your luck. In comparison, an adult-orchestrated soccer practice seems positively sterile. Likewise when comparing an afternoon playing in nature with time spent in a playpark.

These stories correlate very closely with my own childhood experiences, and with the parenting I see around me today. Fortunately, Rosin's voice, and that of a cadre of others, including Lenore Skenazy[74], Richard Louv[75], the late A.S Neill[76] and Johann Hari[77], have given me the courage to allow my own children the same freedoms that I grew up with. The ways in which these carefully crafted freedoms can mould children mesh well with the ideas of Winnicott and Erikson. Sadly, what we are tending to see today is much more like the image below:

Image 3.6 - Hong Kong Now & Then (origin unknown)

---

[74] Free-Range Kids, Lenore Skenazy, Jossey-Bass (https://bit.ly/3fu7E6F)

[75] Last Child in the Woods, Richard Louv, Algonquin Books (https://bit.ly/3T4eYnb)

[76] Summerhill School, A. S. Neill, St. Martin's Griffin (https://bit.ly/3T11UPt)

[77] Stolen Focus, Johann Hari, Crown (https://bit.ly/3h79D1h)

This begs the vital question "where have all the children gone?". It also invites us to ponder what is left of childhood when children stop playing freely together.

Bodies Before Minds

Education, and its impact upon our values, has a large part to play in the answer to this question. The late Ken Robinson, in his seminal TED talk[78], touches upon our culture's growing obsession with the pursuit of specialised and abstract knowledge. This, he contends, is borne out in the fact that "the whole system of public education around the world is a protracted process of university entrance". Here he highlights a very good point, which is the way that we have collectively come to focus on university as the only really acceptable goal for our children.

Young people used to have a wide range of ways to proceed into the world, including apprenticeships, technical schools, the armed forces and learning a business from the bottom up. My own father left school aged fifteen to become a trainee golf pro at the feet of a master. This vista has narrowed dramatically, with university often seen as the only really respectable option. This in turn has corrupted the entire process of education, and childhood more broadly, to be a time of intense cognitive work, at the expense of many other skills, pursuits and ways of being. This dynamic is particularly acute in my home city, Hong Kong, where certain professions, including medicine and law, are fetishised at the expense of all others. This seems to go hand-in-hand with a child's joyless and technical acquisition of Grade 8 Piano as a must-have for any self-respecting

---

[78] Do schools kill creativity?, Sir Ken Robinson, TED (https://bit.ly/3DuyCDb)

parent and their university-bound progeny.

As Robinson goes on to point out, universities, which can be caricatured by their professors, risk producing a very unhealthy kind of human being:

> "There's something curious about professors in my experience — not all of them, but typically, they live in their heads. They live up there, and slightly to one side. They're disembodied, you know, in a kind of literal way. They look upon their body as a form of transport for their heads. Don't they? It's a way of getting their head to meetings."[79]

And whilst Robinson's remarks are offered in jest, they underscore a very serious point: ought we really be spending so much time disconnecting children from their bodies?

To me, the answer is a very clear "no", based on the fact that to disembody ourselves is to dehumanise us. In fact, I see a very clear relationship with the way we've disembodied our children, and the ease into which they've slipped into the very artificial act of staring at screens with intense focus. Education has, to my mind, an awful lot to answer for.

In writing on the importance of free play, Johann Hari[80] mentions the work of Dr. Isabel Behncke, a play expert from Chile, who offers three key positive impacts of such play: creativity and imagination, social bonds and aliveness. Whilst all three are important, it is the last one that really hit me hard. I remember my childhood as a time of great energy and activity, precisely a feeling of being alive. I often wonder

---

[79] Do Schools Kill Creativity? transcript, James Clear (https://bit.ly/3UgDT7S)

[80] Stolen Focus, Johann Hari, Crown (https://bit.ly/3h79D1h)

at the ways in which adult life stymies this, and whilst as an adult I can handle the change, it seems tragic to prevent a child from ever knowing the feeling in the first place. This is exactly what we as adults do, however, when we inhibit play, and thus disconnect our children from themselves.

Summary

It is not surprising that we see considerable overlap in the various needs described above, which we can recapitulate as: a balance of attention and autonomy, emotional awareness, positive transactions and scripts, physical freedom and hands-on experiences. This list will be expanded in Chapter 8, which focuses on school, to also include values, connections, risk and boredom. The social structures and beliefs that variously enable or inhibit the satisfaction of these needs are where we should concern ourselves, for it is these that shape our children.

On reflection, it is not difficult to see the great degree to which these essential elements are absent from contemporary childhood. To place the blame entirely at the feet of screens would be myopic, which is why it is so important to consider the broader picture of childhood development. However, screens clearly play a significant and growing role.

Childhood happens in the spaces left by adults, and for many children, these spaces have all but disappeared. What remains has been colonised by gigantic tech monopolies and the shareholders they need to keep happy.

With a scaffold in place to understand childhood and the ways in which it has changed, we are almost ready to return to the issue of screens. However, first it is useful to spend some time thinking about what it means to be human, and how we got to where we are. With these major pieces in

Screens That Eat Children

place, we can continue to ask critical, thoughtful questions about what screens are doing to us. But let's not rush.

CHAPTER 4
HOMO TECHNOLOGICUS

Human Evolution

In evolutionary terms, our distant ancestors endured a series of trade-offs as part of life's greatest game: survival-of-the-fittest. In this context, "fittest" can be taken to refer to those who are best able to adapt to prevailing circumstances and thus survive long enough to reproduce.

At many separate intervals, spread across millenia, our ancestors sacrificed physical strength and instinctual ways of surviving in order to build larger and more flexible brains. With these brains we discovered and created a vast array of tools, many of which enabled us to expand the range of conditions in which we could survive. Blades, for example, allowed us to turn forests into grasslands, whilst fur-lined clothes allowed us to endure colder climates. Other tools, such as levers, wheels and pulleys, enhanced our physical power, allowing us to depend less on our own muscles, which gradually withered away.

Of key import is the way in which our cognitive and social tools, such as spoken language, enabled us to begin accruing culture, which in turn accelerated the accumulation of knowledge. No longer was knowledge confined to a single individual, available only through experimentation: instead, it could be embedded in ritual and orally transmitted.

Within this complex of interrelated changes to our biology and our tools, we moved from being just another animal to becoming *Homo sapiens*, via a set of intermediary steps, including *Australopithecus* and *Homo erectus*.

There is no reliable way to delineate the exact sequence of events in this protracted transition, but we can make suppositions based on evidence. For example, one set of changes is believed to be related to walking upright, which freed our hands from the arduous and non-stop task of interfacing with the ground. Instead of deeply calloused and hardened front feet, we ended up with supple, subtle hands, perfect for knapping flint blades and starting fires. In using these hands for new tasks, our brains generated new structures and pathways. The domestication of fire allowed us to cook and preserve food, releasing a greater store of nutrients into our bodies and allowing us to spend less time gathering food, and more time tinkering. In addition, it allowed us to survive with shorter intestinal tracts, weaker jaws and smaller teeth. Over time, this freed up more energy for greater brain development. Interestingly, it is also believed that the decrease in jaw muscle mass, which reduced the need for restrictive anchoring across our skulls, allowed us to develop yet bigger brains.

These evolutionary considerations inform a modern understanding of what it means to be human, and can deepen and enrich many of the arguments found within this book. For now, they allow us to see ourselves primarily as tool developers and users. More specifically, they also allow us to conceive of "tools" as not just material technologies (e.g. those that we can touch), but as any human invention. In this schema, spoken and written languages are technologies, body language is a technology, prayer is a technology. In fact, almost every facet of human life is a technology, or has in some way been technologised. Here we can draw a distinction between instinct, which drives the behaviour of most animals, and technology, which has to quite some degree replaced instinct in humans.

Human Technologies

The approach described above is known as Human Technologies[81], and was developed by Toby Newton at International College Hong Kong (ICHK), the school I am fortunate enough to teach at.

Human Technologies is an effort to reframe technology not as merely physical tools, but as all elements of human invention. Part of this work involves reclaiming the term "technology" itself. For most of us, most of the time, the term technology is used to connote the most recent, novel and exciting of our material tools: smartphones, the Internet, electric cars, medical imaging devices and flat screen TVs. Most of the time, older technologies such as clothes, roads, houses and antibiotics do not figure in our thinking. They've become part of the background. As the technologist Alan Kay very succinctly put it, we act as if[82] "Technology is anything that wasn't around when you were born".

Considering older technologies is a good start, but there is more to Human Technologies than just that. In addition to material technologies, Human Technologies invites us to consider those tools that allow us to think (cognitive), communicate (social), find meaning (spiritual) and manage

---

[81] Human Technologies, ICHK Secondary (https://bit.ly/3h72HRI)

[82] Alan Kay quotation, BrainyQuote (https://bit.ly/3E6S2j7)

and maintain our bodies (somatic). Within this framework we can start to think of elements of human practice as diverse as logic, body language, prayer and dieting as technologies. Each of these was invented by humans, and represents a matrix of values, choices, priorities, world views and goals. Each is open to interrogation, each can be negotiated, each can be changed.

Whilst some technologies can be considered to be of one kind or another, most technologies fit into multiple categories. Importantly, all technologies fit within the somatic envelope, which reminds us that all technologies have a bodily dimension, because we are embodied animals. The Human Technologies Venn diagram[83] helps us to consider these overlaps:

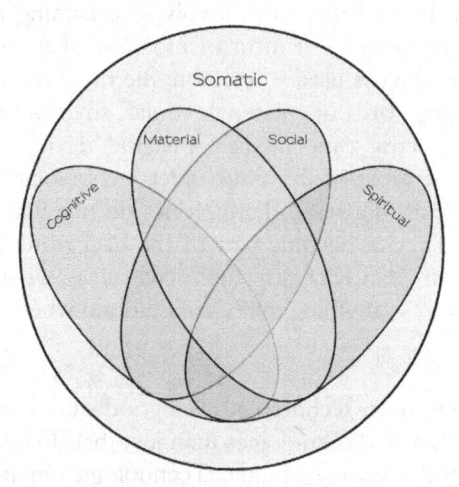

Image 4.1 - Human Technologies Venn Diagram (Toby Newton)

Incense, for example, can be considered a material and

---

[83] Human Technologies Venn diagram, ICHK Secondary (https://bit.ly/3h72HRI)

spiritual technology, as it is tangible yet connects us to something larger than ourselves. It fits into a wider array of technologies, the temple, which introduces social aspects to its use. And without a nose, we wouldn't smell it, which explains the inevitable, all-encompassing somatic dimension.

Some of our inventions, such as deep breathing, might initially not seem to be technologies at all. It would be entirely false to claim that humans invented breathing, as it is a natural instinct. However, whilst we did not invent breathing, we have technologised it, bringing it under our own control and directing it to our own ends. And so we find that we can position deep breathing, when it is used for meditation, as a spiritual and somatic technology. Likewise, humans did not invent fire, but by controlling it we have technologised it, allowing it to be meaningfully considered a human technology.

On deeper consideration, there is little in contemporary human life that is not a technology of some kind. This insight is significant, as it allows us to reframe our lives, and to reconsider many things that we had taken for granted or assumed were "natural". It gives us licence to think and act in ways that might previously have gone unconsidered.

Further, in thinking about technology more deeply, we might not be surprised to discover that not all inventions are created equal, and that it is fair to say that some technologies are considerably more influential and disruptive than others. Symbolic representation, the control of fire, agriculture, the wheel, steam power, the moveable type printing press and electricity are all examples of massively influential and disruptive technologies.

If we were to search for exactly those kinds of technologies, we would likely find ourselves drawn to the centre of the

Venn diagram. And exactly there, I would posit, is where we would find screens. In their current form, we use smartphones to manage our bodies (alarm clock, sleep tracking), to scaffold our thinking (Internet search, calculator) and to socialise (email, social media and sometimes even phone calls!). Sitting comfortably in our hand or pocket they are clearly material. Given the anxiety we feel when separated from them, and the way they place us at the centre of the action, it is hard to argue that they do not have a spiritual dimension.

Significant to the story unfolding here is the way in which phones, through social media, technologise "friendship". What is the difference between a friend in real life and a "friend" on Facebook? How have our devices altered the cognitive scripts through which we understand this word, and how has this impacted the way in which our friendships function. In other words, we might ask to what extent have phones trivialised, monetised and skewed the meaning of friendship? We can see hints of this when we compare how many "friends" we have online, with how many we have in real life. The former are easy to count: just look at your favourite social media platform. Before I stopped using Facebook I had somewhere between 300 and 500 friends listed. In real life, counting friends as those people that I actively seek to spend time with and on whom I can rely when the going gets tough, I would estimate that I have around 30 to 50. What does this ten-fold difference reveal, and is the quality of friendships inversely related?

It is no wonder that these technologies have proven to be so disruptive to our lives: there are few aspects that they do not touch in some way. It is in this insight that we might start to grasp the true power of Human Technologies: it awakens us to the very extreme degree to which our lived experience is of our own making. In reflecting on our lives we tend to think that they are playing out along natural and even pre-ordained lines, where in fact, they are very much shaped by the totality of our technological appendages. Fortunately, we have the power to variously prioritise or de-emphasise the technologies through which we define ourselves. Almost all of the identities available to us hinge upon the careful selection and deselection of technologies: the vegan, the punk, the teetotaller, the recycler, the cyclist, none are immune from the influences of technology.

The lens of Human Technologies invites us to reconsider every facet of our lives. Money, for example, is an interesting place to start. For many of us, especially our young, money is inseparable from life. It has no start or end, it just is. Yet, of course, money is a human invention, and a very useful one at that. Before money we had to deal with the inefficiency of barter. In order to turn my dozen eggs into a loaf of bread, I had to find someone with a loaf of bread who wanted eggs. Even worse, I might have to negotiate with a string of intermediaries to make my exchange work. With money, I can simply exchange a number of tokens for the goods I desire.

Given its utility, why would we possibly want to question the concept of money? Well, it turns out that, like phones, money is not that simple, for it sits right in the centre of our Venn diagram. Allowed free rein, money comes to suggest that everything has a value, that everything is open to exchange. How much for that house? How much for that kidney? How much for that person? How much to pollute that river? Money, it turns out, has had a massive impact on the way we view the world, and is one of the things that separates modern, destructive humans from some of our more naturally-attuned ancestors. This is in no way a descent into reverie about the "noble savage", nor a suggestion that all pre-industrial societies lived sustainability: rather it is an invitation to look more critically at our own choices.

When the world is viewed through the lens of Human Technologies, much that is taken for granted becomes available for critical evaluation.

Human Survival

When it comes to our choice of technologies, we need to take great care, for in a very real sense these decisions lie at the very heart of our survival. At one level, such decisions are about individual survival within a given landscape, but at a point they also come to determine our collective survival as a tribe, nation or species.

Joseph Henrich[84] offers an apt illustration of the power of technology through the study of lost explorers. In a surprisingly large number of cases, seemingly well-prepared Western explorers have perished in foreign lands, simply because the suite of technologies that they brought to bear proved ill-suited to their current circumstances. Often they died in close proximity to indigenous people who, with a different set of technologies, were managing to survive under the exact same conditions. As an example Henrich offers us the case of the Burke and Wills expedition, which crossed the interior of Australia in 1860. On the return leg they, and their two fellow travellers, began to run out of food. After shedding equipment and starting to eat their pack animals, they then missed a rendezvous with a contingent of their support team and the supplies they were carrying.

Running out of food, they were aided by the

---

[84] The Secret of Our Success, Joseph Henrich, Princeton University Press (https://bit.ly/3NyJsfK)

Yandruwandrha people, indigenous hunter-gathers who introduced them to a sporocarp[85] called nardoo, which they mistook for a seed. Finding plentiful nardoo, they managed to consume sufficient calories, but died of malnutrition. As the Yandruwandrha knew, but were unable to make understood, nardoo is nearly indigestible, and potentially toxic, unless properly processed. Specifically, nardoo contains an enzyme which breaks down thiamine (vitamin B1), leaving those who do not properly process it susceptible to beri-beri[86]. The multi-stage work of making nardoo edible is part of a set of technologies that Burke and Wills lacked, and without which they perished. In reflecting on the Burke and Wills expedition, I find it incredibly sad that so many post-industrial humans still treat indigenous peoples as ignorant and uncivilised, despite the great wisdom and knowledge held by tribes the world over. This strikes me as yet another symptom of our misplaced priorities.

I've come to wonder if our adoption of smartphones will, in retrospect, seem as ill-conceived as the packing lists and required reading of various dead explorers. Ultimately, we are individually and culturally the sum of the technologies that we choose to use and discard. Our various choices within this field reflect our values, and come to define who we are and how we live. With this in mind, are we able to say with any certainty that smartphones represent a wise choice? As we will explore in the coming chapters, which build on the concepts sketched out above, I don't believe we can.

In moving forward, it is worth keeping in mind that

---

[85] The fruit body of a fungi

[86] Burke and Wills, National Museum Australia (https://bit.ly/3fu2CXE)

technologies are critical to the human story, to the extent that we ought really refer to ourselves as *Homo technologicus* (technological man). Certainly this seems a good fit for a species as instrumental, short-sighted and self-destructive as our own, especially when contrasted to Carl Linnaeus' *Homo sapiens*[87] (wise man).

---

[87] Systema Naturae, Carl Linnaeus

CHAPTER 5
BECOMING WHOLE

In terms of the process of becoming a viable, healthy individual living in a complex world of others, we might well ask what it means to live with an insistent, inescapable, 24/7 popularity contest in your pocket?

Psychology, as a field, is almost as large and sprawling as human experience itself. In considering the question above, there is no way that a book such as this can seek to capture the full psychological impact of screens. This is especially true if you subscribe to the view that the way we each understand and engage with the world around us is predominantly constructed by our own experience. If this is the case, and I believe it is, then screens can be claimed to have changed everything, just as Steve Jobs predicted they would[88]. To take but one example, we see the scope of this change in the intrusion of advertising into every part of our lives, as Matthew B. Crawford artfully explains[89]:

---

[88] Planet of the Phones, The Economist (https://econ.st/3ssufmQ)

[89] The World Beyond Your Head, Matthew B. Crawford, Farrar, Straus and Giroux (https://bit.ly/3NxuLcT)

> "The ever more complete penetration of public spaces by attention-getting technologies exploits the orienting response in a way that preempts sociability, directing us away from one another and toward a manufactured reality, the content of which is determined from afar by private parties that have a material interest in doing so."

This situation is bad enough when the adverts are in the space around you: so much worse when you hold them in your hand. Worse again when it applies not just to advertisement in the pre-digital sense of billboards and posters, but to more or less every aspect of your lived experience. When the "friends" you follow on social media are paid influencers, you have come, in a sense, to live a life of fiction.

Given the potentially limitless scope of this section it is best to avoid attempting any kind of grand synthesis. Rather, I'll limit myself to a small set of hopefully useful observations, each of which speaks to the challenges that children face in becoming whole on the Internet.

Reality

On the surface, the lens of Human Technologies[90] invites us to expand our conception of technologies to encompass a much wider range of human invention. We move from a consideration of just material artefacts to include creations that are somatic, spiritual, cognitive and social. If we take a further step we can see that each of these inventions has the power to change who we are as individuals: they change the way that we think, the way that we relate to others and the

---

[90] Encountered in Chapter 4

way that we seek meaning within the world. These technologies are clearly powerful.

However, it is in the next intellectual leap that we really start to appreciate the power of technology, and how radically contingent our lives are upon it. Rather than simply changing who we are, technology changes the reality within which we live, not just materially, but in almost every single way. Up, down, left, right, good, bad, beautiful, ugly, right and wrong: these subjective descriptors of reality are all human technologies. Many of these concepts have physical counterparts, but the way we experience them, the way they operate in our minds, is a construct of our own collective making.

For some readers this may feel comfortable, for others it might sound too liberal, too airy fairy, or simply too anthropocentric. The latter it is definitely not: it in no way puts us at the center of life, it simply highlights the degree to which we have, one technology at a time, shaped our own experience of the world.

As a concrete example, consider numbers. For modern humans it feels natural to live in a world where everything is enumerated. I have 12 apples, the stock market is down 37 points, 100 people died in an earthquake, she's a perfect 10. The fact that everything has a numerical value, and that these can be compared and evaluated, is something that we rarely question. However, consider for a moment the Amazon's Pirahã tribe, whose number system includes only the concepts "one", "two" and "many". Given this particular technology, their experience of the world will be vastly different to ours. They may accept that their home has many trees, but they could not conceive of them as a commodity to be totalled up, chopped down and sold on the international market. The cost of this destruction, they would not be able to convert to a money value. This is not just because they don't have the material technologies for the job, it is because their cognitive and social technologies have not made available a world view in which everything converts to numerical, and thus financial, value. We might find living without numbers to be abhorrent, unthinkable: I sometimes wonder if the Pirahã might view our world the same way.

The important point here is that we are almost entirely unaware of how numbers, in this case, shape the way we experience reality. That is, until someone points it out.

Intimate relationships provide us with another interesting example. Traditionally, many societies have conceived of marriage as something to be arranged by parents, in order to ensure a good match for impetuous and unwise youth. By contrast, the contemporary notion of romantic love is a relatively recent invention, stemming from the 18th century[91]. The set of overlapping technologies that we call "love" makes available to us an entirely different conception of marriage: one based on feelings, and fate and individual autonomy. It ties in much more nicely with the West's cult of individuality. It shapes our experience of the world, as we wonder constantly "are they the one?". As a system, it is neither entirely good nor bad…but it is a system, and we can be critical of it. Although romantic love might feel natural to us, it most certainly is not.

Modern technology is making new claims on this conceptual space. In the age of Grindr, Tinder and Bumble, love is something that we find through swiping. Presented with an algorithmically generated menu of willing (and

---

[91] The unromantic reality of love, Johann Hari, Independent (https://bit.ly/3srGOPj)

hopefully able) sexual partners, arranged by location for our convenience, we experience relationships very differently. We gaze upon the latest offering, and lazily swipe left (goodbye!) or right (hello!), essentially up and downvoting individuals as we might Instagram posts, political candidates or cattle in a marketplace. If someone on whom we swipe right happens to return the favour, then the next step is unlocked.

Gone is the visceral, gut churning excitement of approaching a crush in person. No longer do we need to gradually come to terms with finding someone attractive enough to risk our self-esteem in approaching them. We simply swipe. Efficient and "frictionless" as this system is, I've rarely met anyone my own age who actually enjoys it: the few that do are generally more interested in sexual conquest than long-term relationships. And yet it is fair to say that this technology is not likely to disrupt my reality to any great extent: my views on love, for better or worse, were founded long ago. However, my own children, and the generation that follows them, will live in a different world, with their reality constructed in part by these new technologies. The very way that they experience reality, the colours, flavours, sights and sounds that their brains choose to draw out of the constant flux of experience will be shifted.

These ideas are not mere speculation, but form an established part of the study of linguistics. Known as linguistic relativity, and more commonly as the Sapir–Whorf hypothesis[92], the suggestion that language impacts our experience of the world has its roots in the 1920s. Some

---

[92] The Sapir-Whorf Hypothesis Linguistic Theory, Richard Nordquist, Thought Co. (https://bit.ly/3zH5NSJ)

aspects of the original formulation of this idea may have been superceded, but as a foundational conception of human experience it offers genuine insight. Where we might wish to exceed the Sapir–Whorf hypothesis is to move beyond its focus on language, and to encompass the wider range of human technologies, including all symbols, schema and other tools of abstraction, that human invention places between us and reality.

A key insight that stems from this is that it would be easy for me to idealise the version of reality in which I grew up, and in some ways I do just that. However, in many other ways, I understand that the reality I know is deeply unhealthy and far from natural, especially in terms of the indirect experiences that have been foisted upon me by the media. Many of my ways of understanding the world stem from the dominant political and economic paradigms into which I was born: colonialism, imperialism, patriarchy, capitalism and individualism. Far from an ideal start, I know. However, despite the fact that I have no strong desire to preserve many elements of these systems, I also don't want my experience to be hijacked by a newer and more powerful set of corporate and financial interests, emboldened as they are by lax regulation and the most invasive technologies we've ever created.

Emotion

Given this constructed nature of our reality, it is worth considering the connection between experience and the emotions that we feel. Traditional and intuitive understandings suggest that when we experience something it triggers within us an emotional response. This classical view of emotion teaches us that these responses come in a number of basic, universal flavours, including fear, anger, joy and sadness. These responses, we are told, map to various hormones and neurotransmitters, which make our emotional range relatively predetermined. We see a tiger, and we feel fear.

Modern neuroscience has, however, strongly challenged this view, flipping the order on its head. As explained by Lisa Feldman Barrett[93], new evidence tells us that it is our intellectual concept of the tiger, which we have learned to associate with fear, that causes our bodies to release the chemicals that make us feel afraid. We perceive the order of operations incorrectly because it all happens so fast. This makes a lot of sense when we think about the formation of phobias, and how variable such intense fears can be between individuals.

In other words, we are starting to understand that emotion is like our experience of reality, something that we construct to quite some degree. It is our knowledge of the available responses to any situation that informs the emotions that we feel. We believe that emotion is automatic and inevitable, but in fact it is actually variable and manipulable. A good example of this is how we might react to public speaking. On the face of it, for many of us, standing in front of a crowd can be nerve-wracking. Look a little more closely, and it becomes hard to tell if we are scared or excited, as many of the physical manifestations of these emotional states overlap. Given some practice, some coaching and some positive feedback, and we might well come to experience excitement and pleasure rather than fear. Eventually, we might become inured, through experience, and feel nothing much at all. Objectively the situation has remained the same, but the subject and their emotions have changed.

---

[93] How Emotions Are Made, Prof. Lisa Feldman Barrett, Mariner Books (https://bit.ly/3sTCrg2)

Although the difference between these two viewpoints might seem slippery, and perhaps even trivial, they actually represent a fundamental shift in how we conceive of ourselves. It invites us to review our own life story, and to ask ourselves at which points we came to identify certain external stimuli with certain internal feelings, and why. Most likely, as previously discussed, this happened when we were too young to be rational: yet these understandings form the foundation of everything we can and will become, especially if left unchallenged. Were we to be trained from an early age in this new way of thinking, we might come to have a much more subtle palette of emotions to draw on, and to be less direct in leaping from input to output. A stimulus that might previously have incited rage might now simply be seen as irksome, tricky or a trigger for empathy.

Sadly, my instinct tells me that a childhood spent in front of screens, which tend to trade in and stimulate the classical model of emotion, will have the opposite effect. Losing at a video game will lead to a "rage quit", rejection will lead to revenge, fear will lead to hate speech. This tightening loop between cause and effect will not only colour the way we construct reality, it will also further codify and constrain our emotional responses to that reality. Much of my teaching and parenting experience points to these psychological shifts being well underway, with the children I encounter relying evermore reflexively on the stock responses transmitted to them via their phones. My favourite current example of this is the deliberately ironic and low-key use of "meh", and more recently "bruh", in response to anything that is difficult, annoying, confronting or surprising. Rather than technology leading to an expansion of expression, it seems in this way to be leading to a narrowing.

Narrowing

Worryingly, I sense that in many ways humans welcome this narrowing of experience. Contemporary life presents us with a fundamental paradox: on the one hand our ideological beliefs tell us that we have agency and freedom, that we can become anything our hearts desire. On the other hand, the lives that we live are so unbearably complex, so very technologically constrained and so vastly unequal, that reality tells us the opposite. We are presented with a constant stream of perfect lives, of those who have achieved, who are wonderfully glossy, and what we see in the mirror simply cannot compete. We are told that we possess unlimited power, but in reality we know that we are merely tiny cogs in an impossibly large machine. This grinding tension, this daily dose of cognitive dissonance, is more than most of us can bear, even if we know that it is an illusion.

And so it is that the simplicity and predictability of smartphones offer us succour in a complex and troubling world. They allow us to revel in an illusory sense of choice, safe in the knowledge that, because we can only ever choose from a limited menu, the choice is never overwhelming. If I can download the right selection of apps, apply the right filters, deploy the right hashtags, then I can be the director of my own life, and it can have genuine meaning. Likewise, if I learn the rules of a video game, challenge myself to excel in it and vanquish my foes, then I can have a real sense of agency and control.

Of course, the choice, whatever form it takes, is an illusion, crafted to manipulate us for the financial gain of others. Behind the scenes it is programmers, and the algorithms and data sets that they craft, that drive our actions. Their choices are in turn dictated by the emerging parameters of the attention economy, and the whims of the billionaire nerds who ride recklessly astride it.

However, if we can push these thoughts below the surface, then perhaps we can use smartphones as a survival aid in an inhospitable world. The unpalatable alternative seems to question the status quo, and see with terrible clarity the cultural quagmire in which we have found ourselves. Such an insight would put us at odds with everyone we know and everything we think, leading us to read books such as this. And who would want that?!

If, as Marx suggests, religion is the opiate of the masses[94], then perhaps smartphones are the more infantile equivalent: the dummy[95]. Faced with an unbearable world, the few adults in charge are at least kind enough to let us suckle on the false teat of the digital breast. Thus pacified, we are calmed into thinking that we can construct and broadcast a unique and meaningful identity, when in fact we are simply being cast in the image of a limited selection of prefabricated moulds. The alternative is to live in the analogue world, with its abundance of frustrations and failings, with decay and death, with love and loss. And this, it turns out, is no easy feat. In the place of Marx's tranquiliser, what we are offered by digital technology is in fact infantilisation.

Self-Esteem

At the heart of all the energy we pour into our lives is a search for meaning in a brutal, arbitrary and uncaring world. The only thing we can take for granted in life is our own

---

[94] A Contribution to the Critique of Hegel's Philosophy of Right, Karl Marx (https://bit.ly/3FfQHra)

[95] pacifier

death, and in the face of this we feel the need for our lives to have counted for something. Ernest Becker, the American cultural anthropologist who we met earlier, suggests that, within this struggle, it is our self-esteem that is key. For many of us "self-esteem" will seem passé, and closely associated with the "everyone's a winner" mentality in which we are protected from losing at all costs. However, writing in the 1960s, Becker's take on self-esteem[96] is considerably more impactful:

> "Self-esteem becomes the child's feeling of self-warmth that all's right in his action world. It is an inner self-righteousness that arms the individual against anxiety."

Initially self-esteem is derived from parents and caregivers, whose love and attention enables the child to feel a physical "warmth". Over time positive, nurturing input becomes less of a given, requiring the child to cultivate certain behaviours, whilst avoiding others, in order to earn parental approval. Gradually we become subsumed by familial and societal norms, with symbolic language and thought gaining primacy over the use of our bodies. Ultimately, especially as we move through adolescence, it tends to be those outside the family to whom we look for our self-esteem. This may take the form of culture (especially subculture) more generally, or friends and colleagues more specifically. Were we to be strong enough we might not need this external validation...but few of us ever achieve such independence.

Whatever the source, what we each need is a sense that we are of value, that we matter, that we are the hero of our own

---

[96] The Birth and Death of Meaning, Ernest Becker, Free Press (https://bit.ly/3h7vk18)

unique story. And so, we carefully gather our self-esteem, telling ourselves artfully curated tales about our lives. We work hard to do the "right" things, those that lend appropriate meaning within our own context. In a fluid and complex world this proves perpetually tricky, and so it occupies much of our mental energy.

Whether we do indeed have meaning is often arbitrated in the social arena, where our worth is reflected back to us in the words and actions of others. And so it is that engaging with others is fraught with challenge. We carefully scrape together our scant supply of self-esteem, and then allow others to assay it, knowing that there exists, at every moment, the chance of having it all torn apart. The social world, whilst entirely necessary, is also rather frightening. The contemporary philosopher Alain de Botton refers to our fragility in this arena as "status anxiety", the perpetual worry that others believe us to be failures, to be not good enough[97].

What we find on the Internet, when seen through this lens, is the largest challenge to self-esteem that humans have ever constructed. Here we are offered a vast array of platforms on which to produce and share some version of ourselves. Each has its own conventions, and as Marshall McLuhan rightly put it[98], the medium is the message: each platform brings to the fore a particular set of ideologies, styles and customs. Ergo, much of Instagram feels Instagramy, and most YouTubers repeat the mantra "Don't forget to like and subscribe. Leave a comment". We strive to fit in by emulating the allowed conventions, whilst differentiating

---

[97] Status Anxiety, Alan de Botton, Vintage (https://bit.ly/3gXC6Gw)

[98] Understanding Media: The Extensions of Man, Marshall McLuhan, The MIT Press (https://bit.ly/3U4A0mS)

ourselves in ways we hope to be socially "right".

In the end, little of it matters, as each platform is populated by a massively diverse range of people, all of whom are operating under the Internet's disinhibiting anonymity. We enter the fray in an arena with a significant number of trolls, scammers, misogynists, sextortionists and other assorted bad actors. We come to inhabit a space devoid of normal ethics, in which it is okay to be mean, in which we rarely get to see the negative consequences of our actions.

Behind every tragic tale of Internet-cruelty-leads-to-suicide, from Amanda Todd[99] to the thousands you've never heard of, lies a tsunami of devastated self-esteem that has swept us all in its wake. In doing so, it has solidified a culture in which being cruel is normal. Into this hellscape we cast our children, with devices we purchase, and connectivity we procure. That rates of adolescent depression and anxiety are rising, should, in this context, not come as a surprise.

Unlike the playground bullies of yesteryear, the victim now has no escape, not even within their own home. For most, cutting all ties to social media is not an option as it would be akin to social suicide. Our children thus put up with constant emotional pain in order to avoid losing what little status and connection they have. Their tormentors travel with them always and are completely inescapable. Is it a surprise that suicide offers an escape route that growing numbers are desperate enough to take?

---

[99] The Story of Amanda Todd, Michelle Dean, The New Yorker (https://bit.ly/3h4OKUg)

Friendship

Sadly, in my experience, no part of our lives is immune from the influence of digital technology, and indeed we see that this culture of cruelty has profound impacts on childhood friendship. In school I see the many ways in which young friendships, already a volatile domain, are threatened by digital connectivity. As a teacher whose role involves directing a school's use of digital technology, I've seen a dramatic increase in the number of disputes arising from social media.

In a typical case, two or more students will have engaged in some act of unkindness towards each other online. Without an adult to calm the mood, nor the inhibitory forces of face-to-face interaction, a small slight turns into something bigger. Ugly words are typed, disinhibited responses follow. Screenshots are taken and shared, rumours begin to fly, sides are taken and battle fronts form. By the time the incident comes to light in school, it has been blown out of all proportion. These kinds of out-of-school blow ups, which were once anomalous, now account for at least 40% of the behavioural and pastoral issues that I deal with at school.

Such phenomena have come to add increasing complexity to the already challenging task of working with and parenting young people. If we are honest, they simply reflect the norms set by many of the adults who engage in online dialogue.

My own children, much to their chagrin, live in a home whose norms and rules reflect the lessons learned through my own experiences. At times this is the cause of friction, as they can't get what they want, but in general we started down this road early enough that they mostly understand and follow the lead we provide. In order to balance out these rules, we offer our children a very healthy dose of physical independence and freedom to roam, which complements the screen time that they do receive. We realised when they were quite young that 45-minutes of moderated device time allowed them some quiet relaxation, but that any more would lead to rapid mood changes, outbursts and refusal to relinquish the device.

There are no guidebooks for travelling in such terrain: given the only-very-recent emergence of mobile devices there has scarcely been time to assemble a picture of good practice, let alone publish it. It is easy for parents to blame themselves, but in reality it is structural forces beyond our control to which fingers should be pointed. As parents and educators, we simply need to respond as best we can.

Aggression

Studies of rats confirm what many of us already intuit about aggression, which is that it is a reaction to fear, stress and anxiety. At a biological level, it has been confirmed that acting out aggressively towards others is a reliable way to relieve our own tension. Given this, it should not be surprising that in an environment that robs us of self-esteem, our only guard against anxiety, we see a spike in aggressive behaviour. The irony, of course, is that this is a vicious cycle, in which one person's aggression becomes another's fear, which becomes aggression, which becomes yet another's fear. As noted by Robert M Sapolsky[100]:

> "pain does not cause aggression: it amplifies preexisting tendencies towards aggression. In other words pain makes aggressive people more

---

[100] Behave, Robert M Sapolsky, Vintage (https://bit.ly/3Upnkab)

aggressive."

In a world that has always struggled with aggression, the last thing we need is a global machine for weakening self-esteem and amplifying aggression. Taking a look at the kinds of comments people leave for each other on the Internet suggests that this is exactly what we have created[101]:

> "Trayvon's mum is a crack ho"

> "i don't remember giving you permission to speak lowlife nigger. no tender pieces of fried chicken for you nigger. bad nigger. bad nigger"

> "I hate women like this... You know, the kinds of women, you know, the ones that are alive and breathing, and speaking"

> "We hate you. I wish you die. Fuck you bitch. Fuck you."

Godwin's Law[102], which states that the odds of someone being compared to a Nazi approach one the longer an Internet thread continues, recognises this central tendency of disinhibited online speech to spiral towards unkindness. Even the most mild-mannered divergence of opinion online can rapidly lead to hateful responses. We know this, and yet we keep coming back for more. Even more strangely, we invite our children into this very same space, and then seem surprised when they imitate its mannerisms.

---

[101] Comments drawn from a variety of Google Images searches

[102] Godwin's law, Oxford Reference (https://bit.ly/3Wpn1xL)

FOMO

Often our persistence in using screens is closely linked to the fear of missing out (FOMO): we put up with the bad because we are sure that everyone else is having a great time, and we don't want to be left behind. It's the equivalent of staying at a terrible party because it is preferable to being alone, only much, much more powerful. The conventions of many platforms, which focus on creating narratives around living endlessly happy, shiny and glamorous lives, actively promote such feelings.

I've recently been conversing with a very sociable, kind and thoughtful teenager, who attributes some of her own struggles with anxiety to mobile phone ownership. She explains herself as follows:

> "From buying myself my first smartphone at the age of 11, to having bought my 4th phone at the age of 16, I have always been consciously aware of my phone usage. On all my phones I have had a screentime monitor. Like most people nowadays, I carry my phone around with me the majority of the time. I try my best to leave it for longer periods of time without thinking of it. If I turn my phone on for a second to check something, I always end up checking social media or something else then find that I have wasted a lot of time."

Whilst she values the connectivity her phone brings, she struggles to find a balance in using it. There is always something new and enticing there to draw her in, to take her away from other activities. Were she to not check her phone she would miss out on these things, and thus risk disconnection from her peers, both in terms of experiences they share directly, but also through the shared cultural understanding that comes from media consumption. In response to these feelings, she has recently deleted social media from her phone, in the hope that it will improve her mental health. This is something she's tried before, before relapsing into old habits, but for now, it is working out. This is a story that I believe many of us can relate to.

When, as part of my job, I suggest to parents that they do not give their child a smartphone until age thirteen at the very youngest, I hear a lot of positive responses. Yes! the parents say, that is great advice, we could not agree more. A few years ago, in having such conversations, I would walk away convinced that we were on our way to raising children without phones. Imagine my surprise, when, months down the line, the children of those same parents all seemed to own phones. Given the disconnect between what was said and what was done, I could not help but ask those parents what had changed. The answer, in one way or another, always comes back to FOMO. Most commonly this plays out as children convincing their parents that they are horribly disadvantaged without a phone. There is no way, they claim, that they can get on with other children without a device. Who would want their child to be a pariah?

In response to this I've tried to argue along the lines used in this chapter, but no matter what stories, theories and statistics I bring to bear, they never seem quite as powerful as FOMO.

Some months ago I was approached by a parent who was concerned that her daughter, aged eight, was being exposed to sexual language online. I asked on what device this was happening, and she said "on my daughter's phone". When I suggested that her daughter was too young to be using such technology, she agreed, saying "yes, absolutely, but all of her friends have a phone, and she insists on having one too". She claimed to monitor all communications, and to be on top of the situation, yet her daughter was still encountering things she did not want her to. When I asked the source of the unwanted language she said "boys in her class". What struck me is how unwilling she was to undertake the most obvious course of action: the removal of the phone. She left our conversation with this option clearly off the table, intent instead on finding a technical solution.

FOMO. Don't underestimate its power.

Key Statistics

There are lies, damn lies and statistics...or so the old saying goes. As one might expect in an area of life that is so important, so economically valuable and so fast changing, there is lively debate over a variety of studies into smartphone use and wellbeing in children and teenagers. These debates hinge around the fact that certain key indicators have been on the move since around 2010, when smartphones started to really penetrate our lives.

For example, during this time, the CDC has reported a significant rise in suicide among US youth, as shown in the graph below:

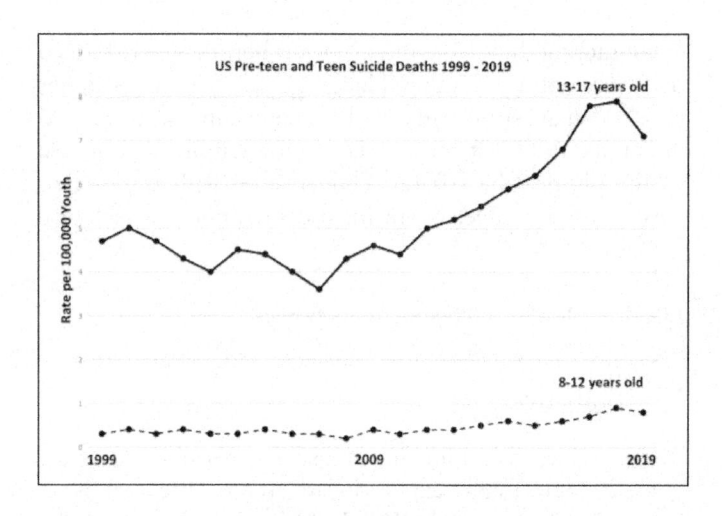

Image 5.1 - US Pre-teen and Teen Suicide Deaths, 1999-2019 (Kaiser Permanente Research)

These changes are mirrored the world over, as documented in excruciating detail by Jon Haidt and Zach Rausch[103].

Whilst there are claims of a cause and effect relationship, it is important to note that such statistics show correlation, rather than causation: the numbers go together, but in a complex world it is hard to say what causes what. In addition, some analysts[104] are keen to show that these changes are offset by other indicators, including decreases in teenage pregnancy, alcohol and drug use and homicide.

Interestingly, I initially encountered these latter trends in a

---

[103] The Teen Mental Illness Epidemic is International (Parts 1 and 2), Zach Rausch

and Jon Haidt (https://bit.ly/46oWAND, https://bit.ly/443deAW)

[104] The Scientific Debate Over Teens, Screens And Mental Health, Anya Kamenetz, NPR (https://n.pr/3gDRhES)

positive analysis suggesting that teenagers were better behaved today than in the past. They are, it is claimed, less likely to engage in the kinds of risky behaviour long associated with adolescence. It was in reading a counter-analysis that I came to see that these changes are not occuring because of improvements in teenage behaviour, but rather are a symptom of adolescent isolation. Where youth used to gather, and engage in some kinds of behaviours, they are now more likely to be spending time alone, due to the kinds of technological and cultural changes described in earlier chapters. Thus isolated, they are less likely to have unsafe sex, do drugs or kill each other. However, out of loneliness and a sense that everyone else is having so much fun, they are more likely to engage in self harm, develop eating disorders and to take their own lives. Screens are not solely to blame for such a shift, but they certainly seem to be playing a role.

Worryingly, many children now seem to be using the Internet to mentor themselves in how to deal with strong negative emotions. For example, online we can easily find supportive, instructional communities based around forms of self-harm such as cutting and proana[105], in which it is all too easy for isolated, lonely young users to find solace. In my work I've encountered parents who have been caught entirely off guard by their child's ability to hide the evidence of self-harm from them. When the self-harm has eventually come to light, the parents learn that not only was the idea of self-harm learned online, but so were the particular strategies for hiding it from them.

As always where numbers are concerned, we find a range of

---

[105] Pro-anorexia: the delusion that anorexia is a good thing, as it helps you become slim and attractive

stories, explanations and agendas. What is probably most telling in this arena is what technology companies' own studies say. Just like the 20th century tobacco industry, they seem to know that their products are not good for us. However, admitting to this would be rather bad for business. As a case in point, it has been claimed[106] that Facebook knows that its Instagram product has negative impacts on the self-image and wellbeing of teenage girls, but has failed to act on this information. According to Facebook whistleblower Frances Haugen[107], Instagram "led children from very innocuous topics like healthy recipes…all the way to anorexia-promoting content over a very short period of time".

Evidence seems to be mounting that the impacts that so many of us feel in our own daily lives are in fact widespread and deeply engrained. The children we see suffering are not outliers, they are the mainstream, and their experiences are a direct result of the ways in which digital technology has been designed and monetised.

Being human has never been easy, and being an adolescent is particularly fraught. Despite the challenges that this phase brings, it has also traditionally been a time of heightened pleasure, of energy, of growth. However, it seems to me that much of the exploratory mystery of adolescence, the sense of discovering the unknown within an unfolding and limitless world, is gradually being eroded. Excitement, adventure and the opportunity to come of age are giving way to simulation, fear and loneliness. How we expect

---

[106] Facebook has known for a year and a half that Instagram is bad for teens despite claiming otherwise, Christia Spears Brown, The Conversation (https://bit.ly/3DtKfeB)

[107] Facebook harms children and is damaging democracy, claims whistleblower, Dan Milmo and Kari Paul, The Guardian (https://bit.ly/3f0ui6i)

young people to grow into whole, sane adults in this landscape is beyond me.

On Covid

In closing this chapter it is worth reflecting on our experience of screens during the Covid-19 pandemic. At the time of writing, a combination of the Omicron variant and widespread vaccinations have helped many countries return to something approaching pre-Covid life. Whilst a very small number of jurisdictions are pursuing a "zero Covid" strategy, much of the world is learning to live with the disease, which more and more seems to be like the flu.

In Hong Kong we have seen the application of a fortress-like approach to keeping Covid at bay: given the city's incredible population density this initially seemed like a reasonable strategy, and indeed, it kept us safe during the first year. However, the strategy has not been adapted to reflect the changing nature of the disease, nor our growing ability to mitigate its effects. This ongoing vigilance has led to a total of 197 days of campus closures at my own school, spanning five separate instances.

During these closures learning was conducted online via Zoom. Other Hong Kong schools, notably in the local sector, have seen even deeper impacts to their schedules. At roughly 37 school weeks of campus closure, however, Hong Kong has had it easy compared to Uganda (60 weeks), Hondurus (58 weeks), Panama (55 weeks) and a number of other countries[108].

---

[108] The Longest School Closures of the Pandemic, Katharina Buchholz, Statista (https://bit.ly/3sY6G5L)

Being a relatively prosperous and high-tech city, Hong Kong has been able to provide a high degree of online schooling during these closures. On the one hand this may appear as a blessing, as learning can continue in some form. However, in reality, what has been observed is a significant drop in student wellbeing due to the massive increase in screen time, coupled with the development of a host of distracting screen habits. Wellbeing is primarily impacted by students sitting still and staring at a screen for much of the school day: time spent exercising and in nature is decreased, in-person social time is almost non-existent, eyesight suffers[109] and ultimately, mental distress becomes more frequent. Hong Kong has seen an alarming rise in adolescent suicide during this time[110].

In terms of screen usage, teachers have observed a rising number of students who are distracted during online classes: a telltale sign is students staring at a second monitor, and thus looking to the side of, or well below, their webcam. And who can blame them, when the alternative is a repetitive carousel of listening to teachers and completing work in isolation. Many well meaning teachers have worked hard to create interesting and stimulating lessons, but there are limits to what can be done. Attempts to get students away from screens can easily backfire, with students using time freed up from class to stare at screens. The most popular culprits? Games, YouTube, memes and social media.

---

[109] CUHK Study Demonstrates a 2.5-fold Increase in Myopia Incidence in Children During COVID-19 Pandemic Due to Less Time Outdoors and More Time on Screens, Chinese University of Hong Kong (https://bit.ly/3z8CCaY)

[110] Alarming rise in Hong Kong young people struggling with mental health issues amid Covid-19 pandemic, experts warn, Laura Westbrook, South China Morning Post (https://bit.ly/3N0nORz)

We know much of this because each return to school has led to a spike in IT misuse in the classroom, allowing us to observe the new-found habits of students as they struggle to prise themselves away from distracting apps and platforms. With each closure and subsequent resumption, the habits seem to be more deeply entrenched and harder to shift. My feeling is that these new patterns are now so deeply ingrained that they will have altered the long-term usage patterns of these children.

This localised trend is placed into global perspective by the acclaimed writer and activist Naomi Klein, who notes that "We were on a gradual slide into a world in which every one of our relationships was mediated by platforms and screens, and because of Covid, that gradual process went into hyperspeed"[111]. Seemingly a golden opportunity for tech giants, Klein detects a silver lining to this rapid shift: rather than gradually acclimatising, we abruptly found ourselves in a new space that was very uncomfortable. For some this brought a sense of clarity in seeing that they did not want to live in a world so deeply mediated by digital technology. Sadly, my students don't seem to be among them: despite the very many negative effects of their newly screen-saturated lives, it is still a struggle to get them off screens.

Covid has also been used to enable a creeping and potentially insidious rise in government surveillance. In Hong Kong, all residents over the age of eleven have, at times, been required by law to use a smartphone app to check into restaurants, sports centres, libraries and museums. Whilst initially this was used to facilitate contact tracing, it was subsequently expanded to include a vaccine

---

[111] Quoted in Lost Connections, Johann Hari, Bloomsbury (https://www.librarything.com/work/book/150094606)

pass. There is no paper-based alternative, and the penalties for evasion are steep. The result is that children, adults and the elderly have all been required to carry smartphones in order to conduct basic life functions, and we have all become habituated to telling the government where we are and what we are doing.

Some people argue that they have nothing to hide, and so need not fear such a broad system of surveillance. However, I would contend that it represents another major step in the erosion of our privacy, which is already under near-fatal assault from surveillance capitalism[112]. Privacy is important, because it allows us to live our lives without looking over our shoulders, without questioning our every move, without being manipulated by others. In this, the experience of Singaporeans is informative: having been told that their government's contact tracing app would respect their privacy, they later learned that it was being mined by the police[113]. Even if you have "nothing to hide", the prospect of government agents sifting through your location data should alarm you, if for no other reason than the potential damage that can be done by false positives.

In many ways Covid has given us a view into our collective future, in which, should we fail to take action now, screens come to dominate our existence to a degree that makes today's collective addiction seem quaint.

---

[112] See Chapter 12 for more on this

[113] Singapore reveals Covid privacy data available to police, Andreas Illmer, BBC News (https://bbc.in/3NtJfe0)

CHAPTER 6
MEMELAND

My work as a teacher has exposed me to the surprisingly high rate at which online culture renews itself. Although this culture is not entirely produced by the young, there seems to be sufficient overlap to meaningfully define it as "youth culture". A number of years ago I made an effort to immerse myself in this space through the use of 9gag, a content sharing platform. For a heady 6 months I was able to understand the subtext of a far greater proportion of student conversation. Eventually, having had enough fun, I removed the app from my phone, and almost immediately fell out of touch. The pace at which the scene moved on caught me entirely by surprise. Things that were fresh and new yesterday were today going extinct.

What this experience exposed me to is something that I've come to think of as "Memeland", a parallel reality that our children inhabit and of which most adults are relatively unaware. Of course, we all see memes, but they don't form the backbone of our culture or identity.

This is not the case for many of the students I work with, for whom laughing at the discomfort of others via doctored images shared without consent is a cultural norm. Even as a teacher I sometimes forget that Memeland exists, as it is often only evident when I am exposed to how and what my students communicate in their personal time.

Of course, youth subculture is always partly hidden from adult view, and this is part of a normal, healthy adolescence. Such scenes represent all of the exciting romanticism that Egan tells us to expect from the young[114]. What seems to have changed is that the Internet lacks our traditional media regulation checks and balances, and that it all starts far younger. My engagement in various subcultures really started at age fourteen: today it is common to see eight-year-olds immersed in Memeland. In my experience all of this positions children more consistently towards Berne's negative free child, long before they have the cognitive capacity and skills to critically deconstruct what they are encountering.

However, to understand all of this, we really need to know what memes are.

Memes

In the 1970s, Richard Dawkins[115] coined the term "meme" to denote the basic unit of cultural transmission. The word itself plays on "gene" as the basic unit of biological transmission. Through this word Dawkins invites us to consider the way that culture is created, resides within us, and is then passed from person to person. Successful memes spread rapidly, colonising cultural space and offering us a pool of common currency and experience. Unsuccessful memes, lacking hosts to transmit and energise

---

[114] See Chapter 3

[115] The Selfish Gene, Richard Dawkins, Oxford Landmark Science (https://www.librarything.com/work/23538)

them, wither and die. Like genes, memes mutate and adapt as they spread.

When I run into my former colleague Sean Moran and he greets me with "Yo dawg, whatsup?!" he is transmitting an existing meme. My response to receiving any meme will depend on my familiarity with that meme, my relationship with its sender, and the context we are in. In this case I will always smile and say "Whatsup?!". Another recipient of the same meme may respond entirely differently, depending on their personality and prior experiences.

In the distant past we encountered memes only from the people around us, and so the level of creativity within our culture was relatively limited. The rate of cultural refresh, or churn, was similarly constrained. The development of mass communication, from the printing press to the radio, to TV, increased the scale of our networks, exposing us to new memes on a far more regular basis. This could be argued to have led to a considerable increase in our collective cultural creativity, and explains why the advent of cheap books in 15th century Europe is seen by historians as such a significant milestone, leading to scientific and industrial revolution as it did.

The Internet has undeniably ratcheted up the level of memetic activity within our societies, and I would suggest that it represents exponential rather than linear growth. For a long time I subscribed to the techno-utopian view that this was undoubtedly a good thing, that the forces inherent in any market would sort the wheat from the informational chaff, and that we would come to inhabit a world of meaningful self-expression. Today, as I witness the memetic churn in which we live, my views are the polar opposite. What floats to the top is the dross, the dreck, the worst.

On the Internet, "meme" has come to mean a very narrow

subset of what Dawkins originally intended. Specifically, it refers to an image captioned with text, generally white with a black border, presented in Impact font. Based on my own experience, I'd advise against trying to convince 11-year-olds that the word meme has any other meaning than this. It generally results in confusion, and the untimely and unfortunate assumption that you are too old to "get it". At this point, all is lost.

At any rate, the "Internet memes" described above seem to serve as a concentrated form of our regular culture. They are memes on steroids, a whole language of their own. Websites have been dedicated to their study[116] [117], and no doubt universities will soon be offering degree-bearing courses in memeology. They are, to use the language of the Internet, most certainly "a thing"[118], and a powerful thing at that.

Most of the content I encountered on 9gag was presented in the form of Internet memes, which have the benefit of conveying a lot of information in a package that is easy to consume and share. These memes share a lot of conventions, and so are easily understood by those in the know. Were you to take a quick survey of memes you'd find a very small number that are clever, funny and insightful:

---

[116] Memebase (https://memebase.cheezburger.com)

[117] Know Your Meme (https://knowyourmeme.com)

[118] To call something "a thing" is itself an Internet-driven meme

Image 6.1 - I Don't Think That Memes (origin unknown)

And many, many more that are cruel, divisive and overtly xenophobic:

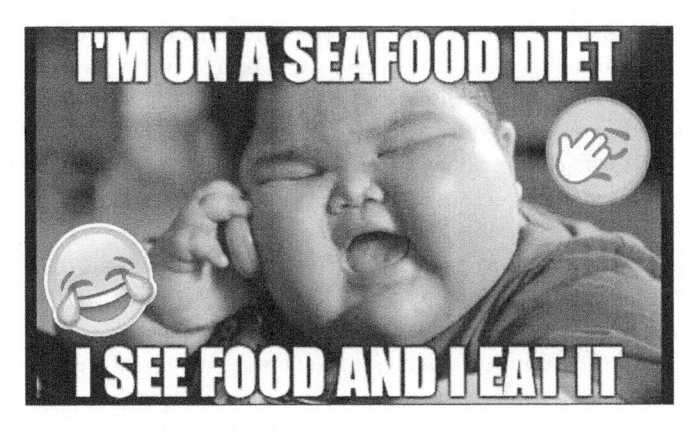

Image 6.2 - I'm on a Seafood Diet Meme (origin unknown)

Recently, for example, I've noticed the rise of a new meme known as "emotional damage", of which pre-teens seem particularly fond. It takes the form of a short, looping video in which YouTuber/comedian Steven He throws a shoe and says, in a strong accent, "emotional damage"[119]. The screenshot below captures it fairly well:

Image 6.3 - Emotional Damage Meme (origin unknown)

The meme exists in multiple remixed forms on a range of platforms, including YouTube and TikTok: on the former it has tens of millions of views. It is clearly influential, and for the moment at least, I can't escape it at school. At home my own children have been clearly told that it is neither funny nor clever, and so I have some respite. By the time this book is published, this meme may well have been forgotten, only to make a "retro" comeback down the line.

Conversing with children about this meme says a lot about how they think of memes in general. Having spotted an eleven-year-old student with the meme looping in their browser's background, I asked them if they thought it was

---

[119] Emotional Damage, Know Your Meme
(https://knowyourmeme.com/memes/emotional-damage)

appropriate for school. In response I was told that it is okay because "no one in my class has emotional damage, and anyway, all memes are funny, so there is nothing to be offended by". My carefully reasoned argument about the hidden nature of mental illness, of racial stereotypes and of the importance of being kind were waved off with the roll of an eye.

Esteemed Others

One reason why Memeland is so significant is that some of the most effective learning comes from observing and imitating esteemed others[120]. And on the Internet, for our young, it often feels like memes have taken the place of tribal elders, parents and teachers as the source of useful knowledge and behavioural cues. The tedious and repetitive work of explaining to children why any given meme is based in out-moded, offensive and xenophobic thinking rarely delivers results: you just end up, as in the story above, seeming out-of-touch.

Bo Burnham's tongue-in-cheek song, Welcome to the Internet[121], gets straight to the heart of this problem:

> "Welcome to the internet
> Put your cares aside
> Here's a tip for straining pasta
> Here's a nine-year-old who died
> We got movies, and doctors, and fantasy sports
> And a bunch of colored pencil drawings

---

[120] The Secret of Our Success, Joseph Henrich, Princeton University (https://www.librarything.com/work/book/174554247)

[121] Welcome to the Internet, Bo Burnham (https://www.youtube.com/watch?v=k1BneeJTDcU). Thanks to Wren Merrett for this gem.

> Of all the different characters in Harry Potter
> fucking each other
> Welcome to the internet"

And so, it often seems to me that today's children are fated to grow up awash in a sea of low grade, unfiltered and ever-changing culture. I find myself grateful to have grown up with a more fixed set of cultural signposts, even if they were themselves flawed in many ways. Yes, the media of my childhood was horrendously consumeristic and awfully Anglocentric, but at least I was not consigned to constantly chasing an unattainable target. I could get a handle on the world, critique it, and make decisions accordingly.

As a teacher I find myself working to fill a narrow and precipitous niche: pushing back against this cultural tide where I can, without crossing the line to curmudgeonly old timer. Staying knowledgeable and relevant, yet maintaining a sense of perspective. It is an exhausting battle, but at least my social capital is not at stake. My students and children are not so lucky.

More and more I feel that I am losing this battle: that my esteem within the world of children is being eroded, that I am being replaced by memes. It is disheartening and alarming in equal measure, and it starts so young. When I asked my daughter, who was ten at the time, about the emotional damage meme, she rolled her eyes and complained that all the boys in her class are constantly imitating it. If this is the cultural North Star by which our children navigate their world, then we are all in trouble.

Truth

Another impact of Memeland is its relationship to truth, through which we can perceive the vitally important role of information in our lives. Memes are a form of information, and, are in turn, also human technologies. However, where Internet memes are designed to mostly entertain, what we are considering here is a wider spectrum of information types.

Traditionally there has been a belief that it is not possible to have too much information. More information would always lead us to be better informed about the world around us, helping us become wiser and more enlightened. The market, we were promised, would ensure that the information we received would be of high quality, with its invisible hand punishing bad actors with reduced revenue and reputational harm.

It turns out that this view, to which I long subscribed, is rather naive, based as it is on the false axiom that the market cares about information quality. What we have come to learn is that the market actually cares about clicks and shares, not truth. Clicks because they generate advertising revenue, and shares because they increase clicks. To extend the genetic metaphor further, we could say that what we see with memes is a case of the "survival of the clickiest".

The key problem here is that negative and divisive information is far more potent than reliable and truthful information. Jaron Lanier notes[122] that "Negative emotions such as fear and anger well up more easily and dwell in us longer than positive ones". Or, as the old aphorism has it "A lie will go round the world while truth is pulling its boots on.", which, in a beautifully ironic twist, is commonly misattributed to Mark Twain[123]. Despite the established

---

[122] Ten Arguments for Deleting Your Social Media Accounts Right Now, Jaron Lanier, Henry Holt and Co. (https://bit.ly/3DTycrf)

[123] Quote Investigator (https://quoteinvestigator.com/2014/07/13/truth)

nature of this idea, the framers of the conventional narrative, and those of us who followed them, failed to foresee this vital wrinkle.

And so, in an economic paradigm that rewards sensationalism, the attention seekers have come to realise that they can deploy exaggerated and false information to drive negative emotions, converting them into clicks, shares and revenue. This applies on an individual level, where the loudest, most obnoxious and most shocking YouTuber becomes the most popular. Sadly, it is also just as applicable at the national level, where the loudest, most obnoxious and most shocking candidate becomes president (Trump, Bolsonaro, Duterte, etc).

Of course, this is nothing new, which is why shock jocks[124] like Howard Stern, and tabloid newspapers like The Sun, have long had a place in our culture. What limited these voices was a strong regulatory framework designed to curtail the power of the media. Under techno-utopianism such regulation is anathema, and it is exactly the promise of this unlimited individual freedom that drew so many of us to the Internet in the first place. With regulation being more generally passé within our dominant neo-liberal economic doctrine, it is not surprising to see the vital pillars of media regulation crumble. In their wake we are facing a crisis of confidence in the information that we have access to.

In reflecting on the early Internet it is clear that what many of us mistook to be a workable system that did not require adult supervision, was in fact a relatively small club in which everyone knew the rules. As Danny Hillis's TED Talk reminds us, in 1982 there were very few Internet users,

---

[124] Radio broadcasters who aim to shock and upset

many of them knew each other, and all of them were listed in a directory containing their names, and both their email and office addresses. Most of them were well versed in the generally-polite behaviours of academic discourse and commercial correspondence. As the Internet grew, the culture laid down by these early founders was enough to keep new users within certain bounds. The fact that most Internet access happened through universities and corporations meant that new users themselves came from a relatively well-educated slice of society. We stopped and marvelled at how well all of these strangers could get on without rules. Perhaps this really was the technology that could elevate us beyond the human condition!

However, before most of the Internet's earlier settlers realised what was happening, their ranks had swollen to the point where the old cultures, the old assumptions, were no longer viable. By then, steeped in the myth of being unregulatable, it was too late. The die was cast. As Lanier rather crudely puts it[125] "With nothing else to seek but attention, ordinary people tend to become assholes, because the biggest assholes get the most attention". A quick trip to the comments section of YouTube should be enough to convince any of us of the clarity of Lanier's observation. It is also a good reason to use a browser extension to block such comments from sight. Under our watch the Internet turned from a haven of self-restraint to a land of insult and denigration.

Living through the second half of the 2010s has provided us with an abject lesson in the dangers of building systems that give everyone a voice, whilst completely lacking the

---

[125] Ten Arguments for Deleting Your Social Media Accounts Right Now, Jaron Lanier, Henry Holt and Co. (https://bit.ly/3DTycrf)

ability to gauge, control and modulate quality. This is most starkly evident in politics, in which we've seen the rise of a fundamental conservatism that has delivered new leaders to power on the back of verifiably and demonstrably false claims. The consequences have been disastrous for civil society and global stability. Donald Trump led the pack with 30,573 false or misleading claims in 4 years[126], but the story runs much deeper. The slaughter of the Burmese Rohingya, our confused and misdirected response to Covid-19 and Britain's exit from the European Union have all been powered by low quality, misleading and deliberately false information, knowingly sown by those with their own agenda.

If this wasn't worrying enough, Pizzagate, QAnon and the storming of the US Capitol building on January 6th, 2021 are unmistakable signs that a lack of trustworthy information is tearing at the fabric of our societies[127]. In case you missed it, Pizzagate is a conspiracy theory whose many followers have been led to believe that pizza parlours in the United States are trafficking child sex slaves through their basements. This particular belief led one heavily armed assailant to storm the Washington, D.C. restaurant Comet Ping Pong, on a mission to forcefully free the captives from the Democrat politicians said to lead the ring. Naturally, he found no paedophiles, no ring leaders and no sex slaves. In fact, he failed to even find the basement, as the establishment did not have one. This would all be rather funny if it were not so deadly serious.

QAnon, one of the conspiracy cults that fueled Pizzagate,

---

[126] Trump's false or misleading claims total 30,573 over 4 years, Glenn Kessler, Salvador Rizzo and Meg Kelly, Washington Post (https://wapo.st/3stcDHA)

[127] From Pizzagate to the Capitol Riot, Matt Gertz, The Progressive Magazine (https://bit.ly/3U0uFgh)

does not deal in anything close to objective reality. However, its many followers seem not to have not noticed. Fed on filter bubbles, in which the only audible voices conform to existing beliefs, a growing tide of (mostly) white men have come to exist in a parallel, and largely fictional, reality.

To think that liberal democracy can exist under such conditions is wishful at best. This much was evident before QAnon followers attacked the US Capitol building, joined by their Proud Boy, Oath Keeper and Boogaloo Boy cousins. Since that event, the conclusion that the Internet is destructive has become inarguable.

It is important to note that this is not just an American or European phenomenon. The BBC recently reported[128] on the growth of hate speech amongst young Hindu males. Often the victims are Islamic women, but Hindu women with alternative political views are also targets. The common theme, and this should not surprise anyone who observes young men using the Internet, is a strong sense of misogyny. What is telling in this particular BBC article is that the problems for the antagonist started when he got his first smartphone:

> "Mr Jha was 14 when he got his first smartphone. He says the content he accessed then was his introduction to the right-wing world. 'On it, I saw memes, heard speeches of politicians who screamed that Hindus were in danger' he says."

In this context it is not surprising that China has worked so

---

[128] Trads vs Raytas: The young Indians spreading hate online, BBC News (https://bbc.in/3h8AQQS)

hard to regulate access to the Internet and to video games. Sadly, their approach is misrepresented in the West as being a simple case of authoritarian censorship, and so is easily dismissed as antithetical to Western-style democracy. Whilst I don't deny that Chinese controls go too far, they show that Internet content can be regulated, and as inflammatory as this claim may be to some, I believe that it must be if we are to curb its worst excesses.

Media Regulation

What is interesting, shocking really, is how quickly we have accepted the abandonment of media regulation. Prior to the rise of the Internet, Saturday morning for many children meant watching cartoons on TV. Whilst the programming might have been far from ideal, it at least existed within some reasonable bounds set by knowledgeable and thinking people. Even the advertisements were regulated. On the whole one could trust that children would not be subjected to anything too terrible. Compare this to the mind-bending range of content available to children on YouTube, and you might think you'd gone backwards in time, not forwards. In one example, illustrated by James Bridle[129], the quest for viewership has led to the rise of imitation Peppa Pig videos "which tend towards extreme violence and fear, with Peppa eating her father or drinking bleach". These videos have appeared high enough in YouTube's search results that they can easily be found by young viewers. Given the way that YouTube's video recommendation algorithms work, it is all too easy to imagine parents finding suitable content for their children, only to have them wind up watching such harmful derivatives.

---

[129] Something is wrong on the internet, James Bridle, Medium (https://bit.ly/2E9EuGV)

Platforms like YouTube are not required by law to be responsible for the content they distribute. This allows them to publicly disapprove of such content when it is highlighted, whilst simultaneously failing to take meaningful, systemic action. Such content will be suppressed on an individual basis when it is reported, but ultimately there is little incentive to prevent it. When action is taken, it is often through the application of fallible artificial intelligence. Such solutions generally move the problem elsewhere, as they don't tackle the fundamental issue of responsibility. It is easy to dismiss the kinds of cases described by Bridle as outliers, or minor problems to be solved, but I believe that they are in fact endemic.

The adverts that platforms tie to children's content can be even more disturbing. I recall a Saturday morning on which our children were enjoying some suitably curated content on YouTube. As I pottered around the house I kept an eye, and an ear, on what they were watching. Much to my surprise, in an intermission on a Paw Patrol video, they were exposed to a video game advert in which a man clubbed a woman over the head. As she staggered to her knees, he then shot her. My children were a little too young to get it, but I was left feeling surprised, angered and entirely unsure where to turn. It certainly challenged my own sense of well-informed vigilance: as an IT professional, I'd assumed I could handle things on the home front. Apparently I was wrong.

The intrusion of such content, which is chosen for us by inscrutable and opaque algorithms, poses a major problem. It puts us, collectively, in a situation in which we cannot control the information to which our children are exposed. Of course, to some degree such control has always been illusory. I recall, for example, finding a pornographic magazine as a young boy. However, as confusing and exciting as the nudity might have been, it was relatively mild, lacked violence and positioned women as people to love. Yes, it was objectifying, but it still seemed to inculcate love rather than hate. The kind of pornography a child might stumble upon today is far more likely to demean and humiliate women, to feature violence, and to assert male dominance. It is far more likely to include incest, harmful racial stereotypes and kinks to which children are best not exposed. It is designed to shock, in order to increase clicks and engagement, and so represents a cultural race to the bottom.

If you are not convinced by these arguments, search for "porn" on Google Images. Scanning down the page you'll find everything described above. Google offers no guidance, no sense of the intense pleasure and love that can accompany sex, no intimacy. Rather, it confronts us with larger-than-life penises, enhanced breasts, pained female countenances, domineering males, squirting bodily fluids and a lot of anal sex. Peek behind the scenes and you'll learn about anal bleaching, vagioplasty and the various other practices used to make porn stars' genitals look more attractive on camera. Several of the thumbnails will contain children, and all of the women will look like girls, except those styled as MILFs and grandmas. To consider, for just a moment, that this is how our children might be introduced to the wonders of sex is to stare into a cultural abyss. It is the equivalent of raising children solely on Hollywood movies, and then expecting them to grow into positive, whole, functional adults.

To me, pornography is particularly pertinent as it directly instructs young boys on how to treat women, whilst teaching young girls what to expect from men. When boys and girls watch pornography that includes men hitting and choking women, which is most definitely a big thing in contemporary porn, they learn that this is normal and okay.

Any nuance around kinks, consent, trust and love are lost, and violent sex goes from the fringe to the mainstream. We should not be surprised, under these circumstances, to find exactly the kind of rising hostility to women that we witness elsewhere on the Internet, and in real life. Sadly, current practices around sex education in school are not fit to tackle such challenges.

Asides from the violence inherent in modern pornography, there is another insidious lesson about what and who sex is for. In his incredibly brave TEDx talk "Why I stopped watching porn"[130], Ran Gavrili describes pornography as "no hands involved" sex. He reasons that because hands get in the way of the camera, obscuring the real action, we rarely see porn stars being sensual. This positions sex as a performative act, carried out for an audience, rather than for the pleasure of a partner. In being taught to think and act like a porn star, such content risks making us the audience of our own sex, turning an act of giving into one of taking. Such are the cues that our young will subconsciously take from Internet pornography. This is unfortunately reinforced by our broader culture of taking selfies, which falsely suggest that our value lies solely in being viewed positively by others.

To be clear, I am no prude. I love nudity, sex and physical affection: they are some of the most wonderful pleasures of being human. They are pleasures that we can give, and that we can receive. Our bodies are a gift, and we should enjoy them in all sorts of ways. Unfortunately, modern pornography is concerned primarily with male domination of the female body and soul, as a means to make money.

---

[130] Why I stopped watching porn, Ran Gavrieli, TEDx
(https://www.youtube.com/watch?v=gRJ_QfP2mhU)

This I have no interest in.

When I first encountered Neil Postman's claim[131] that "a family that does not or cannot control the information environment of its children is barely a family at all", I thought he had overstated things. However, as I peruse today's Internet, I think he was entirely accurate in his assessment, and far ahead of his time. This is in no way to make parents feel bad. Rather, it helps us to understand why it is that contemporary childhood and parenting are so hard: it's because we've totally lost control over our information environment. This points to the urgent need for a reassessment of the media regulation framework, or lack thereof, that the Internet operates within.

Despite the promises of the conventional narrative, the Internet has not saved us from human nature. Instead it has skewed, amplified and accelerated it. The good, the bad and the ugly still exist, it is just that the bad and ugly are far more prevalent, and can enter your home and mind at any time. The fact that companies can make a lot of money by enabling this is at the heart of the issue. Most worryingly, thanks to fake news and the many online scams we encounter, it is now harder than ever to distinguish between good and bad, right and wrong, true and false. Fear, in this context, abounds, explaining the rise of political polarisation, nationalism and fundamentalism.

---

[131] Technopoly, Neil Postman, Vintage
(https://www.librarything.com/work/46821/book/161568159)

It's Not Just Kids

Whilst this book is ostensibly about children, it will not escape the attention of the observant reader that each of the issues outlined thus far also relates to adults. Very few are the adults that can claim a healthy relationship with their screens: the technology is simply too compelling. When presenting to teachers and parents I often ask for a show of hands from those who feel that they control their device usage effectively. Very few raise their hands.

We feel it when we reflexively take out our phone whilst simultaneously realising that we did so without a specific goal in mind. This action, we realise, happened unconsciously, below the level of our awareness, and beyond our control. We feel it when we ignore our children at the expense of some trifling digital distraction. We feel it when the first thing we look at upon waking is a screen. We feel it in the anxiety that attends a lost phone. We feel it in every phantom notification. Most of the time, like any true addict, we refuse to admit that we have a problem. But we do.

Screens, and the software that run them, are, as promised by Andressen, eating everything. Including childhood and adulthood, our customs and our culture. This set of problems is one that impacts us all, and to whose solution we can all contribute. As we'll see in the following chapter, this problem is so all-encompassing that not even the physical world is immune.

CHAPTER 7
THE ENVIRONMENT

As a species, the range of technologies that we bring to bear has allowed us to bend the natural world to our will in many ways. We generate electricity, fell forests, move mountains, split atoms, clone animals, traverse the skies, plumb the ocean depths and launch vessels into orbit. Whilst we might have been smart enough to achieve dominance over much of the planet, we have certainly not been wise enough to carefully husband our only home. Dangerously, many of us seem to have equated harnessing nature to overcoming nature, forgetting that we cannot exist without the productive and protective bounty of the natural world. We forget that we ourselves are fragile systems, and that we also dwell within fragile systems.

It is hardly surprising that we live in times of environmental degradation so severe that our own survival is under threat. Climate change, resource depletion, air pollution, plastic waste, plummeting biodiversity, water shortages, deforestation, loss of topsoil and overflowing landfills are just some of the problems that we have created for ourselves.

Some choose to downplay these issues, others to suggest that better, newer technologies will fix the legacy created by our existing technologies. However, it seems to me that to live in the 2020s and deny the existential threat that humans pose to life on planet Earth is only possible if you are heavily invested in maintaining the status quo. Only by valuing life-as-we-know-it over life at all, can we bury our heads in the sand.

Writing in the 1970s, James Lovelock[132] posited that planet Earth behaves like, and can be conceived of as, an organism. Given the subsequent popularity of systems thinking in our lives, this no longer seems like a bold statement, but at the time it was revolutionary. How could a place as large and complex as the earth possibly resemble something as small and insignificant as an amoeba, a mouse or a human? If this thinking does not come naturally to you, then consider the example offered by the inverse gaseous needs of animals and plants. The former inhale oxygen and exhale carbon dioxide, whilst the latter require carbon dioxide and provide oxygen. These opposing needs exist, in general, in a harmonious balance that brings equilibrium to the whole.

In this metaphor, which is not without its critics, we can place humans in the nefarious role of parasites, dining on a host which they slowly disable. It might be a stretch to thus claim that the steady warming of our atmosphere is a fever, although ultimately it might serve the same purpose: ridding the host of its parasite.

Into this already unbalanced equation, in which humans take far more than we ought, we've introduced a new factor: power-hungry and rapidly obsoleted digital technology.

---

[132] Gaia, James Lovelock, Oxford University Press (https://bit.ly/3zFB2gV)

Although estimates vary, new research[133] suggests that the IT industry is responsible for between 2.1 and 3.9% of global greenhouse gas emissions. Whilst some argue that IT leads to efficiencies in other industries, it is hard to imagine those efficiencies offsetting the move towards having a device in every hand. As of 2021 we had collectively built an estimated 6.37 billion smartphones, a number that is expected to grow to 7.33 billion by 2025[134]. With the average smartphone lasting just over two years, Greenpeace expects average lifetime phone ownership to run to 29 devices per person[135]. Each of these devices contains a mix of exotic and rare minerals, as well as more common materials, each of which must be extracted, refined and shipped, prior to manufacturing and distribution. Each device will be charged every day, and, more significantly, will be constantly reliant on the colossal data centres that make up the ever-so-lovely sounding "cloud" (a stroke of marketing genius if ever there was one). Ultimately some of these devices will be responsibly recycled, but many will end up in landfills or shipped to developing nations for unregulated and highly dangerous processing[136].

The United Nations estimates that global e-waste production amounts to 50 million tons per year, of which only 20% is formally recycled [137].

---

[133] The real climate and transformative impact of ICT: A critique of estimates, trends, and regulations, Freitag et al, Patters, (https://bit.ly/3sVH3Te)

[134] How Many Smartphones Are In The World?, bankmycell.com (https://bit.ly/3DWKDm4)

[135] What 10 years of smartphone use means for the planet, Elizabeth Jardim, Greenpeace (https://bit.ly/3TARGpZ)

[136] Electronic waste is recycled in appalling conditions in India, Eco-Business (https://bit.ly/3SwKpGr)

[137] Time to seize opportunity, tackle challenge of e-waste, UN Environment Programme (https://bit.ly/3SyePbo)

Within the ideology of neo-liberal economics we refer to this process of waste generation as "growth" and "progress". Under this doctrine it makes no sense to extend the life of such devices, or to enshrine in law an individual's right to repair: instead, companies seek to design obsolescence into their products, whilst bringing consumers an endless stream of enticing innovations, all with the aim of shipping the maximum number of units per quarter.

More insidiously, the very lack of truth and trust described in Chapter 6 has made it impossible to build popular consensus around the reality of climate change. This, despite 97%[138] of all publishing climate scientists agreeing that climate change is not only real, but has its roots in contemporary human activity. Those most invested in the status quo, particularly the fossil fuel companies and their executives, have used their power to cast doubt where none should exist. And so, we are faced with a bizarre situation, in which screens contribute to climate change, yet result in it being almost impossible to tackle.

Of all the existential threats that face us today, the vast majority have been created by educated minds: technically adept individuals working on isolated problems at the expense of the whole. There is no grand design at work, and no evil geniuses pulling strings behind the scenes, yet the damage is no less real for being emergent.

Alarming proof of this can be found in the form of Thomas Midgley Jr., the Cornell-educated mechanical and chemical engineer responsible for not only adding lead to petrol, but also for using chlorofluorocarbons in refrigeration. Both of

---

[138] Scientific Consensus: Earth's Climate Is Warming, NASA (https://go.nasa.gov/3DFghDA)

these innovations were technically brilliant, and both turned out to be terrible for humans and the planet. The former caused wide-spread lead poisoning, the latter a hole in our planet's protective ozone layer. Likewise, I believe, is the case with the very many innovations that make up our beloved screens.

The roots of how we've come to live with such disregard for the environment that sustains us are deep and tangled, and much has been written on this topic. Whilst we won't pause long on this theme, it is worth a small detour. Consider the way these roots are characterised by Australian regenerative farmer Charles Massy[139]. In his writing, Massy offers us the distinction between the "organic mind" of ancient human tradition, and the "mechanical mind" generated by the enlightenment and resulting industrial revolution. In becoming more scientific, more rational and more reasoning, we have also become less attuned to nature, more extractive, and less spiritual. This shift has freed us in some ways, whilst enslaving us in what Massy describes as "a powerful and suicidally destructive belief system" in which we plunder our home planet merely to keep our economic engine purring, our shareholders happy. He goes on to quote Thomas Berry's The Dream of the Earth[140] to link these ideological foundations to the moment of crisis we currently face:

> "For peoples, generally, their story of the universe and the human role in the universe is their primary source of intelligibility and value…The deepest crises experienced by any society are those

---

[139] The Call of the Reed Warbler, Charles Massy, Chelsea Green Publishing (https://bit.ly/3T2OD98)

[140] The Dream of the Earth, Thomas Berry, Counterpoint (https://bit.ly/3DWJf2R)

moments of change when the current story becomes inadequate for meeting the survival demands of a present situation."

This seems to be the exact moment in which we find ourselves. We have crafted a fictitious story of ourselves as the rational masters of nature, the creators of wealth, the ultimate arbiters of truth and value. Almost all of our actions stem from the dominance of these beliefs. The tools that we have constructed in reaching this point, far from enshrining this position, have entirely undermined it. We've unsettled the earth's equilibrium, and our current story cannot undo that. Our very beliefs are now inimical to our survival. In this process, screens represent the next ratchet click of the great intellectual and industrial machine that divides people from nature.

Massy calls on us to actively develop what he calls the "emergent mind", that blend of the organic and the mechanical which will produce human flourishing in a sustainable manner. His hope, and it is one that I share, is that in producing this mind we can create new stories, that lead to new tools, which deflect us from our current trajectory.

Unfortunately for us, and the other organisms with which we share our home, our dominant economic paradigm promotes growth above all else, and this means that the environment will always play second fiddle to profit. That is, until we learn, or are forced, to make it otherwise.

CHAPTER 8
WON'T SCHOOL SAVE US?

Schools are funny places for many reasons, but to me, most notably for their singular obsession with cognitive development above all else. Of course it is easy to justify the intellectual development of our young, because we closely associate education with progress, and progress with the safety of our species. As H.G. Wells wrote[141], "Human history becomes more and more a race between education and catastrophe". This is a sentiment which educators will gladly back, given that it places us front and centre in the fight for human survival.

It is, also, at face value, rather hard to argue with. The logic that education drives progress is so deeply engrained that we rarely question it. However, we gain a rather different perspective when we stop and consider the fact that most of the extinction-level threats that we now face are, in fact, created by educated minds. Climate change, collapsing biodiversity, plastic in our food supply, nuclear war, terrorism, cyber warfare, financial collapse. None of these

---

[141] The outline of history: Being a plain history of life and mankind, H. G. Wells, George Newnes

were invented by under-educated minds.

In fact, it is distinctly over-educated minds that are at play here. As Gambeta & Hertog[142] have shown, a disproportionate number of Islamic jihadists have backgrounds that include university-level engineering. Likewise the Zyklon B that was used to kill six millions Jewish people during World War II was created by highly educated chemists rather than fortuitous alchemists.

The more I think about it, the more convinced I am that Wells was, in fact, 100% wrong. It is the pursuit of disembodied, dismembered, abstract and siloed technical knowledge that is the threat to our survival. A purely intellectual education is the problem, not the cure. What we need is to be more connected with our bodies, as a way to become more connected to the world around us, in order to live more sustainably on this planet.

Just because the world of commerce requires ever greater specialisation, does not mean that education should fold to its needs.

Just because we are technically smart, does not make us wise[143].

At the individual level, this disconnection from our bodies and our hands is also deeply unhealthy. As Matthew B. Crawford[144] has made agonisingly clear, schools have gutted their ability to teach traditional crafts in order to pursue an

---

[142] Engineers of Jihad, Gambeta and Hertog, Princeton University Press (https://bit.ly/3T00Fjt)

[143] A point that my Head of School, Toby Newton, has drilled into my thinking

[144] Shop Class as Soulcraft, Matthew B. Crawford, Penguin (https://bit.ly/3UjF2vB)

ever-narrowing curriculum that revolves around literacy and numeracy. The result is the loss of a time-honoured means of engaging children, and their bodies, in the physical world. One might argue that such skills are no longer needed, but as Crawford makes clear, it is how the experience impacts our way of being in the world that is key:

> "The satisfactions of manifesting oneself concretely in the world through manual competence have been known to make a man quiet and easy. They seem to relieve him of the felt need to offer chattering interpretations of himself to vindicate his worth. He can simply point: the building stands, the car now runs, the lights are on. Boasting is what a boy does, because he has no real effect in the world. But the tradesman must reckon with the infallible judgment of reality, where one's failures or shortcomings cannot be interpreted away. His well-founded pride is far from the gratuitous 'self-esteem' that educators would impart to students, as though by magic."

The furniture maker Peter Korn[145] puts his finger on the result of this shift when describing people he meets beyond the walls of the carpentry school he operates:

> "The banquet of work, leisure, and consumption that society prescribes has left some essential part of them undernourished. They are hungry for avenues of engagement that provide more wholesome sustenance."

---

[145] Why We Make Things and Why It Matters, Peter Korn, Godine (https://bit.ly/3JDjirL)

We produce ourselves, it seems, through the physicality of the things we make and fix. Whether it be woodwork, welding, sewing, cooking, or damming a river with stones, we have a need to act on the world with our hands. Doing so at a distance, through the application of advanced technologies such as computer programming, is all good and well, but simply does not have the same impact upon us.

None of this ought to surprise us, given our evolutionary background as tool makers and users. And yet, it is wisdom that our leaders in politics, commerce and education seem to have forgotten.

Should you happen to be a hard-nosed lover of only "relevant" contemporary skills, and thus unmoved by these lines of argument, perhaps the news[146] that overuse of our brains is leading to a loss of fine motor skills in surgical students might sway you. When next you come under the knife, I would imagine you'd opt for the most manually dexterous surgeon available. The solution proposed in this particular article, attributed to one Professor Kneebone, is "a more rounded education, including creative and artistic subjects, where they learn to use their hands". As Professor of Surgical Education at Imperial College London his seems to be a voice we can trust on this topic. In school we encounter many adolescents who cannot reliably tie their own shoes, operate a cable tie or colour neatly. Clearly something is amiss.

By way of a final piece of evidence on this point, consider

---

[146] Surgery students 'losing dexterity to stitch patients', Sean Coughlan, BBC News, (https://bbc.in/3NLkfiF)

the observation made by Scottish psychoanalyst R.D Laing[147], that a common underlying theme among schizophrenics is a disconnection from their own body. A sense of unreality, of dismemberment. One might well wonder at the connection between this adult state, and the ways in which childhood is arranged and then experienced. One would imagine that a greater level of embodiment within the world would serve us well.

My own children were lucky to spend their formative years at the Sai Kung International Preschool (SKIP)[148], which embodies so many of these themes in their approach to early childhood education. Indoor learning time is restricted to a little social singing, sharing and talking, with the majority of learning taking the form of semi-structured outdoor exploration. Digging in the mud kitchen, arts and crafts, scooting on the mini-road, bouncing on the trampoline, cooking, climbing, chasing, sliding and spotting bugs. Nature walks and excursions. All of this accomplished with a modest site and budget, thanks to the dedication of some very thoughtful and considered educators.

It is no wonder that my daughter was, on discovering that her primary school would only allow her to paint once a week, both dismayed and outraged.

Despite the challenges of finding open space in Hong Kong, and its very traditional educational scene, the educators at SKIP are not alone. Danie Strydom's wonderful Hong Kong Forest Adventures[149] offers another inspiring case study in how education might be organised in a sane society.

---

[147] The Divided Self, R. D. Laing, Penguin Books (https://bit.ly/3U0vwxv)

[148] Sai Kung International Pre-school (https://bit.ly/3DAYXzt)

[149] Hong Kong Forest Adventures (https://bit.ly/3T7avQt)

If only our governments would finance this kind of learning to make it universal, rather than leaving it to the market, where it is restricted to only those with the financial means.

Sadly, most children today are not so lucky: they receive exactly the kind of education that led us to this moment in history, rather than the kind of education required to save us from it. What we need is not more individuals skilled in very specific sub-domains. Instead, we need a generation who can see the big picture, who understand how our lives are dependent on nature, and who can steer for us a more thoughtful and sustainable path.

Values

Unfortunately, schools also play a large part in preparing us to live our lives as good, modern consumers, in part by consistently focusing our attention on the economic imperative of getting a "good" job, in order to participate fully in consumer society. Of course, having a job that pays the bills is important, but the meaning of "good job" as understood by schools is far more likely to be based on a career spent behind a desk than working more holistically.

Consumerism, the dominant religion of our times, assails us incessantly with the belief that purchasing the right combination of goods and services will enable us to live the life of our dreams. Whilst many of us instinctively know that this is simply not so, our children, raised on a steady diet of adverts, product placement, celebrity endorsement and YouTube surprise egg opening videos[150] are not so lucky.

If we are to grow to be healthy, balanced and thoughtful

---

[150] Search for "surprise egg openings", YouTube (https://bit.ly/3DwYuy8)

human beings, we have to see that there is more to life than simply earning and consuming. What we choose to value instead is open to debate, but it would be hard to go wrong with the age-old foci of honesty, hard work and being kind to others. Best of all would be for our adults and businesses to model these traits to our young, and for schools to then subtly reinforce them. Sadly, this is not how the system currently works.

In this arena there are plenty of sages to whom we might look. To choose but two, we could do far worse than Paul Tough and Erich Fromm. The former's work highlights the importance of developing values such as self-control, curiosity and perseverance during childhood. Tough's contention is that it is these traits which underlie success in life, much more so than cognitive ability. Meanwhile, Erich Fromm invites us to consider the difference between authoritarian and humanistic ethics. In the first case, we do the right thing because we fear the consequences. In the second case, it is because we value doing the right thing.

Another source of values, often overlooked in the West, is the Chinese tradition of filial loyalty, in which family duty is more important than individuality. Where the West has pioneered philosophies that place the individual at the centre of experience, Chinese belief is centred around the importance of family. This was illustrated to me recently in a conversation with a Chinese friend. I was complaining about the impossibility of entering the Hong Kong housing market, and having resigned myself to eternally renting from my in-laws. In response my friend remarked "but your parents-in-law own this house, and so you are already in the housing market". My Western "I" encompassed myself and my wife. Her Asian "I" extended to include a far wider circle.

Exactly what values we decide to teach, model and live is a

discussion for another forum: the key point here is that this is a discussion that needs to happen. Within families, within schools, within communities and through and across nations. One of the dangers inherent in post-modern intellectualism is that everything becomes relative, and so nothing can ever be said to be good or bad. I appreciate that the aim here is to avoid the kind of dogmatic moral certainty that infected previous times, and to replace it with a critical rationality. However, without some values to guide us, we are lost.

Connections

An illustration of the need for such values can be found in the disintegration of interpersonal connections in the face of rampant capitalism. Although it is not often discussed, one of the failings of contemporary capitalism is its tendency to replace vital social bonds with goods and services. Why take the time to cook a meal with family and friends when you can simply purchase it? Why ride the bus with others when you can drive yourself? Why look after your own children when you can outsource them to a nanny? In each of these situations we pay for convenience, but end up losing meaning.

The irony here is that the destruction that capitalism visits upon our lives ends up providing opportunities for capitalists to sell us new solutions to the very problems that they have created. This is neatly (and very sadly) encapsulated in the concept of selling hugs[151] to console those individuals who modern living has left bereft of human connection. Believe it or not, this is a real

---

[151] Service with a cuddle at little shop of hugs, Will Pavia, The Times (https://bit.ly/3TAS7AD)

phenomenon, a business opportunity that has already been exploited.

Without a firm values-based foundation, how can one make meaning in such a world? If our only lodestar is economic growth, how can we possibly find our way?

Another capitalist solution to the problem of lost connection is social media. One might reasonably expect such platforms to help us connect to others, but in reality we find that the bonds they generate are far weaker and less robust than those that we really need. In fact, evidence abounds[152][153][154] that social media has the opposite effect of deep social bonds, leaving us feeling alone, fearful of missing out and overly concerned with our own affairs. The systems we build reflect our values, and transmit them to future generations, and so we should view these trends with concern.

Risk & Boredom

Another area in which schools, and society more broadly, fail our children is in the balance and type of risk and boredom that they offer. In being immersed in the physical world we are constantly exposed to risks, each of which we must weigh before committing ourselves to action. In adulthood these risks are often social, but in childhood they can be more profoundly physical and existential. Should I wade across this stream? Should I climb this tree and jump

---

[152] How tech and social media are making us feel lonelier than ever, Leslie Katz, CNET (https://cnet.co/3Uk9aXB)

[153] Is Facebook Making Us Lonely?, Stephen Marche, The Atlantic (https://bit.ly/3ftuzyS)

[154] Does social media make you lonely?, Jeremy Nobel, Harvard Health Publishing (https://bit.ly/3Dy547E)

off that branch? Should I tease that child? Should I set this on fire? The outcomes of these decisions can have very real physical consequences. They are also the ways in which we measure ourselves against the world, finding our limits and understanding our place. Anyone who makes it to adulthood ought to have successfully navigated such risks repeatedly.

As if to compensate for all this excitement, childhood can also be a time of deep and sustained boredom. Not yet deemed worthy of agency and self-determination, children seem fated to spend time waiting for things to happen. We wait for our parents to play with us, we wait for dinner, we wait for friends, and we wait for the ringing of the school bell. We wait to be tall enough to see over the counter, and to be old enough to do adult things. Tiresome as this boredom may be, it serves a vital purpose, for boredom is the source of much introspection, reflection and creativity. Without boredom we'd never have to imagine, we'd never have to build. There would be no dens, no imaginary tea parties and no crazy dancing. Everything would happen when and how we wanted, and so nothing would have value.

Sadly, school removes the distinction and contrast between these two states: risk is simultaneously abstract and diffuse, boredom is associated with the teaching of adult people, and seen to be relieved by screens. Organised play, academic tutoring[155] and adult-directed sports dovetail with school to enhance these negative outcomes.

What we need from our schools is the opposite: in-person schooling needs to be filled with exciting but well managed risk, with boredom based less on sitting still and listening to

---

[155] Discussed in Chapter 3

adults, and more on empty time that can be filled by choice. The on-going educational obsession with colonising children's time through homework also pulls counter to what we need.

In modern life we are exposed neither to healthy risks nor to genuine boredom. This is characterised to some degree by the kind of screen-based learning to which schools are turning, and far more by social media. In this kind of usage we enter a limbo state, in which we simply scroll and scroll, occasionally amused and engaged, but mostly apathetic. For our young, teenagers especially, this listless and empty engagement seems to invite the kind of unhealthy risk taking that causes adults concern. It is the opposite of the immersive, turbulent and intermittent real world excitement that children need.

In raising children without physical risk, we also deny them the opportunity to learn to effectively assess the risks they will face as adults. Just as we learn to communicate over many years, so it is with risk assessment: it is a skill we must practice and develop. I strongly suspect that a childhood of learning physics in a classroom and playing racing games on a screen will leave you less well suited to judging risk on the road than a childhood spent on a bike.

In sum, given the traditional ways in which we educate our children, it seems unlikely that school will save us from the dangers posed by screens, nor from the other social ills that we currently face. If anything, schooling seems more likely to open the door to compulsive screen use by offering children risk-free experiences with all the wrong kinds of boredom. Only those lucky enough to attend really progressive schools are protected from this.

CHAPTER 9
EARLY COMPUTING

Having spent a certain amount of my twenties thinking about how computers work, I started to grow curious about where they came from. How did we ever come to create such complex and elegant machines, and how did they become so computationally and culturally powerful? This chapter, and the one that follows, chart this course in the hope of demystifying some of what happens behind those inscrutable screens[156]. They seek to give a more positive view of computers than previous chapters, offering balance to what has come before.

Amplification

The real magic of any technology lies in the ways in which it extends and augments our powers. In many cases this is a purely physical process. A classic example of this is the spear thrower, an ancient device which effectively lengthens the human arm, and thus increases the power of a throw. The

---

[156] Although important to the story we are developing here, some readers may wish to skip these two chapters: despite my best attempts to make them light and accessible, they are still somewhat technical.

same principle of amplification applies to the plough, the lever, the Archimedes' screw, the axe, the pulley block, the wheel and many more of our most fundamental human technologies.

This amplification has been massively extended by fossil fuels, which explains why human society has changed so much since the start of the industrial revolution. Our current standard of living, which is exceptionally high, is not evidence that we have become irreversibly better at looking after ourselves: we simply have much more energy to spend. Of this we are often only dimly aware. It was not until I learned that 1 barrel of oil equates to roughly 25,000 hours of human labour[157] that I really started to comprehend just how powerful this subset of technologies is, and why we have become so dependent upon it. A barrel, however, is hard to imagine, and so let's convert to teaspoons: 1 barrel contains 32,256 teaspoons which means that *a single teaspoon of oil provides the equivalent of around 46.5 minutes of human labour.* That's an absurd amount of power.

At this level of amplification we can make possible the wholesale reconfiguration of the landscape, construction with concrete, refrigeration, long-range high-speed transport, mass production and a host of other epoch-making outcomes.

Applying the lens of Human Technologies we can discern that all of these are material technologies, and whilst many are underpinned by cognitive technologies, we are for all

---

[157] The figure of 25,000 hours is based on a range of assumptions, and is by no means definitive. It has been cited in congress (https://bit.ly/3N1AvLQ) and is explained well at https://bit.ly/3h2hg93. Some cite lower figures, such as 7,000 hours (https://bit.ly/3sSETUn), but in this case the article admits that they are using a work rate that humans can't sustain, and so the figure is on the low side. No matter the final figure, oil is and incredibly potent energy source.

intents and purposes only considering the physical. However, we can easily apply the same kind of analysis to our technologies for thinking.

Humans have gradually augmented their intellectual powers, starting with spoken language and moving into the application of cause and effect to produce logic. This process was vastly accelerated through the acquisition of symbolic representation, in which symbols come to stand in for ideas. Under this banner we can include written language, mathematical notation and manipulation, and also symbolism more broadly. When we see the colour red, and subconsciously associate it with passion, for example, we are being symbolic.

It is worth noting that in the realm of symbolic representation, analogous systems are not equal in their affordances and power. Take for example number systems: Roman numerals are useful for counting, but make for tedious and limited mathematical manipulation. With the combined inventions of the number zero and place value, our modern decimal number system offers us considerably more numerical dexterity.

Where this story has its farthest reaching consequences is in humankind's various attempts to use material technologies to directly extend our cognitive powers. Written language and mathematical notation are early examples of this. The abacus, the astrolabe and the slide rule pushed us further down the path towards modernity. The typewriter, the punched card and the mechanical calculator added the early seeds of automation. And, most recently, the programmable computer has provided the intellectual equivalent of fossil fuels, pushing us into entirely new ways of living and moving us closer to the realm of science fiction.

It is in precisely this sense that Steve Jobs offered us the personal computer as "a bicycle for our minds"[158]. In the same way that a bicycle turns us from merely good to super-efficient at moving around physical space, computers, Jobs believed, would turn us from merely good to super-efficient at thinking. Interestingly, and this may be beyond what Jobs had in mind, both the bicycle and the computer only work when a whole host of other technologies are available, including roads for bikes and electricity for computers. At any rate, it is clear that in many ways Jobs was right in his analogy. However, Jobs did not forsee the many ways that modern computers, most notably smartphones, would come to threaten our ability to focus and think. Ultimately it might be more accurate to say that the computer is a car for the mind: amazingly powerful in many ways but destructive in so many more.

Jobs was far from the first modern thinker to express the ways in which technology might usher in a new and better future, as the following French comic, drawn in the early 1900s, makes clear:

Image 9.1 - En L'An 2000 (Jean-Marc Côté)

---

[158] Steve Jobs, "Computers are like a bicycle for our minds.", Michael Lawrence (https://bit.ly/3DWmTyw)

In this drawing we see a most dazzling future, in which technology allows us to convert book knowledge into personal intelligence with minimal effort on the part of the learner. I often marvel at this picture not simply because it correctly predicts certain elements of online learning, but because of the eerie accuracy with which it shows school students in the year 2000 learning in sedentary rows.

In many ways, given how much digital technology has amplified our powers, it is not surprising that its emergence is known as the "third industrial revolution" (the first being steam and the second being electricity). Neither is it surprising that the advent of a new generation of technologies, including artificial intelligence and quantum computing, are already being heralded as the fourth industrial revolution[159].

Where previous chapters aimed to showcase the ways in which screens do us harm, these chapters seek to investigate and expand upon the story of how we got here, tracing some of the key elements in the development of modern computing. As with so many technologies, its founders had in mind the many miraculous positives that their work would bring to our lives, and they were often not wrong on this score. In fact, I believe that they were generally thoughtful and well-intentioned individuals, and so it was natural that their excitement at pushing boundaries and pioneering new domains helped shape the foundational narratives by which we came to know their work. I don't believe for a moment that these thinkers meant harm, and in reading this section you hopefully feel a sense of the best of humanity: their brilliance, creativity, boldness and energy.

---

[159] The Fourth Industrial Revolution: what it means, how to respond, Klaus Schwab, The Word Economic Forum (https://bit.ly/3TXn9md)

I offer this as a counterpoint to some of the challenging and depressing ideas that have occupied the first half of this book, but also as a reminder of the need to constantly revisit the stories we tell ourselves. For ultimately, technology is less about the thing that is invented, and much more about the culture within which it comes alive. And these cultures, living in their own way, are constantly evolving.

What is a Computer?

In 1962 Arthur C. Clarke rather presciently stated[160] that "any sufficiently advanced technology is indistinguishable from magic". Despite having spent years studying computer systems, when I reflect on what they are, and how they work, they do indeed seem just as Clarke described: magical. Sometimes this feeling is blunted by familiarity and overuse, but it is easy enough to reconjure.

To understand how computers work, it is useful to consider why computer scientists refer to their devices as "machines". This is not done for effect, nor to make the device seem more relatable, it is simply a statement of fact: at heart, every computer is an information processing machine. Just like more conventional machines, computers take inputs, transform them in some way, and then offer the results as outputs. With early computers, inputs and outputs were numbers, and the processes were complex calculations. As computers have grown more sophisticated, the inputs have come to include mouse gestures, voice commands and network data packets, whilst the outputs might be as varied as text, images, audio and haptic

---

[160] Profiles of the Future, Arthur C. Clarke, Holt, Rinehart, and Winston (https://bit.ly/3zH5UOl)

vibrations. In the middle, however, the processes working on these inputs remain, as in older computers, combinations of complex calculations.

Understanding exactly how this works can be a lifetime of study, and it is not an aim of this book to provide detailed blueprints. In short, however, we can consider computers to be extremely flexible calculators. Their power is derived from our collective ability to portray the world mathematically, which allows us to offer our computers models that they can operate on and manipulate. These can then be presented back to us in ways we can understand.

By way of a concrete example, imagine a photo. In traditional film photography light is directed through a lens and allowed to fall briefly onto a sensitive piece of plastic film. The varying intensities and colours of light burn the film and thus capture the image. Once the film is developed and printed onto photographic paper, we can recognise it as a two-dimensional rendering of the original scene.

Consider now the digital camera on a mobile phone. The process is exactly the same, except that the single-use plastic film is replaced by a very precise light sensor. On a modern phone, this light sensor might be able to simultaneously capture 12 million points of lights. These points, known as pixels, are arranged in a grid 4000 pixels wide by 3000 pixels high (for a 4:3 landscape photo). At the moment of capture, each of these 12 million pixels is stored as a mathematical representation, each of which specifies the colour and brightness of that point within the picture. Collected together into an image file, these points can be stored on the phone, displayed on the screen or sent over a network.

The processing work here consists of collecting, organising, error-checking and transporting each individual element of the image. Each of these tasks consists, within the computer, as a set of mathematical manipulations. When you apply a filter to this photo, or rotate it, or replace someone's face with the 💩emoji, these actions also consist of mathematical manipulations. It is for these reasons that I always know that any student who "hates maths" but loves computers has yet to really understand the true power of numbers.

What allows computers to pull off the seemingly magical feats of image capture and manipulation is the speed at which they run. Whilst most computer processors support only a few hundred in-built mathematical and informational operations, they can be combined (through programming) and performed quickly enough that they give the appearance of being far more complex than they actually are.

How fast is fast? A modern smartphone will have a processor capable of executing between one and two *billion* such operations per *second* (e.g. 1-2 GHz). This is so fast that even though the machine has no visible moving parts, the friction produced by the particles within it cause it to heat up. The more intense the processing work being conducted, the hotter it gets. This is why, for example, gamers love computers with big fans. It is also why your mobile phone heats up when you watch videos. These tasks demand a lot of calculations, and so the processor has to work harder than normal, consuming more power to run more operations in a given amount of time. This also explains why your phone or laptop battery drains faster during processor-intensive operations.

By way of a further example, consider the text that you are now reading. At some point in the past I entered this text into a computer. During this process I depressed a series of keys on my laptop's keyboard. Each keystroke temporarily closed an electrical circuit, allowing a particular signal to be sent to the computer. The computer received these signals and converted them to a format used for representing alphanumeric characters (ASCII in older computers, Unicode in more modern ones). Once thus represented, they were stored in a file, which I continued to build upon and refine. Sometimes I added text, sometimes I removed it, and sometimes I changed its formatting or location. Each of these actions consisted of a series of mathematical manipulations.

It is important to note that within each of these manipulations there are elements that are physically built into the structure of the machine: these instructions, the computer's basic mathematical operations, constitute its "instruction set". We call this "hardware", because it has a physical permanence, and is thus hard to change. Built on top of this foundation are collections of calls to the hardware's instruction set, which allow computers to perform more complex tasks. We call this "software", because it is intangible and relatively easy to change. When we talk about "computer programming", what we are generally referring to is the process of writing software.

If you like analogies, you can think here of cooking. The physical setup of the kitchen, the various equipment and utensils are like a computer's hardware. The way they are combined in the following of a recipe is the software. Raw food enters the system as an input, is processed (cooked) and a meal leaves as the output. A major difference is that the chef has to be in the kitchen to cook the meal, where the computer programmer can be remote, but such is the joy of imperfect analogies!

Whilst each individual element of computer systems, from physical hardware to intangible software, is incredibly complex, the overall schema is simple enough, and can be defined as follows:

> "A computer is a programmable mathematical machine that allows for the manipulation, storage and transfer of data".

It's hard to imagine that so simple an idea could change the world.

Mechanical Computing

Once you understand what a computer is, it is hard to avoid wondering how it is that we ever came to invent such a machine. The answer, as with so many things, is slowly, over time, without prior planning and through a cumulative series of many individual conceptual, mathematical and engineering breakthroughs. A historical study of such devices reveals a progression of increasing automation and complexity, from the ancient abacus to Napier's Bones (1617) to Pascal's mechanical calculator of 1642 and onward to Babbage's difference engine. Each of these devices, and the many others that lie between and beyond them, shared the same aims: allowing humans to perform complex mathematical calculations faster, more accurately and with less effort.

A pivotal moment in this story relates to a conceptual leap taken by Charles Babbage, an English engineer and mathematician. During the 1820s and 30s Babbage worked to design and build a mechanical device for calculating mathematical tables. This machine, known as the difference engine, would be flexible enough to perform a range of mathematical manipulations on a variety of inputs. Whilst Babbage was certainly not the first to build such calculating machines, his work pushed the art to new levels of complexity.

With investment from the British government, and the manufacturing skill of engineer Joseph Clement, Babbage worked to bring to life a number of iterations of his idea. Whilst he achieved some success, and part of the work was ultimately exhibited, limitations in manufacturing techniques caused delays and drove up costs, causing the project to be abandoned. Some of the problems can be attributed to developments in Babbage's own thinking, the pace of which far outstripped the means of his age. With inspiration drawn from the Jacquard Loom (1804), Babbage's ambitions evolved, and he started to design a more complex and ambitious machine, which he called the analytical engine. This was not merely a relatively flexible mechanical calculator, but rather a programmable mechanical computer. It would, like any modern computer, feature input (punched cards), storage, processing and output (in the form of a printer). In his correspondence with the English mathematician Ada Lovelace, daughter of Lord Byron, Babbage's thinking was pushed further, with some observers coming to view Lovelace's contribution as significant enough to earn her the title of world's first computer programmer.

Like the difference engine, the analytical engine's sheer complexity meant that it was not built during Babbage's lifetime. In fact, it has never been fully constructed, and in looking at those parts of it that have been built, it is easy to see why not:

Image 9.2 - Babbage's Analytical Engine (Wikimedia)

In learning about Babbage's work, one cannot escape the feeling that he was born a century premature, and indeed one hundred years would pass before his insights were turned into practical reality.

Theoretical Computing

It is notable that Babbage did not use the word "computer" itself, opting for the more industrial sounding "engine". In keeping with the age of steam, he referred to the processing component of his machine as the "mill". These terms reflect the spirit of Babbage's time, and are echoed in the contemporary use of the word "machine" described earlier.

Historically speaking, the term computer was used to refer to an individual hired to perform calculations. This kind of computational work, which was laborious and repetitive, formed a considerable part of the fields of astronomy, geology, surveying, census taking and artillery firing. As the practice of science became more statistically-oriented, and engineering projects grew more ambitious, the need for reliable and scalable computation grew. As late as the 1930s, NASA's Jet Propulsion Laboratory utilised teams of human computers, most of whom were women:

Image 9.3 - Human Computers At Work (NASA)

As the film Hidden Figures (2016) makes evident, NASA's computers included a number of African-American women. Sadly, the work of all of these industrious women was undertaken in the shadow of their male counterparts, to whom credit for NASA's achievements was unfairly perceived to belong.

Beginning in the late nineteenth century[161], the term computer began to be applied to calculating machines, which were the mechanical and analogue forebearers of today's electronic and digital computers. By the 1940s, with

---

[161] Computer, Oxford English Dictionary (https://bit.ly/3fpTraY)

governments and companies generating and recording ever more data, calculation gave way to computation, and the modern computer was born.

For a time the two usages of "computer", the human and the material, seemed to co-exist, but from the 1940s, the latter became pre-eminent. In viewing the changing usage of a variety of related terms, as shown in the following Google Books Ngram, it is evident how quickly interest in this new subject picked up:

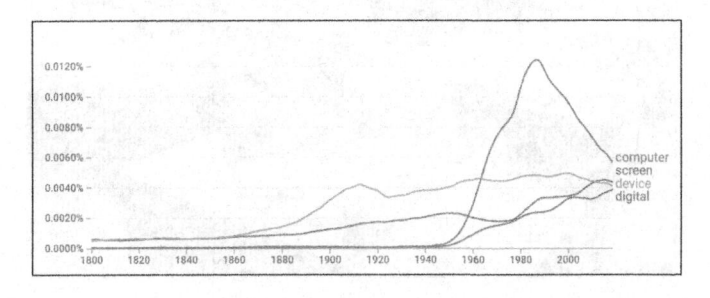

Image 9.4 - Google Ngram (Ross Parker)

A key figure in this transition was Alan Turing, the British mathematician, philosopher and cryptanalyst, who laid the theoretical groundwork for the construction of the first modern computers. As a child, Turing was interested in scientific inquiry, but only in those areas that sparked his curiosity. He had a distrust of authority, and, as the school report below makes apparent, he clearly did not impress his teachers[162]:

> "I can forgive his writing, though it is the worst I have ever seen, and I try to view tolerantly his

---

[162] Alan Turing's Early Life, The Alan Turing Internet Scrapbook (https://bit.ly/3gXd4Hy)

unswerving inexactitude and slipshod, dirty, work, inconsistent though such inexactitude is in a utilitarian; but I cannot forgive the stupidity of his attitude towards sane discussion on the New Testament."

Bottom of his class in English, and only one rank higher in Latin, he did better in science and maths. Described by his headmaster as "the sort of boy who is bound to be a problem for any school or community", he was nearly prevented from even sitting the School Certificate[163]. Despite these challenges, Turing's approach to school underwent a transformation in sixth form. This change seems to have been ignited by his friendship with classmate Christopher Morcom, an outstanding student. The pair applied to Cambridge, with Morcom receiving a scholarship to Trinity. Tragically Morcom passed away before he could take up his place. Deeply affected by his friend's death, Turing became engrossed in a range of intellectual pursuits, before gaining a scholarship to attend King's College, Cambridge.

King's seems to have been the first place in which Turing, as a homosexual man living in intolerant times, found a sense of belonging. Under the liberal thinking inspired by renowned economist and King's fellow John Maynard Keynes, the college was open minded in many ways. This safe and stimulating environment was, ultimately, to be the seat of Turing's most inspired work. After completing his undergraduate studies in 1934, Turing became a fellow in 1935. During these years he encountered the work of mathematical giants John von Neumann, Betrand Russell and Kurt Gödel. In particular, Russell's work on logic and

---

[163] Later to become Ordinary Levels and then the GCSE

provability seemed fruitful to Turing's intellectual and personal interest in the nature of matter and mind. Where Bertrand's multi-volume Principia Mathematica (co-authored with A. N. Whitehead) sought to bring a sense of completion to mathematical thought, Gödel's incompleteness theory pushed back, opening up new horizons[164].

Within these esoteric and generally inaccessible schools of thought, there remained an elusive mathematical puzzle, generally known as Hilbert's Entscheidungsproblem, or the decision problem. This centred around the search for a method through which it could be decided whether or not a given mathematical proposition was provable[165]. Turing worked in isolation throughout 1935, searching for a solution, and by April 1936 he had managed to produce one. Although Gödel and another mathematician, Alonzo Church, both independently arrived at their own solutions, it was the nature of Turing's work that would prove pivotal. Rather than using mathematics directly, Turing's seminal 1936 paper, *On Computable Numbers, with an Application to the Entscheidungsproblem*[166], proposed an imaginary machine, which used instruction sets to operate on numbers. By drawing logical conclusions about the functioning of this machine, Turing was able to attack the problem.

Now universally known as the Turing Machine, the model developed in this paper forms the basis upon which every modern computer is constructed: a machine that uses tables

---

[164] Bertrand Russell & Alfred North Whitehead – Principia Mathematica 1+1=2, Story of Mathematics (https://bit.ly/3h9NzTG)

[165] Alan Turing, Stanford Encyclopedia of Philosophy (https://stanford.io/3NuHgG8)

[166] On Computable Numbers, with an Application to the Entscheidungsproblem, Alan Turing, Abelard (https://bit.ly/3sTbGbJ)

of rules (programmes) to manipulate (process) symbols (data) in a logically consistent fashion. What is striking in reading Turing's work is the way in which he conjured up and manipulated a fictitious machine, in which the roots of today's computers are so clearly evident, but for which there was almost no historical precedent, save for the work of Babbage. Where most invention takes the form of improvement, Turing's insight was a leap into an almost entirely uncolonised space.

The fact that *On Computable Numbers* contains 16 uses of the word "computer" offered a sign of things to come.

Having completed his PhD at Princeton in 1938, under the supervision of Church, and in the company of von Neumann, Turing chose, in 1939, to return to a Britain on the verge of war[167]. Back at King's, and already interested in cryptography, Turing worked on cog-based machines to solve mathematical functions. By September 1939 Turing was employed at Bletchley Park, the British government's code-breaking headquarters. It was here, in working to decipher messages encoded with the German Enigma machine, that Turing began to put his intellectual powers to practical use. Working in the now-famous Hut 8, he led the team responsible for building the Bombe, an electro-mechanical codebreaking machine based on prior work by Polish cryptologist Marian Rejewski[168]. This work, as well as further intellectual input from Turing, helped to inspire Bletchley's Tommy Flowers in his construction of Colossus, the world's first programmable digital electronic computer.

---

[167] Beyond the Turing machine, The Alan Turing Internet Scrapbook (https://bit.ly/3t05PkM)

[168] Bombe, Wikipedia (https://bit.ly/3NtwHmZ)

Screens That Eat Children

The work of Bletchley's Government Code and Cypher School (GC&CS) consisted of analysing intercepted messages from Axis forces. These messages were routinely encrypted (scrambled) with the Enigma machine, which used three rotors to produce variable outputs for any given input. Although a range of different cryptoanalytical strategies could be used to attack the messages, and thus unscramble them, doing so in a timely fashion required automation. This was particularly true after the Germans added a fourth rotor to the Enigma in 1942[169], exponentially increasing the number of permutations in every encrypted message. It was through such automation, using the power of Bletchley's various computers, in conjunction with the expertise of their codebreakers, that the British managed to consistently read secret German communication. The intelligence gained through these means, known within the British forces as Ultra, is believed to have shortened the war by between two and four years[170].

Interestingly, in order to prevent the Germans from discovering that the Enigma had been compromised, Allied forces had to disguise the source of their intelligence. For example, given the knowledge of the whereabouts of a submarine via Ultra, a pantomime spotting of the already-known enemy position would be performed before it was attacked. In this way, the commanders of the enemy submarine would note that they had been "spotted" by an Allied plane or boat prior to being attacked, thus covering up the true source of the intelligence.

Despite Alan Turing's incredible service to his nation, he

---

[169] Enigma Machine, Wikipedia (https://bit.ly/3fzVPvx)

[170] The Influence of ULTRA in the Second World War, Sir Harry Hinsley (https://bit.ly/3FIdfRs)

was convicted of gross indecency in 1952, having been caught in a homosexual relationship with a man named Arnold Murray[171]. Given the choice of chemical castration or prison, Turing chose "treatment" with stilboestrol, which rendered him impotent and resulted in the growth of breast tissue. With a criminal record to his name, Turing also lost access to his security clearance. Although much uncertainty remains, it is believed that a combination of these factors led Turing to take his own life by ingesting a cyanide-laced apple[172]. The year was 1954, and Turing was just 41 years of age. Through fear and ignorance, the world had lost one of its sharpest minds.

Programmable Computing

As so often happens when an idea's time has arrived, other engineers around the world were busy working on their own computers. Whilst Turing's writing was freely available, the work being undertaken at Bletchley remained classified until the 1970s. This makes the history of early computers somewhat challenging to untangle, as does each country's tendency to highlight their own work at the expense of others.

In 1941 Konrad Zuse, a German civil engineer, completed work on the Z3, which used 2,300 relays[173] in order to perform floating-point arithmetic on binary numbers. Although it is possible to build computers that can deal with more complex digits, computer engineers settled on binary

---

[171] Alan Turing, Wikipedia (https://bit.ly/3sSm2sm)

[172] A persistent urban legend explains the bite in Apple's famous logo as a ode to Turing's death, but alas it is not true (https://bit.ly/3hb1AAB)

[173] A Complete History of Computers: From the 1800s to Now, Mara Calvello, G2 (https://bit.ly/3WpqRHc)

due to the relative simplicity of representing only two states: zero and one. A zero could be represented as the absence of electrical current: one as the presence of electrical current. Likewise, these two states could be stored in a switch with two positions: off and on. In early computers it was the electromagnetic relay, in which the flow of electricity would trigger a magnet to flip a switch, that performed this function.

Zuse's Z3 was destroyed in a Berlin bombing raid in 1943, but a later recreation is now exhibited in Munich's Deutsche Museum[174].

Another early machine was the Atanasoff-Berry Computer (ABC), built by Professor John Vincent Atanasoff and his graduate student Clifford Berry at Iowa State College[175]. Completed in 1942 it was to be at the heart of a later legal battle, through which the courts confirmed that Atanasoff had pioneered a number of computing techniques that were then utilised by others. However, these techniques were not considered to be patentable, and so became freely available for others to use. Whilst important to the development of other computers, the ABC was not programmable, nor was it Turing-complete, meaning that its place in computer history remains contentious.

1943 saw the launch of what can arguably be described as one of the most important computers of all time: the Electrical Numerical Integrator and Calculator, or ENIAC for short. Designed and built by John W. Mauchly and J. Presper Eckert at the University of Pennsylvania, it could

---

[174] Computers – the History of the Calculating Machine, Deutsches Museum (https://bit.ly/3UnGrRI)

[175] Timeline of Computer History, Computer History Museum (https://bit.ly/3WqWlXU)

perform roughly 500 floating point operations per second (or FLOPs): each FLOP represents a single mathematical operation. Interestingly, FLOPs, as a unit, replaced the earlier use of "kilo girls", which was the combined computing power of a thousand female human computers[176]. This is akin to the use of horse-power to rate internal combustion engines, and although quaint in its way, has thankfully fallen out of use.

Image 9.5 - ENIAC (Wikimedia)

ENIAC used vacuum tubes instead of the older electromagnetic relays, which made it faster, but considerably larger, hotter and more power hungry. In total the machine used nearly 18,000[177] of these tubes, each of which consisted of electrical components contained within a glass vacuum chamber. These early tubes had a tendency to burn out[178], and a single failure would disrupt the entire

---

[176] The incredible evolution of supercomputers' powers, from 1946 to today, Sara Chodosh, Popular Science (https://bit.ly/3NxHsET)

[177] History of Computers, The University of Rhode Island (https://bit.ly/3sSGCJI)

[178] What do you know about ENIAC?, Pandora FMS (https://bit.ly/3UDGY2n)

machine whilst a search for the culprit was undertaken. It was eventually noted that most breakdowns occurred when the machine was switched on or off, and so, by leaving it running at all times, the interval between breakdowns could be extended from minutes to days.

Interestingly, our modern use of the word "bug" to denote a problem in a computer programme stems from these early vacuum tubes. In 1947 Harvard University's Mark II computer broke down: upon inspection, engineers discovered that a moth had shorted out relay 70 on Panel F. They attached the moth to a piece of paper, noting it as the "First actual case of bug":

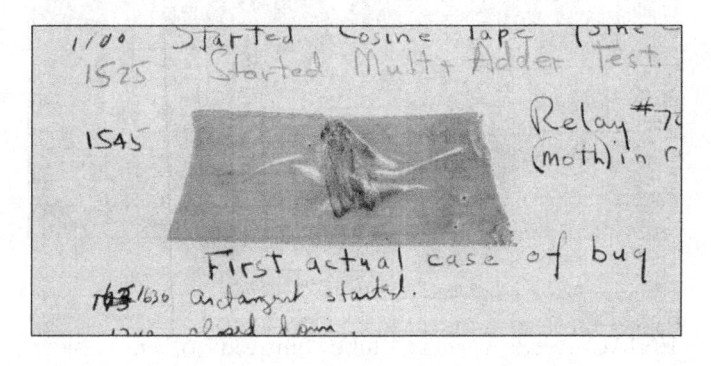

Image 9.6 - First Actual Case of Bug (Smithsonian Institute)

What is surprising to modern computer users is the scale of ENIAC, which took up 167 square metres (1800 square feet) of floor space. At a cost of USD $500,000[179], or $7,283,000 in 2020 money, and requiring a team of trained experts to operate it, the machine was clearly a far cry from our current understanding of "computer". It is in this context that Thomas J. Watson, president of IBM, predicted

---

[179] ENIAC, Wikipedia (https://bit.ly/3zI7nDX)

that the combined global market for computers was a total of 5 machines[180]. It was 1943, and the world was on the brink of a revolution.

Whilst ENIAC seems archaic from today's perspective, it was in many senses a modern device. Its design conformed to a concept now known as the "von Neumann Machine", named after the mathematician John von Neumann, with whom Alan Turing worked at Princeton in the 1930s. Based on von Neumann's incomplete *First Draft of a Report on the EDVAC*[181], the concept refers to a computer which stores both instructions and data in the same location. Almost all computers built since have followed this same pattern, despite massive changes in the underlying technologies used. As is so often the case with invention and innovation, some feel that credit for this insight ought not to lie solely with von Neumann, working as he was with Arthur Burks and Herman Goldstine on Mauchly and Eckert's EDVAC machine (a precursor to the ENIAC). Nonetheless, history has fallen in von Neumann's favour, and so his name alone adorns the design of almost all modern computers.

What certainly has changed over the intervening years is a steady and dramatic drop in the price, size and energy usage of computers. These changes have been accompanied by an even more dramatic rise in their performance. All of this has occurred one innovation at a time, and is work that has involved millions of individual scientists and engineers, working at universities, governments and corporations across the world.

---

[180] Worst tech predictions of all time, The Telegraph (https://bit.ly/3D80wVa)

[181] First Draft of a Report on EDVAC, John von Neumann, IEEE (https://bit.ly/3zHqLkp)

As a practical example, consider that early computers accepted data and programmes via punched cards. These sheets of stiff paper arranged data into columns and rows, with each column generally representing a single character, encoded into binary digits. Each individual cell on the grid represented a single binary digit, with zero denoted by a blank spot, and one denoted by a hole punched through the card. When placed in a card reader, electrical contacts would probe for holes, allowing the computer to read the data as a series of zero and non-zero currents. The process of punching cards was slow and error prone: there was no backspace key, and errantly punched cards had to be scrapped or fixed with tape. Stacks of completed cards were bulky to store and needed to be kept in sequence. Reading the cards was relatively slow, and their capacity was limited.

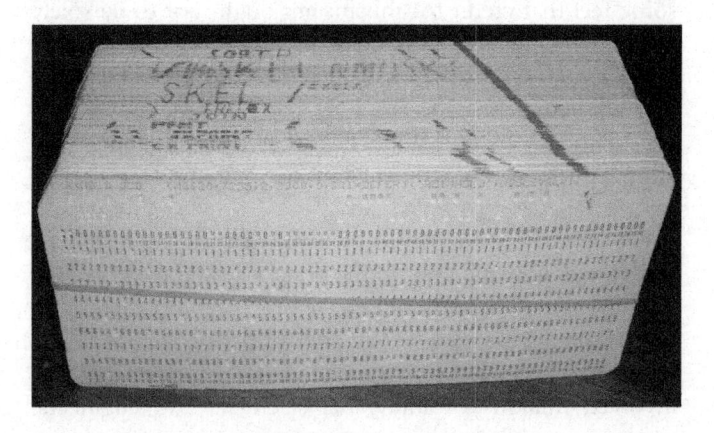

Image 9.7 - A Deck of Punched Cards (Wikimedia)

In considering punched cards as a data store, it is easy to understand why early computers could not, for example, play music. A typical three-minute song, represented in a modern MP3 file, requires roughly 3 megabytes (MB) of storage. These 3 megabytes would contain 25,165,824 individual binary digits (zeros or ones, also known as bits). Given that a standard IBM 12-row/80-column punched card could store 960 bits, it would take a stack of 26,215 cards to hold and play our single song. At roughly 50 cards per centimetre, our stack would run to just over 5 metres in height.

The fact that in 2020 one could purchase a 256 gigabyte (GB) music-playing hand-held computer, at a cost of less than USD $450, would have been inconceivable to anyone working on computers in 1943.

These changes are reflective of the massive improvements in the nature and density of the devices used to store and manipulate binary data within computers. As seen already, there was over time a transition from the mechanical gears of Babbage to the electromagnetic relays of Bletchley to the vacuum tubes of ENIAC, with each new innovation bringing some distinct advantages, as well as certain disadvantages. What came next would have a profound impact on all of our lives.

In May 1954 Texas Instrument's Gordon Teal unveiled, at the end of an apparently dull and uneventful conference session, a milestone of 20th century engineering: the silicon transistor[182]. This tiny device, which superceded the vacuum tube, would go on to transform electronics and computing. In a moment foreshadowing Steve Jobs' famous on stage revelations, Teal produced from his pocket a handful of silicon transistors, sending the attendees of the Institute of Radio Engineers' National Conference on Airborne Electronics into a veritable frenzy.

The transistor itself was not new, having been theorised by

---

[182] The Lost History of the Transistor, Michael Riordan, IEEE (https://bit.ly/3FDKi99)

Julius Edgar Lilienfeld in 1926[183], and later produced by Bell Labs' John Bardeen and Walter Brattain in 1947. Working under William Shockley, the Bell team's transistor used germanium as its semiconductor. At the time it was appreciated that whilst germanium was easy to work with, limitations with its thermal and electrical properties made it far from ideal in terms of performance, especially at temperatures beyond 75 °C.

Much of the foundational work on silicon transistors also took place at Bell Labs, and it was here that Teal did his early work on the topic. Intense dedication, with little interference or support from management, enabled him to pioneer new ground and gave him considerable credibility within a field still very much in its infancy. Lured back to his native Texas by the offer of a better job with Texas Instruments (TI), he took with him a range of insights, and set about assembling the team of scientists and researchers required to bring them to fruition. Teal's unveiling of the results of this work, that handful of silicon transistors, signified that TI had beaten Bell at its own game. As it turns out, Bell's own Morris Tanenbaum was already producing such devices, but his team's work was being kept under wraps. TI's visible head start allowed it to lead the new silicon transistor market from the start, turning it into an internationally significant enterprise.

Being smaller and less power hungry than vacuum tubes, transistors began to appear in a range of existing products. Most notably, they allowed for the creation of the "transistor radio", helping to make radio entertainment portable for the first time. The first commercial transistor

---

[183] Transistor, Wikipedia (https://bit.ly/3WwqYB0)

radio[184], the TR-1, was produced by Regency in collaboration with TI, who were looking for a way to generate public interest in their groundbreaking innovation. When the initially limited manufacturing run of these devices had sold out, a gap in the market was exploited by a young Japanese company, Tokyo Tsushin Kogyo. With their name proving unpronounceable to most Americans, they coined the name Sony as a portmanteau of the Latin "sonos" and a Japanese imitation of the kindly American expression "sonny boy"[185]. Sales of Sony's first transistor radio, the TR-55, helped turn them into a dominant 20th century cultural force, allowing teenagers to listen to the provocative new music of rock'n'roll with far less parental interference.

Meanwhile, in computing, transistors led to what are now known as second-generation computers[186], in which they replaced the vacuum tubes of old. These machines, which include Manchester University's experimental Transistor Computer, Bell's TRADIC[187] and a slew of other machines, were smaller, cooler, more reliable and considerably cheaper. In these computers, transistors were soldered onto printed circuit boards and combined with magnetic core memory. IBM, already a data processing powerhouse, turned its mid-1950s pioneering work on transistor calculators into some of the most successful early transistor computers, starting in 1958 with the IBM 7070.

Over time it has become possible to combine more and

---

[184] Transistor Radios, PBS (https://to.pbs.org/3sSn2N8)

[185] My Last Sony: The Rise And Fall Of The House Of Sonny Boy, John Biggs, TechCrunch (https://tcrn.ch/3FGbPqw)

[186] Topic A: Computer generations, BCCampus (https://bit.ly/3T03QHV)

[187] Transistor, Wikipedia (https://bit.ly/3sR0Umt)

more transistors into a smaller and smaller space, delivering steady improvements in power, size and cost. In the 1960s and 70s these developments took the form of "integrated circuits", in which electronics were built into flat pieces of silicon. Commonly known as "microchips" or "chips", these devices lead to third-generation computers. Further advances in silicon engineering allowed these complex chips to be turned into fully fledged microprocessors, or CPUs, giving rise to what, for many lay users, are the first recognisable computers: the PCs (personal computers) of the 1980s and 90s.

Although technical progress played a key part in the development of modern personal computing, a significant role was also played by culture. The dominance of IBM brought with it a focus on the creation, sale and operation of large, expensive computers designed to be run only by a small cadre of technical experts. These specialist operators, often known as "the priesthood," were responsible for feeding the programmes created by others into computers, monitoring their progress, and relaying errors and output back to the requesting user. Although it is hard for us to imagine today, users in the IBM paradigm never touched the computer. In fact, they were often required to stand in a roped-off area, to keep them at a safe distance.

To a small group of students at the Massachusetts Institute of Technology (MIT) this approach was anathema. These prototypal nerds, now known as the original "hackers", believed that to really understand a computer you had to use it yourself. By hanging around a number of smaller, non-IBM computers, including the Lincoln Laboratory's TX-O and a DEC PDP-1, the hackers managed to scrounge and blagg actual hands-on computer time. Their familiarity with electronics, gained through their studies as well as their participation in MIT's now-legendary Tech Model Railroad Club, allowed them to understand the hardware: their extreme dedication to all-night programming sessions would in-turn allow them to become experts in software too.

Through the late 1950s and into the 1960s, this core group, who later found a more official and permanent home at MIT's AI Lab, worked to exploit and extend the powers of these exciting new machines. They built innovative new systems, learned to display information graphically and produced some of the first computer games, learning all the while how to solve a wide range of technical problems. More significantly, they produced a unique culture, which we now know as the "hacker ethic". As documented by Steven Levy[188], this set of values emphasised an "inquisitive intensity, skepticism toward bureaucracy, openness to creativity, unselfishness in sharing accomplishments, urge to make improvements, and desire to build". These beliefs put them at odds with the centralised, top-down, hands-off approach espoused by IBM, who the hackers naturally viewed as their mortal enemy.

Sponsored by the university and by the government, there was no need to turn ideas into products, meaning that the hackers had no need of keeping secrets. On the contrary, it was, they believed, only through the open sharing of information that they could push the state-of-the-art forward, and thus benefit everyone. There developed a sense that they were challenging the status-quo, and in doing so were producing new ways to live and learn. Over time, through a series of personnel changes, the hacker's hands-on imperative would spread from their East Coast lab to Standford's AI Lab (SAIL) on the US West Coast. From

---

[188] Hackers: Heroes of the Computer Revolution, Steven Levy, O'Reilly Media (https://bit.ly/3Dx1Wc4)

here it would come to influence a second generation of hackers, many of whom participated in the now-famous Homebrew Computer Club, and from which sprang a wealth of nimble new computer manufacturers, including Apple. From these humble beginnings grew Silicon Valley, the innovative engine room of modern computing.

Initially too small to register as a threat to IBM, the hackers and their companies nonetheless managed to bring about a seismic shift in how computers were viewed: everyone could own a computer, and in owning a computer anyone's life could be improved. By the time IBM realised what was happening, it was almost too late, and it was only by shifting their own focus towards personal computing that they managed to stay relevant. By this time, however, it was apparent that the hackers had won the day, and computing was now for the people, not just the priesthood. Against the odds, David had slain Goliath. IBM remained a powerful force for decades to come, but it would never again dominate the way it once had.

This new culture rode the crest of a wave described earlier: the ever-increasing number of components that could be integrated into a circuit. The scale of this kind of integration is hard to imagine, but by the 2010s, so-called "Very-Large-Scale Integration" had delivered coin-size processors containing billions of transistors. Modern mobile phones are powered by the very latest generation of these devices, known as system-on-a-chip, or SoC. These tiny devices contain not only a processor, but also other, formerly discrete, computing elements, such as memory, input/output and modems.

What ENIAC fitted into 167 square metres, we can now fit on a postage stamp, only it now runs billions of times faster, and at a fraction of the cost. By way of example, consider ENIAC's price tag of USD $7,283,000 in today's money,

Screens That Eat Children

and the fact that it ran at 500 flops. In price-performance terms, this means that ENIAC cost USD $14,566/flop. In 2017, Intel announced it's high-end Core i9 X-series chip, priced at USD $2000 and capable of 1,000,000,000,000 flops (or 1 teraflop)[189], giving it a price-performance cost of USD $0.000000002/flop.

In other words, in the 74 years between 1943 and 2017, human beings have improved computer technology by a factor of over 7 trillion.

In this incredible, astounding and entirely unimaginable leap in computational power we begin to see how computing has come to dominate so much of human culture and practice.

Despite the notoriously difficult task of predicting the future, there were some astute observers who could see where things might be headed. In 1965 Gordon Moore, then working at Fairchild Semiconductor[190], observed that the number of transistors that could be built into a microchip seemed to be doubling every 18 to 24 months. Moore published these ideas in a paper named "Cramming More Components onto Integrated Circuits"[191], predicting that the doubling would continue for the next 10 years.

Although Moore never used the term, this pattern came to be known as Moore's Law, and whilst it is not a "law" in the sense of legislation or physical reality, it has nonetheless held more-or-less true for over 50 years. Its demise is constantly predicted, yet the relentless doubling, which lies behind the 7 trillion fold increase noted above, has been

---

[189] Intel's new chip puts a teraflop in your desktop, Rob Verger, Popular Science (https://bit.ly/3UjHYZ9)

[190] What is Moore's Law?, Mike Gianfagna, Synopsys (https://bit.ly/3WDJZBw)

[191] Cramming More Components onto Integrated Circuits, Intel (https://intel.ly/3DuGCoY)

called "the metronome, the heartbeat, of the modern world"[192].

With so much of the action happening at the nanoscopic level, concealed within a chip ensconced within a device, it is hard to get a sense of a computer's machine-like nature. In order to help my students grasp these nebulous ideas, I will occasionally get out a trusty old Dell PC from my classroom's storage cupboard. Opened up and placed on a table top, connected to mains power, and with its cooling apparatus removed, I will ask students how long they think they can hold a finger on the CPU after it is powered up. Most students, perhaps expecting a lesson in the thermal efficiency of CPUs, suggest a time in minutes. Volunteers are invited to step forward and give it a go, and once a few fingers are in place, the power switch is flicked. Inevitably and without fail all fingers are removed, hot and bothered, within seconds.

In that moment, feeling the latent heat within their skin cells, students come to appreciate just what kind of beast a modern CPU is. Later on, as their own computer heats up, they'll better understand that it's the billions of transistors that lie behind the observed phenomenon.

With Moore's Law in mind, we might ask if we are prepared for continuing, exponential increases in power of the very same technologies that we have already fallen prey to? It seems unlikely that we are.

---

[192] The Guardian of all Things, Michael S. Malone, St. Martin's Griffin (https://bit.ly/3zERK05)

CHAPTER 10
THE COMPUTER EXPLOSION

There is more to this story than the steady improvement of hardware, which on its own is relatively unexciting and hard to use. Specifically, the world we live in today was created by the software and networking that this hardware allows, and it is in these areas that we can really chart the explosion of computers into our lives.

Ease of Use

When we use a modern computer, also known as a smartphone, we are generally only dimly aware of all that has come before, and all that goes on within. A large part of this phenomenon is due to the various layers of abstraction that allow these devices to offer extremely intuitive, fast and easy-to-use interfaces. These layers require significant computational power, but as we've seen above, modern CPUs provide this in abundance.

Commonly we refer to this kind of abstraction under the umbrella of "software", which is that part of a computer that is intangible and easily changed. Software is produced through the act of programming. It is software that allows us to move a mouse and see a physical representation of our hand, reduced to a pointer, on the screen. It is software that allows us to use that pointer to pick up a file and drag it into a folder. It is software that lets us take a photo, add filters and upload it to Instagram. In theory we could design hardware that does these things, but it would be very complex, and its functionality could not be changed: instead, we tend to use generalised hardware coupled with specialised software.

In terms of software, these kinds of interactions fall under the umbrella of graphical user interfaces (GUIs), and it is this class of innovation that makes modern computers so easy to use. Compared to the older interface approach known as command line interfaces (CLIs), in which a computer can only display text and every instruction must be typed in as a command, GUIs are a massive leap forward.

As such, we can be more specific and say that it is software-enabled GUIs, running on incredibly powerful, general-purpose hardware, that makes computers so compelling to use. Behind that clean, functional graphical interface, everything still boils down to the extremely fast execution of the small number of mathematical manipulations that are built into the silicon that forms the CPU.

As noted in the introduction, it is software that is eating the world, and this begs the interesting question of what software is, and how we came to rely so heavily upon it.

In the days of relays and vacuums, before software was invented, computers were programmed by reconfiguring cables on plugboards and flicking switches. Advances in computation power, and the advent of "stored-program" computers allowed for software, written as a set of binary commands, to be saved within a computer. This enabled programmes to be loaded from memory, run, and then replaced with other programmes. The process of programming computers using binary commands was tedious, trying of patience and filled with errors. It was only with a Herculean dedication to problem solving that one could become a programmer, and so it remained an obscure and arcane pursuit.

Over time, binary commands were replaced by human readable abbreviations, known as assembly language. Developed by Kathleen Booth of Birkbeck College in 1950[193], assembly is a timely reminder that behind today's stereotype of programmers as white, male college graduates lies a long history of brilliant female computer scientists. Assembly made programming easier and less error prone, a pattern that was to be repeated time and time again in the development of software. Specifically, by combining assembly commands into more powerful functions, and writing software to allow a computer to translate them back to binary, computer scientists developed newer and more supple languages. These "high level programming languages", whilst still requiring specialist knowledge, are much closer to the natural languages in which humans normally speak. They are easier to memorise, perform more work with fewer commands, and represent higher-level abstractions.

Let's consider one example of how using a modern high-level programming language, such as Java, Python or PHP, makes life easier. With such a language, a programmer wishing to send data to a disc no longer needs to labouriously write the hundreds of commands required by older, low-level languages: instead, they can simply use a small number of instructions to open a connection, pipe in the data and then close the connection. In addition to the

---

[193] History of Software, Wikipedia (https://bit.ly/3NuJC7W)

original creators of such programming languages, other programmers using the language will also create their own handy extensions to the language, very often sharing them for free. This process, and the utilities and libraries that emerge from it, act to further reduce the barriers to creating new software.

The steady accumulation of tools, techniques, design patterns, code and culture have gradually allowed for the construction of the kinds of computer interface that we use today. This process has been relatively uncoordinated, taken decades and involved millions of individuals, yet it has delivered incredible results.

Surprisingly, a lot of the pioneering work in this area happened at Xerox[194], the photocopier company, which was behind the invention of many of the elements of the personal computer. This story represents most starkly how much there is to lose and gain in the modern economy.

As a technology company, Xerox had a natural interest in pursuing research and development. It was for these reasons that Xerox founded the Palo Alto Research Center (PARC) in 1969, under the leadership of their Chief Scientist Jack Goldman. For an East Coast company, this centre gave access to innovative work being done on the West Coast, in that area now known as Silicon Valley. It also gave PARC's scientists the freedom to work on new ideas, unencumbered by the views and practises entrenched at head office. The combination of this space, and the judicious hiring of very capable researchers, allowed PARC to become a rarified hub of innovation. Within a few years the scientists and

---

[194] Fumbling the Future, Douglas K. Smith and Robert C. Alexander, iUniverse (https://bit.ly/3fD17q6)

researchers at PARC had produced a string of groundbreaking technologies, including bitmap graphics, the graphical user interface (GUI), Ethernet networking, what-you-see-is-what-you-get text editing[195] and the laser printer.

Combined together, these allowed Xerox to produce the Alto, the world's first personal computer. Featuring the portrait-oriented display you'd expect from a photocopying company, and Douglas Engelbart's newfangled mouse, it is, despite its size, instantly recognisable as a modern computer:

Image 10.1 - Xerox Alto (Wikimedia)

The Alto debuted in 1973, almost a full decade before the PC was "born". On this machine a user could create word processed documents, share them over a network and print them to paper. The machine was an undeniable success, and

---

[195] Which has the charming acronym WYSIWYG

garnered attention throughout Silicon Valley. Sadly, the divide between Xerox's East and West Coast teams meant that the executives back at HQ, although aware of the machine, chose not to bring it to market in any meaningful way. Photocopying was seen to be the company's future, not overpriced and misunderstood computers such as the Alto.

And so, as Xerox failed to commercialise the Alto, others, most notably Apple's Steve Jobs, filled the void. Jobs famously visited PARC in 1979, and although what he saw there mirrored some elements of what Apple were already doing, the visit seems to have helped Apple realise the potential of their almost-cancelled Macintosh project[196]. Today, Apple is one of the world's largest and most profitable companies, sitting at the very centre of the digital technology landscape. Xerox still exists, as a subsidiary of the Japanese firm Fujifilm, but there is no doubt that it let the very future it invented slip through its fingers.

Apple's reputation for the ease of use of its devices is directly related to its current position as market leader in consumer technology. Whilst certainly innovative in its own right, Apple did not invent the majority of what it today receives credit for, with much of that work having been done at companies like Xerox, Microsoft, IBM and the many others that Apple has imitated, partnered with, licensed from or swallowed whole. Apple's embodiment as the corporate face of the early 21st century reflects the sum of a massively distributed and generally underappreciated cultural undertaking focused on making computers easy to use.

---

[196] The Xerox PARC Visit, Standard University (https://stanford.io/3T3hTwv)

As this story illustrates, it is by hook or by crook, through chance and misstep, that we exist today in a world full of rich graphical interfaces, operated by mouse, finger and voice, offering us numerous, abstracted ways to interact with our computers, and the rest of the world.

The Internet

Human communities have long been limited by the impermanence and relatively short range of verbal communication: there are only so many people you can coordinate when language is ephemeral and local. This limitation is expressed neatly in the work of British anthropologist Robin Dunbar, who proposed 150[197] as the maximum number of social connections that any human being can meaningfully maintain at any one time. Exceed this number and the cohesiveness of your connections is impaired.

In the face of the limits suggested by Dunbar, it was the development of written language, initially used for bureaucratic and legal purposes, that allowed for the development of bigger and more complex societies. This is a process that started three to four thousand years ago, and which was significantly accelerated by Gutenberg's moveable type printing press. This single innovation, anticipated but not exploited in ancient China and then Korea[198], led to a huge increase in the availability of books, lowering prices, and unleashing a wave of scientific communication and progress in 16th century Europe.

---

[197] Dunbar's number: Why we can only maintain 150 relationships, BBC Future (https://bbc.in/3zgAEW3)

[198] So, Gutenberg Didn't Actually Invent Printing As We Know It, M. Sophia Newman, Literary Hub (https://bit.ly/3DzNhNq)

Despite these notable improvements in permanence and volume, communication over long distances remained slow for most of human history, with letters and news requiring weeks at sea well into the 20th century. America's Pony Express and France's optical telegraph system provided improvements in certain contexts, but only at great expense.

It is only relatively recently, through the 19th century invention of the electrical telegraph, and the later development of the telephone, that our ability to communicate at a distance has really advanced. Combined with train and then air travel, radio and then television, these developments have fundamentally altered the reality in which we live. As an example, take the weather report, a technology to which most of us rarely give a second thought, but which is only possible with relatively fast, cheap, long-distance communication. Prior to the advent of these technologies, someone living in Rome would probably have spent relatively little time considering the weather in Milan, Munich or New York. Certainly they would not have known about it in real time. Today, such thinking, such perspectives, such information, are part of the fabric within which we live our lives.

The story is the same in regards to coordinated time, in which we've come to expect that our understanding of measured time is exactly aligned with the understanding held by others. Prior to the advent of train networks, with their need for careful scheduling, local time in London and Liverpool could differ by minutes, and no one would have been any the wiser. Nor would it really have mattered. Today we take such global coordination for granted, as it has seeped into our expectations of how the world works. It takes an effort of mind to appreciate that things have not always been like this.

Screens That Eat Children

As a child I marvelled at the speed with which conversation was conveyed from our apartment in Hong Kong to my grandparents in England and Austria. How, I wondered, was it possible that my utterings could make it to their ears quickly enough for them to listen and reply, such that it felt like we were physically together? Of course, the expense of such calls meant I rarely got to linger, but the whole experience left a deep impression. I simply could not imagine a higher level of technology than this.

I was later to learn that these phone calls were facilitated by the interconnection of various copper circuits, through which electricity would flow at more-or-less the speed of light. Our phone would be connected through a local circuit, which would be connected to a Hong Kong-wide circuit, which would connect to various other national circuits, possibly passing under the sea, before being connected, through an inverse process, to my grandparents' phone. By the 1980s the switching of connections to form these circuits was automated, but not too long before it had been performed by human operators working in telephone exchanges (please hold!). The picture below shows women working at a Bell international telephone switch circa 1945.

Look carefully and you can see the names of various locales (London, Paris, Bermuda) on the plaques above the columns that make up the board.

Image 10.2 - Bell Telephone Switchboard (The U.S. National Archives)

In technical terms, what is happening here is known as circuit switching, so called because data flows across the network along the lines of dedicated electrical circuits. Little did I realise, as I spoke to my grandparents, that the successor to circuit switching had already been invented, and was slowly gaining hold in the world of global communication.

In this alternative paradigm, known as packet switching, there are no dedicated circuits. Rather, all data is broken up into chunks, known as packets, which are then placed onto the network. The network, which is self-aware, transmits these packets via the fastest route available at that moment. The various packets in any communication may well all take the same route across the network, but they might equally end up taking a variety of different routes. As long as they arrive in a relatively timely fashion, they can be reassembled into the original message, in a process that is invisible to the user.

When initially proposed by Paul Baran, working at the RAND Corporation in the early 1960s, packet switching seemed, to most network engineers, to be a poor solution to a well solved problem. However, championed by Donald Davies of Britain's National Physical Laboratory in the mid-60s, the concept started to gain attention, before being adopted for use in the Internet's predecessor, the ARPANET. This network, sponsored by and named after the US Department of Defence's Advanced Research Projects Agency (ARPA), was an early attempt to create a robust network through which computers could communicate. At the time of its initial launch in 1969, computers were still large, expensive, heterogeneous and idiosyncratic machines: having such varied computers communicate was a considerable technical challenge.

In much the way as mighty oaks from little acorns grow, the first iteration of the ARPANET consisted of only four computers, each with its own operating system and individual ways of doing things: an SDS Sigma 7 at UCLA, an SDS 940 at Stanford Research Institute, an IBM 360/75 at UCSB and a DEC PDP-10 at the University of Utah[199]. Each of these machines was connected to a specialised machine known as an IMP (Interface Message Processor): built by BBN Technologies, these devices allowed the computers to connect to leased telephone lines and exchange messages in a mutually understandable fashion.

Somewhat dishearteningly, the very first interaction between two ARPANET computers caused one of them to crash. In this first version of the Internet just two characters

---

[199] ARPANET, Wikipedia (https://bit.ly/3Ui25Ha)

had been transmitted before things went dark. A second attempt, performed after an hour of adjustment, proved successful. By 1971 the network had been declared operational, and soon came to support remote login and file transfer, before the later addition of email. The network grew rapidly, and by March 26th, 1976 Queen Elizabeth II was able to send an email from an ARPANET-connected device at the Royal Signals and Radar Establishment in England[200]. The following diagram shows the logical structure and various host computers using the ARPANET in March 1977:

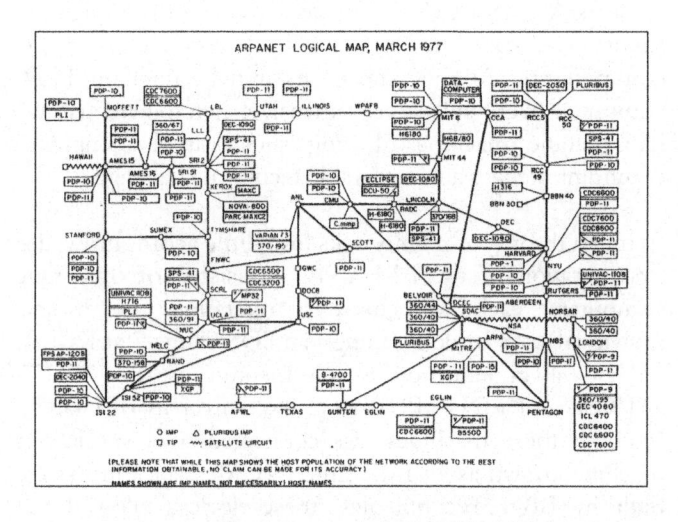

Image 10.3 - Arpanet Logical Map (Wikimedia)

It is worth noting that all of the computers on the network in 1977 belonged to governments, corporations and universities. Computers were, for the most part, still too expensive, too specialised and too complex to be used at

---

[200] Queen Elizabeth Sent the First-Ever Royal Email in 1976!, Monique Jessen, People (https://bit.ly/3stdRma)

home. This situation would, however, soon be changed by the advent of the personal computer.

As the number of computers gradually grew, and the benefits of connecting them into groups became more apparent, ARPANET was joined by a range of other networks, including the National Science Foundation's NFTNET[201], and later, CompuServe and AOL. This led to questions about how to connect these networks into a single massive network-of-networks. It is this concept of *internetworking* which led to the creation of today's Internet, with much of the architectural work being carried out by two ARPANET veterans, Robert Kahn and Vint Cerf in their drafting of the TCP/IP protocol suite. These two sets of rules, TCP for moving information across the Internet and IP for giving computers addresses, are open standards, allowing any company to build hardware and software against them. This openness, long a feature of the Internet, lives on today in the work of the Internet Engineering Task Force (IETF), the body responsible for maintaining the Internet's technical standards, and an organisation to which anyone can apply to join.

Over time a significant number of organisations, companies, individuals and computers adopted the TCP/IP standard, and the modern Internet emerged. The ARPANET was shut down in 1990, but its legacy lives on in today's Internet.

For those who are interested, TCP/IP is defined in two

---

[201] How the Internet was born: from the ARPANET to the Internet, The Conversation (https://bit.ly/3U3QZ94)

IETF publications, known as RFC1122[202] and RFC1123[203]. Running to 115 and 97 pages respectively, these standards describe the minutiae of how TCP/IP compliant hosts (computers) should behave in order to make themselves understood on the Internet. Whilst it can be a lifetime's study to become a TCP/IP expert, the following sections aim to give a little flavour of how they function. For a more extended dive into the Internet's plumbing, with much more character than the two IETF documents listed above, it is hard to do better than Andrew Blum's fascinating book Tubes[204].

Individual computers join physical networks using some kind of medium, such as copper cables, optical fibres, or, in the case of WiFi, radio waves. Each of these individual networks has a globally unique address, known as an IP address, which allows other computers to identify and locate it. Within each network, each computer has its own IP address, which may be globally unique, or just unique to that network. Such networks can be found in offices, schools, universities and homes, and are often called local area networks, or LANs for short.

These LANs are themselves connected to wide area networks (you guessed it, WANs), and it is these connections that form the Internet. In this sense, the Internet does not exist in any one place, but rather is globally distributed. However, there are some places where the Internet is more densely concentrated, such as in the big switching facilities that link many networks to each other.

---

[202] Request for Comments: 1122, IETF (https://bit.ly/3UnIju0)

[203] Request for Comments: 1123, IETF (https://bit.ly/3WkwOVM)

[204] Tubes, Andrew Blum, Ecco (https://bit.ly/3WwsC5E)

In my experience, most lay people when asked how the Internet works, refer erroneously to satellite connections. In reality, the Internet is considerably more earth-bound, with hard-wired connections making up the vast majority of the its infrastructure. In fact, many of the connections between countries run along the seabed, taking the form of dense bundles of high-speed fibre optic cables:

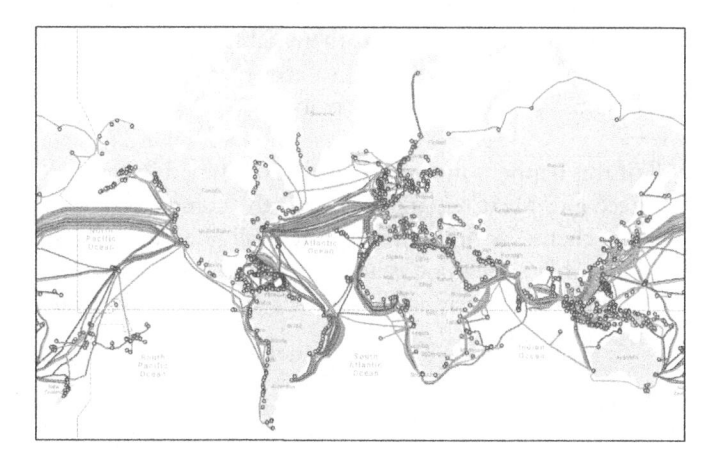

Image 10.4 - Submarine Internet Cables (submarinecablemap.com)

These cables are laid by specialised boats, which spool out the cable as they trundle across the ocean. The cable bundle is allowed to settle, unprotected, on the ocean floor, where it remains for the duration of its operational life. The light pulses projected through these cables diminish in intensity over distance, and so need to be amplified every 50 kilometres or so. These amplifiers, built into the cabling, require a power supply to operate, and so the cable bundles also include electrical power. Clearly some serious engineering goes into making these systems robust, safe and reliable.

In order to communicate, one computer must know another computer's IP address. Often this is communicated via a domain name, such as google.com, which computers can translate to an IP address, like 216.58.200.238, using the Domain Name System (DNS).

Data to be sent across the network is cut up into packets, according to the rules of TCP. Each packet is numbered, such that it can be reordered upon receipt. The packets are pushed onto the network, which routes them to their destination using the fastest path available. Lost packets are resent dynamically as they fail to arrive, and mathematical checksums are used to detect errors.

All of this happens incredibly swiftly, often within fractions of a second. Most remarkable, given the complexity of the whole scheme, is how infrequently it all goes wrong. The odd hint that something is amiss can be found in an image that loads part the way and stops, or a website that lacks any stylistic elements:

Image 10.5 - Website Without CSS (Ross Parker)

The website above is not an example of minimalistic design

work: it is simply that a vital element of the site, its stylesheet, has been lost in transmission, and TCP has not been able to recover it. Generally reloading a page received in this state solves the problem.

For the most part we can count on the Internet to rapidly and reliably transmit information from one part of the world to another, at a cost of virtually zero. It's a miracle we've come to take for granted...but a little scrutiny of its mechanics reveal what a miracle it really is. Occasionally, if we are watching closely, we might catch a glimpse of what is hidden behind the curtain. In such cases it is hard not to be surprised at what we see.

For me, such a moment occurred on December 27th 2006, when an earthquake struck off the coast of Taiwan[205]. At the time I was on holiday in Sydney, and having run out of money, I found myself at an Internet café[206], trying to access my Hong Kong-based online banking. The required web page refused to load properly, with only incomplete chunks displaying. Initially I thought it was a problem at the bank, but a little sleuthing revealed that the problem seemed to be impacting only websites hosted outside of Australia, with local sites loading up relatively fast. Sites in the US were slow, but nowhere near as slow as Asian sites. Checking major news and technology sources, I could find no clues as to the cause of the issues I was observing, suggesting that it was an emerging situation. Eventually, with enough patience, I accessed the needed funds. I left the café with a sense of curiosity as to the root cause of the problem.

The following day I found out, from a newspaper, that the

---

[205] Earthquake shakes the internet, New Scientist (https://bit.ly/3hb3RM9)

[206] Remember them?

earthquake had sheared a series of submarine Internet cables, through which my Australia-to-Hong Kong packets would normally have flowed. The network, behaving as it was designed, started to route around this damage, sending my packets onto various other routes, which themselves quickly became congested by the higher-than-usual volume of traffic. Some packets made it through, others, having taken too long, were deemed lost in transit. As the dust began to settle, with data being more effectively rerouted, some sense of normality returned, albeit at lower-than-normal speeds. All of this I knew in theory, but this was the first time I experienced it in real life.

Cables damaged in this way are expensive and time-consuming to replace, and so, where possible, they are repaired. This involves using submersibles to locate the severed ends of the cable before bringing them to the surface. Secured onto the deck of a boat, they will be repaired by engineers who work to splice together each of the individual fibre optic strands, reconnect the electrical cables and then reinsulate and protect the lot, before dropping it back to the ocean floor. I'd been studying and working in IT for over a decade before I became aware of such heroics, despite this work being vital to the construction and maintenance of the Internet. Such is the complex and often obscure nature of the technologies that we rely on each day.

Interestingly, those old school telephone engineers who worked with circuit switching networks were initially sceptical and dismissive of packet switching, viewing it as inherently inferior. Today almost all of our communication, telephony included, is conducted over packet switched networks, and much of this has been made possible by the vast increases in computational power discussed previously. The shift represents a reminder, should we need one, that every paradigm has its day. No doubt packet switching will itself, in time, be replaced by something that most of us cannot currently conceive of. Perhaps that technology is already under development in some distant lab, to be scorned, in due course, by the current generation of network engineers. As Thomas Kuhn, American philosopher of science, was keen to remind us, scientific progress happens in revolutions[207]: technological progress, being based on science, seems to operate in much the same way.

The World Wide Web

Peering back into the late 1980s, it is possible to see the ways in which the Internet might have been perceived, by an astute observer, as a solution to the generalised problem of how to connect remote computers. A particularly prescient observer might have seen in this the opportunity for convergence of many different types of communication into one system to rule them all.

Despite all of this potential, the software available at that time for making the Internet do useful work was relatively limited. Yes, you could transfer files, send emails and join discussion groups, but there remained an unanswered question: how best to structure the information contained within such a system? For information is only useful if it is organised, discoverable and cross-referenced.

The question of organising information is not new, and in many ways, human progress is told through this particular tale. Written language, it can be argued, has helped us organise our fractured thoughts. Initially written in continuous text known as *scriptio continua*, this kind of writing

---

[207] The Structure of Scientific Revolutions, Thomas Kuhn, University of Chicago Press (https://bit.ly/3sVOSrW)

was read aloud:

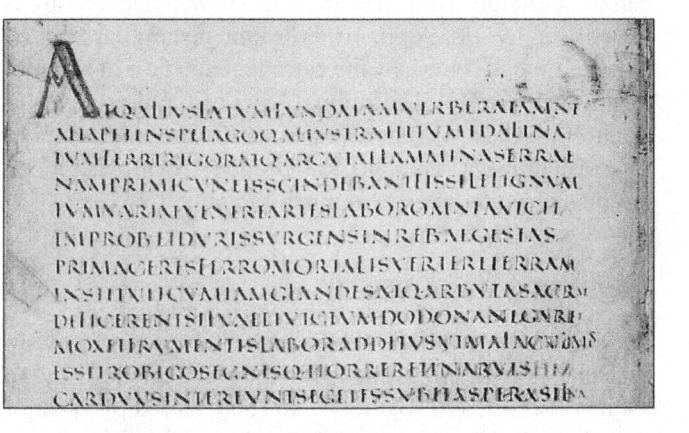

Image 10.6 - Example of Scriptio Continua (Wikimedia)

Private reading (aka "reading in your head") was developed later, offering readers a very different way to interact with the written word. Almost 400 years after the birth of Jesus Christ, St. Augustine met with St. Ambrose in Milan, and in doing so he witnessed such silent reading for the first time. He was moved to comment that "When he read his eyes scanned the page and his heart sought out the meaning, but his voice was silent and his tongue was still." [208]. Clearly, at this time, private reading was not a common phenomenon.

Later innovations, including spaces between words, and the wide range of grammatical conventions and characters that we know today, helped develop writing and reading further. These were joined by paragraphs, chapters, sections, tables of contents and indexes, each of which acted to improve the organisation, and thus the accessibility, of individual texts.

---

[208] The Confessions of St. Augustine, Saint Augustine (https://bit.ly/3DWc4wh)

Calendars, diaries, journals and personal libraries allowed individuals to organise their own lives and knowledge, and these were later supplemented by photos and gramophone records. Meanwhile, dictionaries and library classification systems helped us to become more organised at the book and language levels. Each of these different human technologies helped nudge us closer to the world that we occupy today.

Within this history of informational organisation, the development of the World Wide Web represents, for now, the pinnacle of our achievement. As an application that runs atop the Internet's global communication infrastructure, the Web has enabled us to publish, organise and gain access to an unprecedented wealth of information. It is not without its faults, but it is without doubt, for now, the Internet's killer app[209]. The very fact that most people use the terms "Internet" and "Web" interchangeably, despite their being two distinctly different things, says a lot about the Web's importance in modern life.

The story of the web's development reflects the old adage that "necessity is the mother of invention". In the late 1980s the British computer scientist Tim Berners-Lee was working within the European Organisation for Nuclear Research (known as CERN), investigating ways to organise the massive amounts of data, information and knowledge produced by their research. His proposed solution to this problem drew on the concept of *hypertext*, the power of which, Berners-Lee hoped, would be amplified by the Internet.

Hypertext is the idea that different written elements can be

---

[209] An indispensable feature or function

linked together, to form a web of interrelated meaning. There is no right or wrong way to read hypertext: rather, you start somewhere, and, following a trail of text and embedded links, you end up somewhere else. This no longer seems radical, but emerging from a centuries-old tradition of linear text, which has clear start and end points, it represented a dramatic change. The roots of hypertext can be found in a theoretical machine, called the Memex, proposed by Vannevar Bush in 1945. This electromechanical device would store an individual's ideas, notes, books and communications, allowing them to be quickly found and cross-referenced. This would function, Bush wrote, as "an enlarged intimate supplement to his memory."[210]

Although Bush's ideas were revolutionary, they were beyond what could be built at that time, and it was not until 1960 that they moved closer to reality. In that year Ted Nelson founded Project Xanadu, coining the terms "hypertext" and "hypermedia" to capture his dream of creating a global digital publishing system. Despite its abundant promise, Nelson's Xanadu failed to deliver. Described by Wired magazine as "the longest-running vaporware project in the history of computing", it took a full 38 years to produce and release a partial implementation[211].

Nonetheless, it was to Nelson's concept of hypertext that Berners-Lee turned when seeking to harness the power of the Internet in order to produce the Web. Working on a now-famous NeXT workstation, he programmed both a server to share web content, and a browser to access and

---

[210] As We May Think, Vannevar Bush, The Atlantic (https://bit.ly/3T5qvT8)

[211] Project Xanadu, Wikipedia (https://bit.ly/3T1zq8e)

Screens That Eat Children

display it. In the process, both HTML, as the language used to define web sites, and HTTP, as the protocol for accessing them, were developed. These two protocols remain the central and defining technologies of the Web today. Berners-Lee released the first website on December 20th 1990[212], unknowingly launching human civilisation into an entirely new era.

By this time, other systems for producing hypertext had already been developed, including Apple's much loved Hypercard application. However, it was the key addition of Internet access that propelled Berners-Lee's work to global-scale adoption. It also helped that he released the whole project under an open licence, allowing anyone to get involved without paying fees or royalties.

Gauging the size of the Web is challenging, and so whilst estimates vary, a recent figure of 1.90 billion webpages[213] (and counting) serves to remind us of the massive impact that the Web has had on our lives. The central importance of the Web's dominance is elegantly explained by Nicholas Carr in his book The Shallows[214]. As he points out, the Web's non-linear approach to text has caused us to reconfigure the way that we create and consume written language, which has in turn changed the very structure of our brains. This is, in his words, highly significant:

> "Because language is, for human beings, the primary vessel of conscious thought, particularly higher forms of thought, the technologies that

---

[212] Tim Berners-Lee, Wikipedia (https://bit.ly/3FPkZRw)

[213] Total number of Websites, Live Internet Stats (https://bit.ly/3DWOakl)

[214] The Shallows, Nicholas Carr, W. W. Norton & Company (https://bit.ly/3fwMODI)

restructure language tend to exert the strongest influence over our intellectual lives."

In looking back from the vantage point of the future, it seems likely that the Web will be seen as significant a milestone in human development as was Gutenberg's movable type printing press.

Unfortunately, one of the Web's biggest strengths, its openness, is also its major weakness. Right from the beginning, the standards that defined the Web were open and transparent, meaning that anyone could contribute to and use the Web free of charge. This helped drive adoption of this new platform, but also meant that certain elements like authentication and monetisation, which might have been baked into a corporate network, were entirely absent. Although such features were later added, they were done so in an ad hoc fashion, and people were already used to information on the Web being free of charge. Companies that charged for such information lost customers, and so there was a general movement towards paying for services through advertising and data harvesting. Collectively, we made peace with exchanging our attention and data for access, failing to anticipate just how much of a power imbalance we would ultimately end up with. The result is an economic system that we now describe as *surveillance capitalism*[215], and which underlies many of the phenomena described in this book.

---

[215] See Chapter 12

CHAPTER 11
A FANTASTICAL TALE

Today we find it hard to imagine a time when access to knowledge was restricted, slow or subject to cost. A citizen of the Internet can access far more information than could queens, kings and presidents just a few generations removed. We also find it hard to imagine a time where computers were massive and scary, seen to be evil instruments of war and oppression. These shifts are neither accidental, nor coincidental, but reflect a rather fantastical and deliberate tale: for the steady encroachment of digital tools into our lives has been enabled not just by technical progress, but also by a very skillfully told narrative.

This story has its roots in Europe's 18th century Enlightenment, in which rational thought and the scientific method began to dispel faith, superstition and intuition. With age-old myths being replaced by new explanations for how the world worked, we ran the risk of sinking into nihilistic despair: if everything could be explained by mere cause-and-effect, what meaning did our lives hold? The answer, provided by a combination of science and capitalism, was *progress*. The point of our collective existence was to keep getting smarter, to live better, to march boldly into a new future.

Backed by science, from which new technologies are generally extruded, we were able to extend our lifespans, live more cleanly, eat better, work less and, in general, improve our lot. The benefits of the developed West would trickle down, enriching the world's masses. Old regimes would give way to young democracies, and new economic models would yield untold wealth.

Tarnished by the technologically-driven global devastation of two world wars, and beset by the rise of totalitarian governments on both the left and right, ideas about a newer and more spiritually attuned kind of progress emerged in the post-war period. The 1960s encouraged us to turn on, tune in and drop out[216], to defy authority, to stick it to the man, to live communally for the benefit of all, whilst being our own unique individual self. The Beatles went on pilgrimage to India, Dr. Martin Luther King Jr. had a dream and Americans protested an illegal war. Times, as Bob Dylan so neatly put it, were a-changing[217].

And yet, despite all the youthful, churning energy of revolution, not much of substance actually changed. Instead, the symbols and language of the movement were co-opted in the service of the status quo, business profited, and life rolled on. Becoming a hippie became as easy as purchasing a t-shirt with a peace sign. Counter-culture was pillaged for corporate profit, and, for the most part, governments continued to govern whilst consumers continued to consume.

Except, that is, in Northern California, in and around San

---

[216] Turn on, tune in, drop out, Bionity (https://bit.ly/3FGdTil)

[217] The Times They Are A-Changin' lyrics, Bob Dylan, Genius (https://bit.ly/3Up12Fx)

Francisco, where there co-existed two strong and contrasting cultures: the free loving counter-culturalists, and the nascent, but eminently square, digital technologists. By some strange fate, these two forces, the disruptive and the computational, mated and produced an offspring: the individualistic, anti-authoritarian, capitalist, digital techno-utopian. Best encapsulated by a young Steve Jobs, this was a spirit of innovation in the service of the self, wrapped up in quasi-Buddhist beliefs, offering progress through digital technology. Jobs' 1984 would not, we were assured, be Orwell's 1984[218]: personalised digital technology would see to that. Under this world view we could have our progress cake, and eat it too.

Before Jobs, other Californian techno-utopian figureheads, both native and adopted, led the way. One of these leaders was Stewart Brand, who founded the Whole Earth Catalog, a counter-cultural periodical dedicated to ecology, self-sufficiency and craftsmanship. Despite these interests, Brand also assisted Douglas Engelbart in his famous "Mother of All Demos", the 1968 showcase that, in 90-minutes, introduced many of the features common in today's computers. Brand sensed the connections between Englebart's work and the hippie pursuit of higher consciousness and more sustainable living. These strands came together in 1985, when Brand co-founded The Whole Earth 'Lectronic Link, or the WELL for short. This was a virtual community dedicated to providing "a cherished watering hole for articulate and playful thinkers from all walks of life"[219]. Jobs himself was clearly influenced by Brand's philosophy, as he outlined in his famous 2005

---

[218] 1984 Apple's Macintosh Commercial, Mac History (https://bit.ly/3UoYpDk)

[219] Well.com (https://bit.ly/3sSGnxK)

commencement speech at Stanford[220]:

> "When I was young, there was an amazing publication called *The Whole Earth Catalog*, which was one of the bibles of my generation. It was created by a fellow named Stewart Brand not far from here in Menlo Park, and he brought it to life with his poetic touch. This was in the late 1960s, before personal computers and desktop publishing, so it was all made with typewriters, scissors and Polaroid cameras. It was sort of like Google in paperback form, 35 years before Google came along: It was idealistic, and overflowing with neat tools and great notions."

John Perry Barlow, founder of the Electronic Freedom Foundation and lyricist for the Grateful Dead, expressed much of this newly evolving ethos in his *Declaration of the Independence of Cyberspace*[221], which begins with the words:

> "Governments of the Industrial World, you weary giants of flesh and steel, I come from Cyberspace, the new home of Mind. On behalf of the future, I ask you of the past to leave us alone. You are not welcome among us. You have no sovereignty where we gather.
>
> We have no elected government, nor are we likely to have one, so I address you with no greater authority than that with which liberty itself always speaks. I declare the global social space we are

---

[220] 'You've got to find what you love,' Jobs says, Stanford University (https://stanford.io/3SWVe4J)

[221] A Declaration of the Independence of Cyberspace, John Perry Barlow, Electronic Frontier Foundation (https://bit.ly/3FGgXeb)

> building to be naturally independent of the tyrannies you seek to impose on us. You have no moral right to rule us nor do you possess any methods of enforcement we have true reason to fear."

Barlow's rhetoric, which is based around American notions of liberty from oppression, bled neatly into the MIT-born hacker ethic[222]. These themes were later extended by the free and open source software movements, and eventually became a clarion call for all information to be free. Key thinkers such as Lawrence Lessig[223] and Eric S. Raymond[224] provided a clear and compelling intellectual foundation for this ideology. Those outside the culture might find it unlikely, but such ideas are taken very seriously, and have at times been matters of life and death. The depth of feeling around the freedoms offered by digital technology was tragically illustrated by the premature death of "The Internet's Own Boy"[225], Aaron Swartz, who took his own life following his arrest for disseminating publicly-funded scientific knowledge that had come under corporate control[226]. There is no shortage of irony in the fact that it was MIT, birthplace of the hacker, that was behind the legal action against Aaron Swartz, taken in response to his having "liberated" some of their intellectual property.

---

[222] See Chapter 9

[223] Free Culture, Lawrence Lessig, Penguin (https://bit.ly/3fD2S6G)

[224] The Cathedral and the Bazaar, Eric S. Raymond, O'Reilly Media (https://bit.ly/3h71U3g)

[225] The Internet's Own Boy: The Story of Aaron Swartz, Brian Knappenberger, Luminant Media and Unjustsus Films (https://bit.ly/3U37rX6)

[226] The Brilliant Life and Tragic Death of Aaron Swartz, David Amsden, Rolling Stoen (https://bit.ly/3FeLNdY)

What emerged from this writhing mass of culture is the strange but compelling hodgepodge that drew so many early adopters to the Internet, whether we heard it clearly first hand or vaguely and at a great remove. It is a clear and repeated insistence that digital technology, paired with liberty of expression, freedom from authority and free data, would prove to be a democratising, liberating and enriching force. It would unleash the next wave of human progress, whilst consigning intellectual and moral darkness to the pages of history. Oddly juxtaposed here are elements from both the left and right of the political spectrum: alongside an anti-capitalist, spirit of free love we see the right-wing neo-liberal doctrine that assures us that freedom from government interference will allow the market to sort information by quality, allowing truth to shine its light on all.

As Steven Levy puts it "If *everyone* could interact with computers with the same innocent, productive, creative impulse that hackers did, the Hacker Ethic might spread through society like a benevolent ripple, and computers would indeed change the world for the better."[227].

For anyone coming of age at the turn of the millennium, this was heady stuff. Too young and too naive to know that human nature is pretty hard to shift, I swallowed it whole. Sadly, experience has since proven virtually all techno-utopian claims to be falsehoods.

What would most upset those original MIT hackers is the fact that it was the very culture they built, in working to overthrow the dominance of IBM, which allowed the young

---

[227] Hackers: Heroes of the Computer Revolution, Steven Levy, O'Reilly Media (https://bit.ly/3Dx1Wc4)

upstarts of Silicon Valley to become *big tech*, the world's greatest ever entrenched power, and manipulators of minds on a global scale. The story that sought to set us free has, in the end, been used to enslave us, and the great narrative of computer-as-liberator has been revealed as a work of fiction. Apple, Google, Facebook, Amazon and co. have collectively hidden behind this epic tale, using it to conceal the power that they have amassed.

Turning your back on such a lovely and compelling story is never easy, even when its falsehoods have been laid bare. The process of leaving this particular story behind feels akin to a nasty hangover: gradually it is starting to clear, both individually and collectively, but the pain lingers on.

CHAPTER 12
CHANGING TIMES

A lot of media ink has recently been spent documenting growing concerns around the power of a small number of tech giants, and the impact that they are having on our lives. Governments are starting to awaken to the issue, and 2021 alone saw US congressional leaders learning of Facebook's impact on elections[228] and the bodies and minds of young women[229]. Meanwhile, the Chinese government is pushing to put controls on young gamers[230], whilst also curtailing the power of technology firms in domains as diverse as financial risk, privacy and monopoly-busting[231].

Digital technology has, for all its benefits, had a profound, broad and widely negative impact on individuals and societies. Whether it is hate speech, addiction, narcissism,

---

[228] Facebook's Zuckerberg grilled in U.S. Congress on digital currency, privacy, elections, Pete Schroeder, Reuters (https://reut.rs/3zFjDFp)

[229] Mark Zuckerberg should quit Facebook, says Frances Haugen, Dan Milmo, The Guardian (https://bit.ly/3zdx7Ia)

[230] China cuts children's online gaming to one hour, BBC News (https://bbc.in/3U3uJfg)

[231] TechScape: Xi Jinping's 'Little Red Book' of tech regulation could lead the way, Vincent Ni, The Guardian (https://bit.ly/3Dvz4B3)

polarisation, FOMO, loneliness, self-loathing or disinformation, none of us are untouched, none of us are immune. It has all happened so suddenly, having started off with such promise, and it has left us all scrambling.

Henry Kissinger, elder statesman, sums up this situation as follows[232]:

> "Technology has brought about a means of communication permitting instantaneous contact between individuals or institutions in every part of the globe as well as the storage and retrieval of vast quantities of information at the touch of a button. Yet by what purposes is this technology informed? What happens to international order if technology has become such a part of everyday life that it defines its own universe as the sole relevant one?...Will the rapidity and scope of communication break down barriers between societies and individuals and provide transparency of such magnitude that the age-old dreams of human community will come into being? Or will the opposite happen: will mankind, amidst weapons of mass destruction, networked transparency, and the absence of privacy, propel itself into a world without limits or order, careening through crises without comprehending them?"

Although our politics might diverge, Kissinger and I see eye to eye on the threats posed by the digital technology explosion, as well as the ways in which their use can be positive. His thoughts on "careening through crises without comprehending them" seem to sum up our current situation

---

[232] World Order, Henry Kissinger, Penguin Books (https://bit.ly/3NxQMbl)

rather aptly.

And Kissinger is not alone: the writings and revelations of a slew of insightful, articulate and brave authors invite us to dive deep into the myriad interconnected issues at play here. They alert us to the perils, leaving us dizzied at just how much has changed. The list is long, but for starters includes Edward Snowden[233] on surveillance and privacy, Adam Alter[234] on compulsion by design, Cory Doctorow[235][236] on surveillance capitalism and radicalisation, Diana Graber[237] on raising our young, Michael Harris[238] on the end of absence, Jaron Lanier[239] on the ills of social media, Andrew Keen[240] on the limits of the Internet and Matthew B. Crawford[241] on living beyond your head. Each, in their own way, brings to the fore the particular perils posed by our current digital tools and the wider culture that they have generated.

The question, as with any generation-defining issue, is, once alerted, what to do? Clearly, there is risk attendant to

---

[233] Permanent Record, Edward Snowden, Metropolitan Books (https://bit.ly/3DsIgWO)

[234] Irresistible, Adam Alter, Penguin Books (https://bit.ly/3NDHhYE)

[235] How to Destroy Surveillance Capitalism, Cory Doctorow, Medium Editions (https://bit.ly/3UcCZcK)

[236] Radicalized: Four Tales of Our Present Moment, Cory Doctorow, Tor Books (https://bit.ly/3Uf6QBu)

[237] Raising Humans in a Digital World, Diana Graber, AMACOM (https://bit.ly/3DvCweR)

[238] The End of Absence, Michael Harris, Current, (https://bit.ly/3sTth3d)

[239] Ten Arguments for Deleting Your Social Media Accounts Right Now, Jaron Lanier, Henry Holt and Co. (https://bit.ly/3DTycrf)

[240] The Internet Is Not the Answer, Andrew Keen, Atlantic Monthly Press (https://bit.ly/3zFh1ak)

[241] The World Beyond Your Head, Matthew B. Crawford, Farrar, Straus and Giroux (https://bit.ly/3NxuLcT)

inaction: power tends to accumulate, and bad behaviours tend to persist, until a resistance is mounted.

Yet, there is also tremendous risk inherent in any action, given the complexity of the world we have constructed for ourselves. Each of the many actions that we might take could play out in any number of unexpected ways, cascading and amplifying the effects of other efforts within the same space.

A useful case study of this dynamic is offered by the global distribution of insecticide-treated mosquito nets (ITNs) in a bid to combat malaria[242]. Whilst undoubtedly effective, with millions of lives saved, this programme has triggered an unexpected ancillary behaviour: hungry people using the nets to catch fish. Whilst this behaviour is, at the individual level, rational, understandable and relatable, it has raised concerns about pesticide contamination and depletion of fish stocks: the fineness of the nets catches fish too small to be sustainable, whilst the embedded pesticides leach into the water. Debate rages as to the sum cost and benefit of this programme, but it underscores a vital point: any attempt to help can harm. The educator Yong Zhao makes this point in relation to school reform[243] by invoking the medical notion of side effects, and it has no doubt been felt by countless other well-intentioned humanitarians.

The forces at work in this paradox are wonderfully illustrated by Dave Snowden's Cynefin framework[244]. This

---

[242] Implications of Insecticide-Treated Mosquito Net Fishing in Lower Income Countries, Larsen et al, Environmental Health Perspectives (https://bit.ly/3DsJ7Xw)

[243] What Works May Hurt, Yong Zhao, Teachers College Press (https://bit.ly/3U7LMwT)

[244] Cynefin, Dave Snowden, Cognitive Edge (https://bit.ly/3Dq0R5S)

model distils down the differences between situations that are variously simple, complicated, complex and chaotic.

In simple situations, inputs and outputs are closely correlated, and can be worked out with trivial rules. It is easy to guess what outcomes will stem from an action. Best practice can be defined and used to guide us. We tend to find that rules are effective. As situations become more complicated we find that inputs and outputs are still correlated, but that there are many more variables and interactions. It takes experience, judgement and sense to predict and control outcomes. The unknowns are known, and so good practice and heuristics can guide us.

Things become considerably murkier when we move towards the complex, in which the relationship between inputs and outputs is opaque, confusing and changeable. There is generally no right answer, and clarity might only be gained retrospectively, after action has become outcome. The unknowns are unknown, and so we must fly by the seat of our pants, developing emergent practice as we go. Ultimately, a situation might be described as chaotic when events unfold rapidly and unexpectedly, with input and output seemingly disconnected. The situation is confusing, and planning is not possible: reactive damage control is the only course of action.

Whilst we might casually interchange the words complicated and complex, they are in fact very different beasts, a key understanding that Cynefin helps keep front and centre in our thinking.

The truth is that we live in a world that oscillates, much of the time, between the complex and the chaotic. Never are the affairs of groups of humans merely simple. Under authoritarian rule, such as in a traditional school or some other totalitarian regime, we might be fooled into believing that they are complicated. In reality, this is a short-term illusion purchased at great human expense. It can be comforting to those in charge, but is dismal for those subordinate to their power.

In reality, complexity forces us to reckon with the fact that any societal action we take will only be loosely coupled to the outcomes that are generated. In approaching any change, we need to proceed with caution.

In weighing the risks suggested by the Cynefin model, we have to ask ourselves whether the world we have built is the world that we wish to inhabit. Do our digital tools serve us, or do we serve them and their masters? For me, given the road I have travelled, there is no doubt that the risks of doing nothing far outweigh the risks of doing something. In this vein, I invite you to consider, in big picture terms, where digital technology is taking us.

The Road Just Ahead

At the very highest level of concern is the now well-established view that we are living in a state of surveillance capitalism[245], driven by digital technology. In this new paradigm, which has been pioneered by Google, Facebook, Amazon and others, our every interaction, transaction and digital utterance is harvested by monopolistic firms for conversion into profit. There are no secrets, there is no privacy, and nothing other than profitability is sacred. Every possible data point about us is harvested, aggregated and sold to others, whilst also being used to sell to us. Our world view, our emotions, our friendships…all of these are up for grabs.

---

[245] Shoshana Zuboff on surveillance capitalism, VPRO (https://bit.ly/3U0vCpa)

Within this attention economy, keeping us glued to our screens is a key concern and the primary driver of growth. In this context, Facebook's newly announced transformation into Meta[246] is extremely concerning: not content with current engagement levels, Facebook's founder wishes us to inhabit *his* metaverse, a virtual reality environment where we will live, work and socialise. You only need to have read one techno-dystopian novel[247] to know how this particular story ends. And Meta is not alone here, with a range of companies vying for us to wear their headsets and thus seeking to further disconnect us from ourselves, each other and the world around us.

Although with different ends in mind, the singularity, that state when humans are no longer distinguishable from their machines, is equally concerning. Popularised by Ray Kurzweil[248], this notion attacks the very foundations of our humanity: our embodiedness and our ultimate death. It seeks to diminish what makes us human in order that we can live forever inside a machine. Based on the simplistic notion that intelligence and consciousness can be reduced to an algorithm, it promises that given enough computational power we can be uploaded to a computer and live without our bodies. Alternatively, we might choose to live as cyborgs, as computerised brains housed in mechanical bodies.

Recent developments in generative AI are strongly suggestive of a world in which a large number of educated

---

[246] Facebook changes its name to Meta in major rebrand, BBC News (https://bbc.in/3fwcRLb)

[247] Despite the happy ending, Ernest Cline's Ready Player One (https://bit.ly/3DYitaq) checks this box for me.

[248] The Singularity Is Near, Ray Kurzweil, Penguin Books (https://bit.ly/3UlWMqd)

and creative humans, their jobs having been outsourced to computers, can no longer find work or meaning. We ought to ask where this rapidly emerging technology will take us, and what it will mean for us as a species. Why bother learning to write eloquently when ChatGPT can do it faster and more cheaply? Why employ graphic designers or artists when Midjourney can steal from the world's best to create new works? Why hire any thinking human, for that matter, when a computer can do it better? Of course, "disruptive" technologies are nothing new, but these latest innovations cut awfully close to what it means to be a human.

Our Silicon Valley masters seem to long for a frictionless future, unencumbered by bodies, by nature, by society and by reality. To me, the rise of this world view, this perverse fantasy, which has been codified by a small group of young, white men, speaks volumes about our lack of collective maturity. We clearly have yet to grasp that it is the very real texture of a life well lived that gives our short time on earth its meaning. Without the challenges and the frustrations, without the aches and pains, without intense and immediate interpersonal relations, without meaningful work, life is a dull and featureless terrain. In a digitally curated world, massaged to our liking, there is no pleasure, no wonder, no excitement, simply a flat and lifeless monotony of clicks, views, likes and ads.

In chasing the painless efficiency of digital living, we risk losing everything for which we might wish to live.

Resistance is not Futile

For some, the awesome economic and cultural capital of big tech raises the natural question of "should we even bother to resist?". There is a sense that, having set off on this path, we are now committed, and that there is no way to back out. Is it ever possible, my father recently asked me, to get the technological genie back in the bottle?

Without a beat of hesitation I answer this question with *yes*, it is absolutely possible. Human history is replete with the invention and dissemination of terribly cruel technologies, many of which have been challenged, repositioned and bested. These vanquished demons rarely disappear entirely, but they are certainly defanged. Eugenics, the Atlantic slave trade, leaded petrol, chlorofluorocarbons and tobacco smoking spring immediately to mind. Others are less cut-and-dry, and more work remains, yet the battle has commenced. The oppression of women, the colonisation, exploitation and suppression of many multitudes of people, the spanking of children, nuclear weapons, the internal combustion engine. Each of these once acceptable technologies has been robustly challenged and forced onto its back foot, if not yet entirely conquered.

I don't believe that we really need to get this particular genie entirely back in the bottle, and neither do I think we would want to. Given the number of humans currently living on earth, and the logistical heavy-lifting required to sustain them, I suspect that without our digital infrastructure we would now struggle to survive.

Rather, what we need is to *tame* our digital tools.

With the right story, the right values and the right leaders, progress is possible. Not an Industrial Revolution-style progression to some imagined pinnacle of human production and consumption, but rather progress towards leading better, more meaningful and more sustainable lives. In truth, what is under discussion here is not just screens. This is about a way of life into which we have sleep-walked. It is about the unassailed rise of a mechanistic and extractive world view, the dominance of a torrid neo-liberal capitalism in which everything has a price and nothing is sacred. It is about the way that forces beyond our ken have shoehorned us into a new reality, from which we need to awaken. It turns out that the Wachowskis' era-defining film, The Matrix[249], is a fine analogy for something we experience every day: the only difference is that it is our culture that enslaves us, and not, for now, our machines.

In the course of my work I often talk with groups of pre- and in-service teachers. Through these engagements I try to offer them a sense of the cultural challenges that we face, with the hope that my peers can be positioned to push back, to make their own classrooms and schools just a little better in this regard. Of late I've taken to ending such presentations by posing variations of the following question:

> "Will we help our students live with meaning in a world of others?
>
> or merely
>
> Study, work, consume, reproduce, poke devices...and die."

I've yet to meet anyone willing to back the second option.

From the top-down and from the bottom-up, we need to start imagining and building new ways to live, whilst resurrecting others that we've collectively abandoned and forgotten. We need to build our culture not around convenience, and not around simulation, but around real, lived experience. We need to regain the joy of being enveloped within the world, of living through fewer filters, of having regained, rebuilt and recalibrated our senses

---

[249] The Matrix, Wikipedia (https://bit.ly/3UjoN1A)

gradually over time. Distilled in the following chapters are some ideas, drawn from a massive potential pool, of how we might approach this vital task.

Do be warned, however, that in undertaking the steps that follow, you will start down a path that puts you in conflict with almost all of the major technical, social and political forces of our times. This is rewarding in its own way, but certainly not without its challenges. At times it can feel like a lonely path to tread.

CHAPTER 13
THE INDIVIDUAL

It might seem odd, in the face of such systemic challenges, to start with a section on individual change. The problems we face today are beyond our making, and in no way am I suggesting that this is a challenge that any individual can completely resolve. In fact, some might argue that it is perverse to expect individuals to change when given such long odds. Believing in the power of individuals to overcome such massively systemic challenges is sometimes described as "cruel optimism"[250], which I feel is a rather apt description, and not at all the intention of this chapter. Hiring an expensive consultant to teach underpaid and overworked employees to use mindfulness to control their stress is an example of cruel optimism.

Nonetheless, for most of us, our selfhood is the only entity over which we have any kind of real control, and so, as a unit for change, the individual makes a great place to start. Hopefully the stories and advice contained in this chapter help you to begin chipping away at the problems posed by screens, in the knowledge that much more than this is

---

[250] Stolen Focus, Johann Hari, Crown (https://bit.ly/3h79D1h)

required.

Choice of Technologies

It is claimed that insanity is the only sane response to an insane world, and I often wonder whether my own anxious, neurotic responses to life are simply my mind's way of fighting back against a mad world. This sentiment is neatly encapsulated in Blaise Pascal's sentiment that "Men are so necessarily mad, that not to be mad would amount to another form of madness"[251].

For as long as I can recall, the societies and cultures that I've inhabited have led me to feel a generalised sense of confusion, a slight and omnipresent discomfort. Why do we do things this way, and not that? Why are we here? Why is life so terrifying, and why isn't everyone else scared witless? What ought we to do with our limited lifespans? What does it all mean? What if I turn out to be less powerful than I hope? What if I turn out to be more powerful than I can control? These age-old questions have tormented greater minds than mine, pushing many past breaking point.

As hard as these questions can be, they have ultimately driven me to positive ends. I've read as much and as deeply as I can, I've stopped to reflect on the harms I've caused, and I've tried to live a life of meaning. For me a certain subset of this quest has boiled down to doing things slowly, by hand, repeatedly.

When I bake bread I want to feel the moisture that forms the gluten as I work the dough. I want to make the same dough a thousand times, until I know it intimately, until I

---

[251] Madness & Civilization, Michel Foucault, Vintage (https://bit.ly/3Nw668B)

can sense its composition and state beneath my fingers. When I shave I want to feel the dampness of the brush as it stirs up a lather on the surface of the soap block. I want to know its quality on my cheek, I want to sense the rate at which it dries, offset by the day's humidity. I want to feel a single blade blunting gradually over time until I know, just before cuts appear, that it is time to change it. I want to live in the very practical, very hands on and very real moment that each of these experiences makes available to me. When I make coffee I want to judge the number of beans by eye, such that their grounds fill the mocca to just the right level: not so low as to make gritty coffee, but not so high that they stymy the flow of steam and then burn. I want to feel the sharpening of a knife blade on a stone, I want to repeatedly run up a mountain until I either reach the top or accept my limits. I want to teach until I can reliably sense the mood of the room well ahead of my students, before gracefully deflecting them in a more desirable direction.

And so, I deliberately eschew convenience, as a choice. It's hand made bread, not store bought. It's a double edged safety razor, not a multi-blade or an electric. It's taking the bus, not the car. It's hand ground coffee, not capsules. I judge my sleep by how I feel, not by the readout of a device. I embrace discomfort, not because I enjoy it, but because it brings comfort into sharper relief. I welcome inconvenience, not to go slow, but to avoid missing out on life.

In other words, I choose very deliberately the technologies by which I live.

This is not, I hasten to add, snobbery. I don't believe that the results of my actions are better, purer or more noble than those offered by alternative technologies. Often, as with older methods of shaving, they are worse. But this is beside the point, for the journey is what counts, not the destination, and I happen to believe that my chosen means serve me well.

There is no doubt that I still rush too much, work too hard, and fail to spend enough of my time where it counts. But I try, each day, to push back the relentless cultural tide of personal productivity and live a life less quantified.

Maybe I am insane, but it seems to me unsurprising that our lives leave us feeling simultaneously bored and overstimulated, exhausted yet sleepless. Our wonderful conveniences, contrivances and contraptions have reduced our burdens, and thus removed the life from the living. Without any friction, life offers us no surface on which to adhere. Our creature comforts have left us weak and afraid. I'm no masochist, but a cold shower early in the morning reliably reminds me of how obscenely comfortable my life really is.

Changing Habits

So, as our Californian friends from the 1960s taught us, our first job really is to turn on, tune in and drop out. We need to turn on to simple life ways, tune in to the means by which technology dulls our senses and drop out from the most egregiously blunting tools.

In terms of digital technology this has played out for me in a gradual refusal to add gadgets to my life. For my work I have a laptop computer, and for connectivity I have a smartphone. In my life there is no smart watch, no fitness tracker, no drone, no tablet, no smart TV, no gaming console and no ebook reader.

I spend far too much time on my laptop, I know, but I love to work and I love to create. However, I no longer use social media: no Facebook, no Twitter, no Instagram, no nothing.

I don't play video games, there are no fantasy sports leagues, and I long ago stopped consuming pornography. I read the news a little, and I spend a lot of time supporting the schools and individuals who help build and use Gibbon, the humane, open source software project that I run. I try to be kind, and avoid hostile environments and individuals.

My smartphone, I know, threatens my wellbeing the most. It is in my pocket, and all-too-frequently appears unbidden in my hand. I go to check the time, and end up somewhere else entirely. And so, I've worked hard to defang the beast. Tristan Harris's advice to set your phone to grayscale[252], which initially seems too simplistic to work, has proven a game changer. A black and white screen really is so dull as to reduce the compulsion of the whole experience.

Removing all non-essential apps was another big step, as was turning off notifications for all but direct human contact. I've worked consciously to build awareness of the times that I default to my phone, such as in waiting for a train, or standing at a bar, and to redirect my mind and body to other things.

Recently I have begun a *digital fast* each Friday after work, which I aim not to break until Sunday morning. My phone and laptop are put away, out of sight, and this gives me 36 hours of uninterrupted peace in which to be present with my family, read, bake bread and otherwise be human. Once or twice in that period I will deliberately check my phone's notification screen to make sure that there have been neither family emergencies, nor any blow-ups in our school systems, but I am careful not to unlock my phone on these

---

[252] Former Google Designer Says 1 Simple Trick Can Curb Your Smartphone Addiction, Betsy Mikel, Inc. (https://bit.ly/3TOMqiV)

occasions.

The Social Tax

I've found most aspects of this journey to be relatively easy, partly due to the way I've come to think about digital technology in general, and social media in particular. On this front I had a revelatory breakthrough shortly after I started using Spotify to listen to music. Spotify, being a modern tech company, is keen to make sure their product is as social as possible: listening to music with others makes it easy for them to harvest more data about you, and makes you less likely to switch to other platforms. And so, as I started to use Spotify I also followed some friends. A little time later I was followed by some students, which is odd, as kids hate old music, but oh well. Some weeks later I was sitting at my desk after school, relaxing to a little Rage Against The Machine, when the thought struck me that my students might be seeing my listening habits. What would they and their parent make of the Rage maxim[253] "fuck you I won't do what you tell me"? They would almost certainly take this deeply political song the wrong way, and then I'd be in real trouble.

I sat back in my chair, marvelling at the ways in which digital technology could turn the most mundane event into the most traumatic, when it occurred to me that what I was facing was a kind of *social tax*. In order to profit, a corporation was seeking to exploit my social network, and, as a result I encountered a tax on my time and headspace. I found the required settings to disable all of Spotify's social features, and then spent the next several months slowly

---

[253] Killing In The Name lyrics, Rage Against The Machine, Genius (https://bit.ly/3h5wAlh)

unpicking the various social elements from other platforms that I use. This one concept helped to shift my perception onto a new plane, making change easy. It is exactly the reason that these practical chapters come at the end of this book, allowing you to utilise the new ideas you've encountered thus far.

Every so often I find that some insistently social feature has been added to an app or service that I rely on. One example of this is WhatsApp's Status feature, which appeared a few years ago, and wants to serve as a mini-social network, allowing users to post updates on what they are doing to anyone in their address book. Although many adult users appear not to have registered its presence, it seems to be popular with kids. There is no way to disable this feature, or the little dot that appears when a new status has been added. You might have come to WhatsApp for chat, but it now comes at the cost of a little extra social tax.

Eventually, I came to see much of social media for what it really is: a set of relatively loose and meaningless social connections which companies offer us for their own gain, under the guise of living our best lives. Having seen through this illusion it was easy to pack up and leave.

Most important to me is the fact that, through this process, I have come to minimise the number of times each day that my children and students see me using a phone. I know that in much the same way that I longed to be like the adult smokers of the 1980s, they want to be like the adult phone addicts of the 2020s. What grown ups do, children will esteem and emulate.

I am far from perfect on all of the fronts described above, and many is the day I wish I could jettison my remaining two devices. I try to recognise that this is a journey on which we are all pioneers, that there is only emerging practice, and that digital technologies definitely add value to my life, as long as I can keep them within certain bounds. The odds are certainly stacked against anyone wishing to make individual change, but with thought and commitment it is possible.

At this point I invite you to consider the ways in which you use your own screens, to list the behaviours that you dislike, that waste your time, that make you less friendly, that take you away from the people who matter to you. Set some goals for where you want to go, and apply the ideas above, and any others that you learn along the way, to getting where you want to be.

CHAPTER 14
THE FAMILY

Fortunately, most of us do not live alone, and for all the strife that family life can entail, it also represents our greatest source of strength as we learn to live with screens.

In starting this section it seems worth revisiting Neil Postman's assertion[254] that "a family that does not or cannot control the information environment of its children is barely a family at all".

For me this statement highlights the single hardest aspect of parenting in a digital age: at the very same time that the family is required to create a healthy information ecosystem, digital technology acts to flood the family with unfiltered information. This barrage is present twenty four hours a day, seven days a week on multiple screens within and outside the home. It makes the parental task of bringing some information to the fore whilst keeping other information at bay extremely difficult. I know, from working with families whose children sneak around at night seeking an informational fix, that it often feels like a losing

---

[254] See Chapter 6

battle. How can we compete with the bright, glimmering lights of the digital world?

Matters are complicated further, for just as Winnicott's "good enough mother" needs to withdraw support at just the right times, so the "good enough family" needs to admit different information at different ages. Our judgement calls, already fraught with challenge, require constant revision, with the conflicting needs of older and younger siblings also needing to be reconciled.

As Nicholas Carr points out[255], the stakes could not be higher:

> "And when we hand down our habits of thought to our children, through the examples we set, the schooling we provide and the media we use, we hand down as well the modifications in the structure of our brains."

This is to say, that at every turn, our children are strengthening and weakening the various neuronal brain structures that make them who they are. Although these structures are changeable, through a process known as neuroplasticity, structures that are formed and reinforced tend to turn into habit. And we all know how hard habits are to kick, especially those with an addictive bent.

However, it is possible, with careful planning, to have screens in the home, enjoy their delights, and keep the family intact. Research by the Kaiser Family Foundation[256]

---

[255] The Shallows, Nicholas Carr, W. W. Norton & Company (http://bit.ly/3fwMODI)
[256] See Chapter 1

shows that whilst many parents don't set rules for their children, when they do, they are effective in reducing media consumption considerably.

A great first step in this journey is to do your best to give your children full, fun, playful and independent lives. Screens, like any potentially addictive substance, tempt most strongly those for whom life is joyless, burdensome or fearful. Spend time exploring your local area with your children from a young age, teaching them to move and act safely. Model for them a sense of exploration and wonder in nature, and provide them with the tools to have fun and take risks: rope swings, bikes, skates, and, as they get older, knives, flint and steel. Work to bring them into the company of like-minded children with whom they can roam. Let them know that it is okay to take risks, but that risks have consequences. Allow your children to get dirty, wet and cold, and, within reason, to hurt themselves. Avoid overscheduling their lives, and push back against any school or teacher that gives homework from a young age. Read with and to your children. Ask them probing questions and tease them with riddles and puzzles. Gradually expose them to the wondrous, delectable complexity of life.

All going well your children will grow up without losing too much of their natural curiosity, their sense of wonder at the daily miracle of life on planet Earth. This being the case, you can then use a structured approach to integrate screens with less risk that things will unravel.

This starts with positive role modelling: as my good friend Trent Barrett once taught me, children record everything that their parents do, and from a surprisingly young age. Right from birth, if you have the chance, make a conscious habit to use phones and other screens sparingly within the home. If you already have children, start building new habits, and discuss these changes with your children. Let them know of your own flaws and struggles, your hopes and plans for doing better[257]. However, there is a careful balance here, as devices should not be taboo, and should not be accompanied by moralising: it is enough to note that they are useful and fun, that they can distract us from what counts, and then to model moderation.

As your children get older, invite them to co-view stimulating media with you. Play simple games that encourage cooperation and thoughtfulness. Discuss the positives and negatives of the things that you encounter on your travels. Whilst specifying ages for certain activities is tricky, I would seek to avoid any real screentime until the age of five, after which I would slowly introduce this kind of conversational co-viewing and co-playing.

Early Devices

As children grow older, they will ideally not have their own devices, but rather will have access to a shared screen within a visible and public part of the house. In the 1980s this was easy: there was one TV, it was in the living room and it could not easily be moved. You can recreate this within your own home by choosing technologies that eliminate private viewing. This promotes sharing, consideration, discussion and co-viewing, whilst making screen time less about the immediate satisfaction of personal desires.

In our home, personal devices made an earlier-than-expected appearance, arriving in the form of fifth birthday gifts from well-meaning relatives (no names mentioned). This proved challenging, as it was clear that they were extremely compelling to our children. Reflecting on this

---

[257] Chapter 13 should have helped with this

challenge, my wife and I worked to introduce firm, simple rules, which emphasised self-control on the part of our children. The tablets were not to be used during the week, and on Saturday and Sunday could be used for 45 minutes with on-the-spot parental permission required. From my sister, Nic Parker, we learned the wonderful trick of teaching children to set and manage their own on-screen timers, placing the onus of honesty and self-regulation on their shoulders. Thus constrained, devices were to be used in a public area of the house, where the screen could be seen, without headphones. We set clear expectations and consistent consequences for misuse. Boundaries were breached on a few occassions, and the devices then went away for a period of time. Some mildly inappropriate content was discovered, and interesting discussion ensued around its meaning and place within the family. One grossly inappropriate advert was encountered[258], but having a mindful adult to hand mitigated that hazard as far as was possible, and it seems to have done no lasting harm.

And so, to this day, weekend mornings generally start with our two children (aged 13 and 10) asking to have some iPad time, and being granted 45 minutes. They set a timer, and if they "forget" or otherwise elongate their time, we talk about it. They are in a public part of the house, generally near each other, and mostly not wearing headphones. My wife and I are not always watching them, but we have done so enough in the past, and do so on enough other occasions, that they generally do the right thing. Once the screen time is done, they cook their own breakfast, do arts and crafts, and play with their friends. Often they ask for more screen time, and sometimes this is granted, especially as they have gotten older. During the holidays, they need to exercise or do

---

[258] As discussed in Chapter 6

chores before enjoying screens, just to keep things interesting.

Choice of Media

When allowed to choose their own media, our children used to generally watch traditional TV shows, via YouTube or Netflix. The latter, although paid, definitely provides a more protected and curated environment, and one that is free of advertisement. As they got older, they began to spend more of their allotted time on YouTube. We aimed to offer them guidance, steering them towards content that reflected our values, and away from violence, consumerism and adult language. At times our son would start to mimic the style of various YouTubers, DanTDM being a favourite, affecting a brash and self-centred style, announcing life's every happening loudly. We would discuss the ways in which YouTube and real life are different, and why people act differently in different circumstances. An entire family meal accompanied by YouTube-level hyperbole, with every detail described and narrated, was, we discovered, not to our liking. At times we have enforced embargos on certain content, before relaxing the guidelines at a later time.

As my son has gotten older, his recommended videos list on YouTube has come to provide a useful glimpse into his interests. It also acts as a discussion point, when we notice it filling up with rubbish, allowing us to redirect him to better content.

Much of our family viewing time is spent on film, which we sit and enjoy together as a family. Movie night is always popular, and often accompanied by a meal we make together. It's not always easy to find a film that everyone likes, and which fits our family's values and tastes, and arguments sometimes ensue. Having to think of others, rather than acting in isolation, is, for me, an important part of such co-viewing. Common Sense Media, who do excellent film reviews for families, is invoked when my wife and I are not familiar with a film the children wish to watch.

Gaming

In general there is no serious gaming in our house, in large part because our children lack access to the right hardware and software, but also because we don't allow it. So, with no massively multiplayer online games, our children tend to play simple, pre-vetted mobile games within their allotted tablet time. Gaming culture has previously been alluring to our son: his friends play and talk about games, YouTubers review them, and popular culture and language are driven by them. One minute everyone is getting roasted[259], the next they are flossing[260], and then they are yeeting[261] everything in sight. Today all everyone can play is Fortnite, tomorrow it's Among Us. And, in a surprisingly short time, it's all become passé, and everyone moves on to the next big thing.

I know, from listening to and talking with my older students, that many pockets of gaming culture are extremely adult in nature. Players use very strong language, and the talk is often unapologetically misogynistic and xenophobic. This often seems to stem from games in which strangers play together, but quickly spreads into games played by groups of friends, simply because of the way language is transmitted. Due to the way that culture permeates from older to younger children, our own kids are subtly, unknowingly under the influence of such forces. In response to this we make nothing taboo, discuss things openly, and keep serious

---

[259] Teased or defeated

[260] A dance made popular by the game Fortnite

[261] Throwing

gaming at bay. As our children have gotten older, we have allowed access to some multiplayer games, such as Minecraft and Roblox, but always gradually and with strong social framing and education about why we don't play with strangers, and how we should conduct ourselves online.

I do make sure to gently tease my children for those things that they pick up online, but which seem strangely out of place in real life. When my son offers the standard YouTube greeting "Whatsssss'up guys", I'll remind him to "Like, subscribe and comment below". Sometimes I'll greet him with an unexpected "Whatsssss'up guys". From time to time I let out a frustrated "bruh". He doesn't always appreciate the ribbing, but it's done in jest, and it keeps him honest and on his toes. Occasionally I take out my phone in public and act like a YouTuber: I know from the eye rolls that my kids know exactly what I'm up to, and it certainly helps encourage them to moderate their own behaviour. Dad's are so lame. Bruh.

Chat

As a rule our children had no exposure to chat throughout primary school. However, Covid brought Zoom into our lives, and along with its video conferencing capability came individual and group chat. We've spent time discussing with our children the fact that digital chat is disinhibiting in ways that face-to-face speech is not. Much of this comes down to the fact that you can't see someone's reaction during text chat, as well as the fact that there is zero risk of immediate personal harm when you say something cruel. We came to a compromise where a couple of small group chats are permitted, but only on the laptop, and only for school-related matters. These rules were later relaxed when my son turned 13, but only in small increments and within specific parameters.

When I do observe my son and his peers chatting, it is immediately evident that most of the chat is friendly rubbish ("sup", "hi", "sup", "yo", "what are you doing?", "sup", "yo", "sup", etc.), but it is amazing how quickly this can turn hostile, especially as group size increases.

In my experience as a teacher and school leader, group chat is where the majority of contemporary childhood social drama is born. At home we discuss the difference between being a bystander and an upstander: the former is culpable, the latter makes things better. We explain that standing up for others is not an easy thing to do, but that it is worth the risk, and wouldn't we all like others to stand up for us when we are in need of support? As a general rule, our children know that there are certain things that they won't be allowed to do with screens until they can be consistently nice to others in real life.

Later Devices

The topic of online schooling and chat raises the interesting spectre of school-mandated laptops. As a technology leader at a school with a one-to-one laptop programme, it is part of my job to introduce laptops into the lives of eleven-year-old children. I take this responsibility seriously, and see it as a learning opportunity for children and families alike. This will be considered from a school point-of-view in the next chapter. However, as a parent I can see the ways in which this device introduces new dilemmas and challenges, and how essential it is for school and family to work together to ensure that this learning tool is effectively used.

However, for me the biggest technological challenge of all is the smartphone. For all of the reasons discussed previously, it is just too powerful a tool for children to own. It is too portable, too connected, too insistent, too persistent, and far too warped a lens through which to learn about the world. Both of our children have long known that they won't get any kind of phone of their own until they are thirteen at the very earliest, and most likely it wouldn't be a smartphone until they are older. As with chat, it certainly won't be until they've begun mastering the art of being kind.

For peace of mind, however, we have long kept a feature phone[262] at home, which our son could use on some of his longer and more adventurous forays. We helped him understand that this phone does not belong to him: it lives in a drawer in the parental bedroom, and he needs to ask to use it. As a pre-teen, we allowed him to cycle a long way from home using our district's extensive network of cycle paths. At times he would be gone for two to three hours, covering up to 40km. Given the probability that he would, at some point, have an accident or encounter issues with his bike, the phone was a useful aid to have. With this said, he's encountered such problems without a phone, and always managed to find help and get in touch with us. On a number of occasions he's asked a stranger to use their phone, and this has always worked out well. We feel these are invaluable life skills to develop, provided opportunities and risk are introduced gradually, over time, with plenty of coaching. At any rate, phones run out of batteries, can fail to find a signal or can be lost: as such they should never be used as a safety blanket in the place of real world nous[263].

In the end, Covid and the Hong Kong Government conspired against us when it came to smartphones: by the time we set out to purchase our son his own feature phone, for his 13th birthday, he'd already been carrying an iPod

---

[262] An old-school Nokia, which only has calling and SMS. Also known as a "dumb phone".

[263] British slang for common sense

around in order to use the government's Leave Home Safe app, without which one could not, at the time, use any public facilities. In the end we compromised, giving him an old smartphone with some very strict technological limits applied (as described later in the chapter).

Friends

One area that is tricky to navigate is time spent with friends. When our children go off to other houses we have to accept that they will be exposed to different kinds of screen usage. This is unavoidable, and is part of growing up. I was introduced to alcohol, pornography and smoking at the homes of my childhood friends. We try to make sure that we know the parents of our children's friends, and with most of them we have discussed screentime at some point. They know where we stand on this issue, and sometimes (to my wife's chagrin), I remind them. Often, when checking if he can visit a friend, I'll mention something about screentime (e.g. "I don't mind if they have 30 minutes on the Nintendo, but it would be great if they could spend most of their time outdoors"), although as he's gotten older I've tried to do this less.

When our kids' friends visit us, we have a rule that their phones need to be stashed near the front door, in a specially labelled "Box That Eats Screens". This is especially true during sleepovers, where phones can easily be used, illicitly, in the middle of the night. The potential for young adolescents to create remote social drama and access harmful content is simply too high to not preempt. I discuss this policy with the parents of friends who come over in advance, in order to explain the rationale and make sure they are okay with it, and most parents are delighted with the arrangement.

Porn

Speaking of illicit, middle-of-the-night activities seems to be a good way to introduce the topic of Internet pornography. As the musical Avenue Q very humorously puts it, "the Internet is for porn"[264], and, judging by the amount of it that is available, this may not be an exaggeration.

Although schools and families don't like to discuss this facet of Internet life, pornography is everywhere online, and it has pernicious, negative effects on many of us, including children. I am not a prude: I believe the aesthetic and sensory delights offered by naked human bodies to be one of the greatest pleasures that life confers on us. Given a choice of content, I will always choose nudity over violence, and am constantly confused as to why mainstream media wants to offer me the opposite.

However, modern pornography is not about love, sensuality, human connection or eroticism[265]. It is about violence, power and entertainment. It is about extremes. And, in a world without sensitive digital filters, more extreme content often gets more clicks, moving it higher up Google's rankings. As parents, we have a duty to educate our children about modern pornography, and although this is difficult, it is not a duty we can shirk, should we want our daughters and sons to grow up with a reasonable level of emotional and sexual health. The alternative is that they become totally deluded as to what sex, relationships and gender are all about.

As a parent I am not shy about discussing these issues with

---

[264] The Internet is for Porn, Avenue Q (https://bit.ly/3fyd6FA)

[265] As discussed in Chapter 6

my children, but I do know that they are easily embarrassed. I also recognise that for many parents, this is not something they would feel comfortable or knowledgeable enough to tackle. For this reason, I would like to offer the following letter, which parents can handwrite and customise for their own children, should this feel easier than an in-person conversation. However it is done, this kind of dialogue really needs to be engaged in as children enter their adolescence: the cost of doing this too early seems lower than that of doing it too late.

Dear Daughter/Son,

I know that you find talking about sex with me to be embarrassing, and that is fine and easy to understand. I used to feel the same when I was your age.

However, there are some things that I can teach you in this area, which will save you a lot of confusion and heartache. I've decided to write these things down in this letter, so that you can read them in private, and think about what they mean. You can ask me any questions you want, by return letter or in person. There are no bad questions on this topic.

As you know, human beings reproduce by having sex. In order to help us make as many babies as possible, and thus be a successful species, our bodies evolved to make sex fun. Done correctly, with a partner that you trust, sex feels amazing.

However, evolution also played a trick on us, as it made adult brains think about sex all the time. You know, so we can make more babies! Some kids call this "sick minded", but I call it normal. Biologically, we are always on the lookout for attractive healthy partners, and so we find lots of people around us appealing. Advertisers know this, and so they surround us with images of sexy people, in the hope that we will buy their products.

Historically, families and religions have often worked to control sex, partly because it can produce unwanted babies. This makes a lot of sense, but it has also come to make us feel bad about our bodies, and all those natural desires we have.

From these ideas, there are certain things that I'd like to help you understand:

1) Thinking about sex, and having sexual feelings towards others is normal, and not something to worry about. Sometimes sexual ideas might pop into your head, and you might feel bad about this. Don't! Even if those ideas are weird and unexpected, just accept them as part of who you are.

2) As part of learning about our bodies, humans do something called masturbation. This means to play with yourself sexually, for pleasure. Almost all humans do this at some point or another, and I did it a lot when I was your age. Because no one talked about it, I thought I was weird, and I felt guilty about it. I wasted a lot of time worrying, and it made me doubt my own goodness. As I've gotten older I've come to understand that historically, because many people were afraid of the power of sex, they were uncomfortable with children masturbating, and so made it out to be a terrible thing to do. As long as you are in a private place,

and don't hurt yourself, you should feel okay to explore your body and discover what you like, and what you don't.

3) When masturbating, it is normal to think about someone you find attractive. When photography was invented, people quickly realised that photos could help with this. Many people find photos of naked humans to be exciting, and this makes a lot of sense. Such photos, which we can call erotica, pornography or porn, are a form of art, and invite us to marvel at who we are. They used to be shared in magazines, but are now much more likely to be found on the Internet. Unfortunately, a lot of modern porn is not about loving yourself and others: it is much more about men having control over women. It rarely leaves anything to the imagination, is not at all romantic, and is often violent and demeaning. Acts like slapping, choking, embarrassing and hurting, which most people don't enjoy in sex, are made to seem normal and desirable. Boys think they can do these things to girls, and girls come to expect them from boys. All of this is unhealthy, as it makes sex awkward, painful and scary…the opposite of what it should be. Why Internet porn has become so violent is a conversation we can have at some point if you'd like: it is an interesting story. For now, if you go to the Internet looking to learn about sex, remember that this is like learning about life from movies…unlikely to work! If you search Google for "porn" you'll see a mix of healthy and unhealthy images, many of which will confuse you, and some of which are harmful for your mind. Search for "softcore porn" or "softcore couples" and you'll have much more fun! As with all good things, moderation is key.

4) It can be really scary to think about having sex with someone else. What if you get it wrong? What if they find you to be unusual in some fashion? What if your body lets you down? What if they laugh at you? These kinds of thoughts are all normal, and they are good reasons to not rush into sex. Wait until you find someone you really like, who you trust, who makes you feel good and laugh a lot. Spend time getting to know your own body first. Then spend time getting to know each other. Enjoy the wonderful feelings of kissing, touching, lingering. Be generous, always looking to give more pleasure than you take. Remember that sex can result in unwanted babies, and can spread uncomfortable and dangerous diseases, so it is best to enjoy sex safely and thoughtfully.

5) Some people aren't interested in sex at all, and others have quite specific preferences and tastes. Many people are heterosexual, some are homosexual. Some people feel that their biological gender does not match who they are as a person. All of these variations are normal, although some put you at odds with society in ways that may benefit from talking to those with more experience.

6) Before having sex with someone, you should be clear that you both want to have sex with each other. This is known as "consent", and requires talking about what you are about to do, which can be awkward. However, if you don't feel mature enough to talk about sex, you might discover that you aren't mature enough to be doing it.

If you can keep these ideas in mind, then there is a good chance that you'll grow up to enjoy sex, and to not spend too much time worrying about whether or not you are "normal". You'll be more likely to treat your partners right, and to get on with others in the strange and confusing world in which we live.

Thinking about these ideas might be confusing, scary and exciting…all at the same time…which pretty much describes sex.

Love,

Mum/Dad

As we can infer from the chapters about what children need, and the various threats posed by the Internet, this is an area of life in which children need to engage through safe, gradual, real world exploration. We can give our children permission and guidance to do this safely, without leaving them to rely on exploitative, low-grade Internet porn. I would suggest that it is, in fact, our duty to do this.

Controls

The sections above point to a principle that I feel is very important, which is to avoid relying on purely technical solutions within the family. Whilst there are many useful settings, applications and router-based rules that we might deploy in helping our children manage their device use, they tend to achieve two things. Firstly, they invite children to engage in a race-to-the-bottom game of cat and mouse. Settings are installed, children find ingenious workarounds, more settings are installed, more workarounds are found. This undermines the parent-child relationship, causes much frustration, and wastes a lot of time. Secondly, such solutions can give a very strong false sense of security. They are often seen as "set and forget", and months can go by without a parent noticing that they've stopped working, or been willfully disabled.

In general, such solutions also don't invite children to engage in developing their own self control, and they certainly don't protect against doing silly things on devices belonging to friends.

When the kind of family-based framework described above is used, especially in conjunction with rationale and discussion, the odds are much higher that such software will never be needed. Parents who are present and on the ball will always outperform technical solutions. Surveil in person. Set up your home to make this easy by having devices used where content can be seen and heard, and stored safely and visibly at other times.

My only general exception for this guidance is smartphones, which are simply too compelling to use without controls. Fortunately, smartphone controls are generally harder to circumvent than computer controls, and all going to plan, your child is only taking ownership of a phone after many years of laying a firm foundation of self control. For any parent giving a smartphone to a child under the age of eighteen, I recommend strictly limiting the available apps (no social media, no games, no web browser), limiting daily usage time (we've found that a 45-minute daily total is good) and disabling the phone overnight. In our house, the phone never leaves the ground floor, and lives in a high-traffic location unless it is being used. We constantly remind our son that the purpose of the phone is for "direct, purposeful communication with friends", and although this advice is not always followed, it is a good heuristic.

For children who come to screens without a period of measured training, or for those who fall into really bad habits, then some more general technical solutions might be needed. Even here, my preferred approach is to simply remove physical access to the device, and then, on return, allow it to be used only under certain conditions. If this proves impractical or ineffective, then technical controls might well become part of a workable solution.

Through my work I've known a number of families for whom misuse of screens has become a critical and destructive issue. This is always tragic to see, as inevitably both parents and children end up wracked with guilt. Relations are constantly strained, and despite many attempted solutions, and well intended promises, screens keep getting misused. At times the patterns of behaviour, which include cycles of abstinence, relapse, cover-up and confrontation, have all the hallmarks of addiction. In these cases working with a counsellor or therapist is often a good approach, as it allows underlying issues and tensions to be brought to the fore, examined, challenged and replaced. Pushed to the extreme, some parents send their children to bootcamp for digital detox and rehabilitation[266].

I've engaged in a lot of conversations on this topic, with both children and parents, and although it takes a lot of time, progress is almost always possible. No small part of the motivation for writing this book stems from working with such families, many of whom have been extremely open and honest in response to my input, and none of whom should ever have suffered in the way that they did. My hope is that prevention, based on the kind of ideas presented here, will prove far more effective than post-hoc remediation.

---

[266] 'Electronic heroin': China's boot camps get tough on internet addicts, Tom Phillips, The Guardian (https://bit.ly/3Ucwx5C)

CHAPTER 15
THE SCHOOL

As you might have noticed[267], I am sceptical of the role that schools play in the lives of modern children. And yet, if we are to transform our relationships with screens, schools need to be part of the solution.

Schools and Screens

School is, for most families, the point at which children leave the home to spend a considerable amount of time with others. As such, it is fraught with difficulty, even if you are lucky enough to get your children into a school whose values align with your own.

H.G. Wells' assertion that education holds catastrophe at bay does not stand up to scrutiny. Education, most commonly delivered through formal schooling, seems in fact to be responsible for the creation of many of our woes. This is no less true for screens, the use of which is often mandated by schools. Where technical instruction is offered in the absence of strong values, we can expect to see a wide

---

[267] See Chapter 8

range of creative, inventive and innovative misuse. Even when coupled with solid values, screens and schools can make uncomfortable bedfellows.

However, schools cannot ignore screens, in the same way that they cannot ignore sex, drugs and profanity. Schools need to discuss such issues without moralising, and without coming across as old and irrelevant. This is a very hard balance to find, but without at least trying, schools are doomed to fail their students, leaving them exposed and imperilled.

As the professor of English and social commentator Mark Bauerlein points out[268], modern children are given a huge degree of choice in the way they use technology, often from a very young age, and generally funded by their parents. This means that many children arrive at school with a considerable range of disruptive and distracting digital habits firmly in place. This automatically puts schools on the back foot, and this is a pattern that only seems to get stronger with each passing cohort: Bauerlein's comments were published in 2006, and technology has only become more pervasive since then.

Given the risks that are already packaged with screen use, it seems, on balance, vital that schools take a thoughtful and carefully considered lead. Benjamin Conlon, a public school teacher, notes[269] that often schools are role modelling exactly the behaviour that they complain about in their students:

---

[268] The Dumbest Generation, Mark Bauerlein, TarcherPerigee (https://bit.ly/3tdK4yp)

[269] Middle School Misfortunes Then and Now, One Teacher's Take, Benjamin Conlon, Wait Until 8th (https://bit.ly/3gu4waU)

> "In many districts teachers are encouraged to employ Twitter and Instagram for classroom updates. This is a bad thing. It normalizes the process of posting content without consent and teaches children that everything exciting is best viewed through a recording iPhone. It also reinforces the notion that 'likes' determine value. Rather than reading tweets from your child's teacher, talk to your children each day. Ask what's going on in school. They'll appreciate it."

His point is an excellent one, and exposes one of the reasons why schools often have little impact on student screen use: the contradictions are just too obvious, the scope for calling out our hypocrisy too broad. Yes, it is lovely to have photos of student learning, especially in novel settings such as school camp. But, on the flip side, we need to model to students all the wonders of living in the real world. Many are the "educational" corporations who are happy to profit by providing the hardware and software that enables such constant recording and sharing of student experience, and their motives should not be beyond examination.

Schools and Culture

At ICHK Secondary we spend a lot of time thinking about and discussing such issues, in relation to digital technology and beyond. We frame the environment that emerges from this work as "school culture", and there is little in our school that is more important than it. As the management consultant Peter Drucker supposedly put it[270] "culture eats strategy for breakfast", and it is true: the best thought out

---

[270] Culture Eats Strategy for Breakfast and Transformation for Lunch, Gokhan Guley and Tracy Reznik, Jabian (https://bit.ly/3Un5dBz)

plans are useless in the face of the wrong culture. And likewise, in the right culture, a lot of plans need never be considered.

This culture is, in many ways, the sum of the human technologies that we choose to bring to bear. It stems from all of the seemingly disparate decisions that we make, including those around the subjects on offer, what is "appropriate" for school, the timetable, school uniform, how we deal with student behaviour, assessment, use of language, digital technology and much more.

It is as much about what we choose to exclude from school as what we include.

And we know, from experience, that if we can keep refining the complex *alchemy* that generates the culture, then we can create a stronger and more effective school environment. Along the way we need to remind ourselves that schools are not simple, and that they are not complicated: they are complex. We must never forget that schools can rapidly become chaotic, and that the exhausting job of running a school, or a classroom, is to work at constantly generating the emergent practice that improves culture.

As the British educator Guy Claxton reminds us, the curriculum is not simply what we teach, but the sum total of everything that takes place within the school. He invites us to see education as an *epistemic apprenticeship*[271], a long-term journey in learning how to learn. This is a useful definition to keep in mind, as it keeps our eye firmly trained on school culture, which sets the tone for everything that follows.

---

[271] School as an Epistemic Apprenticeship: The Case of Building Learning Power, Guy Claxton (https://bit.ly/3U48xSj)

It is only from a positive school culture that students can come to value their schooling, and by extension, be interested in building strong teacher-student relationships. And, it is only through such relationships that genuine, authentic, whole-student learning can take place.

Within such a framework, much of the work of encouraging positive screen use can be built into the everyday interactions between students and teachers. That is to say, if the culture is right, the work of strategy becomes much more light-touch. Teachers can model good usage of screens, encouraging students to be thoughtful, intentional and kind. They can be vigilant for misuse[272], and use adult-adult conversations[273] to gently and patiently direct students towards more productive behaviours.

Policy

The situation described above can be facilitated by a digital technology policy that makes use of carefully considered structures to set the scene, with a light enough touch to avoid criminalising all students. Such a policy needs to be robustly researched, thoroughly written and widely consulted upon. Students and parents should be presented with the full text, and asked to sign an agreement that covers the main points. They should also be offered a visual overview, which summarises the few main rules, and which allows teachers to frame conversations on the matter.

Those students who err repeatedly, or whose erring causes serious harm, should be treated as the exception, not the

---

[272] Gamer Spotting For Teachers, Ross Parker (https://bit.ly/3U1CAKv)

[273] See Chapter 3

norm. At all turns the focus should be on learning, remediation and reconciliation, not punishment.

At ICHK Secondary, our policy follows the pattern described above, consisting of a full text policy, an agreement, and a visual summary. These are provided in Appendices 1 to 3. A key point, should you take the time to read these documents, is their deliberate use of language. In general we avoid saying that students "must not" do something, and we try to avoid declaring things as firmly against the rules. Rather we say that things are discouraged, or we focus on the expected positive behaviour.

To an outsider this might seem vague or disingenuous, but it is actually reflective of our school's culture, and the thoughtfulness and flexibility it hopes to inculcate in students, staff and parents alike. I've never before in my life been a member of such an organisation, and I suspect that this is true for most of us. We are used to firm rules, strict discipline and "high standards". Spare the rod, spoil the child, and all of that nonsense. The approach we take makes the school very easy to misunderstand, but it is also what makes it palpably different from every other institution I know of. This approach is not accidental, and in fact it stems from the Cynefin framework[274]: it is a way of acknowledging the complexity of school, and avoiding the kind of simplification that leads to chaos.

Our phone lockers[275] provide a useful case study of this. In an ideal world students would not own smartphones, however, given the reality that most do, it is incumbent

---

[274] Discussed in Chapter 12

[275] Shout out the wonderfully creative Phil Morgan, our colleague who set the ICHK Secondary phone locker ball in motion.

upon us to help them manage the many distractions that follow in their wake. And so, each student is assigned, as part of their pastoral care, a compartment in a bank of phone lockers. This lockable box, made of clear perspex, sits near the door of their form tutor room[276]. Students are very strongly encouraged to power off and dock their phone at the start of each day. They are, however, not compelled to do so, as this is likely to incite a game of "I didn't bring a phone to school, miss". Such a lie, casually and instinctively told, serves only to undermine the student-tutor relationship, eroding trust.

Students who use the box increase the chances that they will enjoy a focused and productive day. Those who opt out know that their phone should be turned off, and remain out of sight in their bag. During the school day, students may choose to retrieve their phone if invited to by a teacher for legitimate learning, such as shooting a video. This may require them to sensitively navigate the challenge of interrupting whatever lesson is taking place in their form room. They know that in using their phone they may be asked by a passing teacher what they are doing. In the same way, a student who has opted to keep their phone in their bag, and who falls prey to temptation, may also be asked what they are doing when seen with phone in hand. Meanwhile, the curriculum has been carefully adjusted to never require a student to own a phone.

This schema is, by design, imperfect. We do not want to run a police state, we do not demand compliance, and we do not want to be in the business of oppression. We simply want to provide students with an environment that is supportive of learning, and to give them the material, cognitive and

---

[276] Also known as a homeroom, this is the room they visit each morning

social technologies that nudge them towards good decisions. Those students who ultimately struggle to use screens sensibly reveal themselves to us through their actions. They will be given the support needed to make better decisions, and this may include a mandate that they begin to use their phone locker.

This is, for many, a strange, inefficient and unorthodox way to do things. As noted above, it is certainly not the way that schools, corporations and societies generally function. What it is, however, is a deliberate and determined response to the bewildering complexity of school life. It is an effort to proceed sensitively, to assume the best, to allow people agency and self-respect. The aim is to avoid falling into a wishy-washy, anything-goes liberalism on the one hand, and a totalitarian rule on the other, as both these approaches risk inciting chaos. It is no silver bullet, no panacea, and it requires attentive energy and charisma on the part of teachers, but it does work better than the other approaches I've tried and encountered.

The policy contains a variety of other similar guides and provisions, each of which aims to point, nudge, manoeuvre and suggest students in the direction of focus, and away from distraction.

Home Life

In approaching the issue of screens, we know that each student's home life will play a significant role in their relationship with their devices. In order to try and shape this aspect of their experience, which is mostly beyond our control and generally outside our field of vision, we provide new parents with an IT information pack several months before their child joins us. This pack includes some of the thinking and guidance provided in this book, and aims to empower parents to engage in positive, confident and knowledgeable discussion with their children. One thing we do encourage is for parents and children to co-create simple contracts to govern their device use. An example of such a contract is provided in Appendix 4.

Over the past few years, however, it has become clear that, even for children joining us in Year 7, at age ten, the horse has already bolted from the stable. By this age 90% of our students already own a smartphone, which they bring to school each day. Many have already taken ownership of a laptop before they join us, and tablets, gaming consoles and smart watches are common too. Based on these observations we've begun working with our partner primary schools to try and reach the parents of younger children. These trends form a significant portion of the motivation for writing this book, and there are some early indicators that our work is beginning to turn the tide.

What is important to keep in mind is that there is no right or wrong way to approach these issues: being complex, we can only rely on a developing sense of the changes around us, using these inputs to intuit and infer emerging practice. As previously noted, there are risks to doing nothing, and risks to doing something. Although we have found our current policies to be effective, we continue to look for ways to refine them, whilst always remaining alert to the fact that totally new approaches could be required at any time. For now we sense that our policies are working: there are few phones visible on campus, laptop use in school is fairly sensible, and social drama caused by screen use, although not infrequent, is lower than we expect it to be, given the social and technological field within which our students operate. What visitors to ICHK will see is students playing games, hanging out, drawing, exercising, eating and otherwise enjoying time spent in the analogue company of others.

The situation is, in general terms, far from perfect: put simply, too many students are getting devices too young, and bad habits accumulate from there. However, given all that is outside of our control, a state of mostly-positive equilibrium has been found.

School Reform

In the more general sense, schooling seems recently to have been moving in the wrong direction, and so is today less well placed than ever to tackle these issues. Through policy initiatives such as No Child Left Behind and international PISA tests[277], many schools have become obsessed with standardised quantitative data. In such schools, students are tested on a regular basis, with the results used to measure the efficacy of instruction, the competence of teachers, the health of schools and the competitiveness of nations. This represents an intrusion of the world of business into education, with a focus on productivity and accountability rather than learning. One result of this has been an explosion in the use of business terminology in schools, including value-added, performance management and KPIs, which have sadly become common currency.

These changes have had two disastrous effects on students. The first is that the range of subjects that are valued, and thus taught, has been significantly reduced. Traits, attributes and skills that are hard to measure, or which aren't compared across nations, are devalued. In their place have risen to prominence those endeavours which are easiest to measure and compare, most notably numeracy and literacy. Whilst there is no doubt that numeracy and literacy

---

[277] Who's Afraid of the Big Bad Dragon?, Yong Zhao, Jossey-Bass (https://bit.ly/3NyaPqv)

underpin modern life, they are not enough to produce the healthy, well-rounded, passionate, resilient human beings we so desperately need.

The second impact is that teachers, fearful for their jobs, are incentivised to teach to the test. So, not only is the range of content reduced, but it is now utterly divorced from reality. There is no impetus to craft authentic, challenging and intriguing content. There is no need to stimulate and engage. There is only a steady push toward test preparation. Break time? Physical education? Shop class? Home economics? Excursions? Fun? Excitement? All of these have been diminished, and sometimes sacrificed entirely, in the race to perform better on tests.

In the face of a lack of genuinely interesting learning, fear is required to motivate students to engage. In the UK the situation is so bad that England's Children's Commissioner, Sir Al Aynsley-Green, has stated that[278] "Children feel under such pressure from endless testing, they do not feel they have the time to enjoy themselves. What is the purpose of education? Is it for the attainment of government targets, or is it to provide children with life skills to become confident adults?"

All of this leaves students bored, untethered and afraid: in other words, perfectly situated to fall listlessly into a life more digital. When the real world gives you lemons, why not bury yourself in a screen?

Calls for school reform are not new, but given the range of social, economic and existential threats we face today, those

---

[278] Walking back to happiness, Anna Bawden, The Guardian (https://bit.ly/3U0EJ93)

calls seem more apposite than ever. We need schools that engage students, that care for them as individuals, not numbers. We need schools that embrace and explore the whole, wide, messy gamut of human experience. We need schools that students want to attend, that excite them about the world, that prepare them to be interesting, passionate and capable adults. We need schools that tell a great story, about a world that is so amazing that life need not be lived through a screen.

CHAPTER 16
THE GOVERNMENT

It is hard to deny that the process of governing has, for most of history, been a process of the rich and powerful controlling the poor and weak. In tribal, feudal, monarchical and dynastic times this process was overt and transparent: kings were kings, peasants were peasants.

Since the dawn of democratic republics, things have become considerably less clear cut. Democracy gives the illusion of control to the people, and in many cases is genuinely better than the alternatives. However, democracy also serves to hide the operation of power behind the rosy narrative of free choice. And, with the operation of power hidden, it is easy for fundamental changes to go unnoticed. In this way, it has come to pass that in many modern, Western democracies, a small number of individuals and corporations control wealth and power at levels without historical precedent.

Going under a range of names, this elite, this 0.01%, this private-jet, Davos-oriented cabal pay almost no tax whilst exerting a disproportionate influence on government policy. Through their lobbyists, the corporations they own and the think tanks they fund, they shape our lives for their own enrichment. Their money pays for the campaigns of the politicians who then go on to support and enable them, often through the vehicle of corporate deregulation.

The primary result of this process, whose roots stem from the 1980s, and the neo-liberal policies of Margaret Thatcher and Ronald Regan, is rising inequality. The graph below compares the share of national income earned by the top 10% of earners (the upper line) with that earned by the bottom 50%. After a period of decreasing wealth accumulation for the top earners, starting in the 1940s and continuing into the late 1970s, we see the divide grow considerably over the past 40 years:

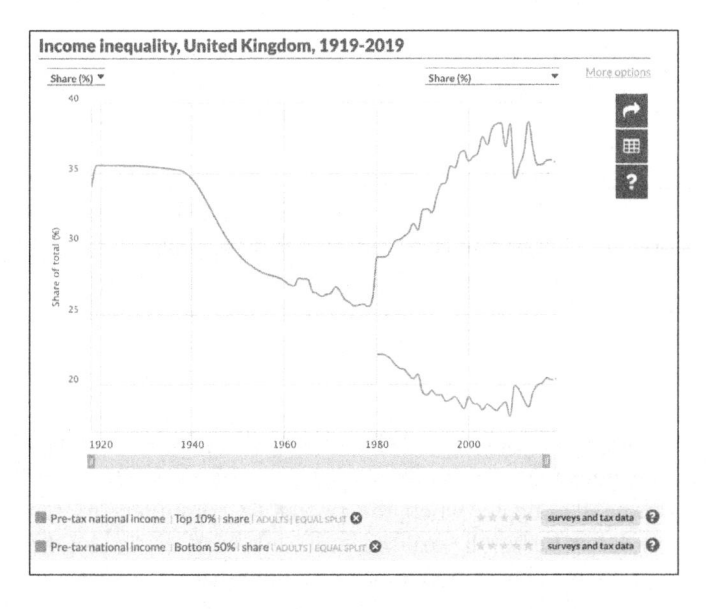

Image 16.1 - Income Inequality, United Kingdom, 1919-2019 (World Inequality Database)

This data shows the deceit inherent in the economic theories, sponsored by the rich, that tell us that their accumulation of wealth will lead to trickle-down improvements for the poor. This is simply not true.

Other than the material and emotional suffering that these policies inflict, they are also a signal that our leaders no longer care about the lot of common, everyday people. You know, like you, and me. We may elect them, but they do not serve us. Perhaps, in the post-war years they really did, but those days are long gone. Owen Jones[279] in the UK, and Lawrence Lessig[280] in the US, have both written persuasively about the mechanisms that lie behind many of these changes.

A Perfect Storm

In many ways, the situation we find ourselves in represents a perfect storm: the emergence of ultra-powerful digital technologies at just the time when governments seem to have lost the will to regulate so many aspects of corporate conduct. This has allowed incredible wealth to be accumulated within a tiny number of tech giants, who now operate almost-unchallenged global monopolies. This has given those corporations, and their billionaire figureheads, tremendous political and economic power, and virtually free reign over our personal data.

Although easy to overlook for its zany, Internet meme-inspired humour, the 2021 film The Mitchells vs. The Machines makes a profound point on this front. It comes during the finale, when the power of computers to run amok has been fully realised, and leads Mark Bowman, the seemingly naive tech billionaire, to quip that:

> "It's almost like stealing people's data and giving it

---

[279] The Establishment, Owen Jones, Penguin Press (https://bit.ly/3U5YI6C)

[280] Republic, Lost: Version 2.0, Lawrence Lessig, Twelve (https://bit.ly/3h5xDBJ)

to a hyper-intelligent AI as part of an unregulated tech monopoly was a bad thing."

As might be expected, the film was produced by Sony, a giant of old media, rather than Netflix or Amazon, who might not be quite so forward in highlighting their own failings, nor those of their founders. Credit to Netflix, however, for distributing the film.

For a long time the progress-through-liberty narrative of technology, peddled by Brand, Barlow, Jobs and company, provided the ideological cover that these companies needed. Now that their power has been consolidated, they no longer require the narrative, and so don't seem too bothered by its threadbare state.

Awakening

Fortunately, there are some signs that governments are beginning to wake up to the dangerous levels of power held by the mega-corporations of big tech, and calls are being made to break them up into smaller units. Europe's General Data Protection Regulation (GDPR) has provided the most robust defence of personal data yet, and although far from perfect, is a step in the right direction.

What we have yet to see, but desperately need, are strong, globally-consistent measures to:

1. Regulate the design of hardware and software in order to limit compulsion;
2. Make surveillance capitalism illegal, demonetising data in order to force a return to products and services that are paid for with money rather than privacy invasion;
3. Support families by making it illegal for children under a certain age to own and operate certain types

of hardware and software.
4. Tackle online hate speech, revenge porn and indecent exposure (aka cyber-flashing), none of which we tolerate in the real world, but all of which proliferate online.

Of course, strong measures such as these would be fiscally painful for those who finance our leaders, and so, without considerable political reform, they are unlikely to happen. In addition, there already exists a culture of calling out nations that regulate aggressively for the social good, labelling them as "nanny states". This view stems from the libertarian belief that governments should be small and unobtrusive, and conveniently ignores the many things that our complex societies require from their government. You know, like roads, drainage, security, law and order, health care and the social safety net.

What is thus needed is a strong grassroots movement that makes these issues so visibly and demonstrably clear that they can no longer be ignored. This process, akin to the 20th century's civil rights and gender equality movements, and the more contemporary #metoo and climate crisis mobilisations, requires thoughtful, educated and impassioned individuals willing to fight for the rights of their fellow human beings. If history teaches us anything it is not only that these individuals do exist, but that they are willing to make personal sacrifices for the greater good...and this fills me with hope.

CHAPTER 17
THE CORPORATION

Unfortunately, whilst corporations hold almost all of the power within our societies, they are also the entities least likely to change themselves. On the one hand we see from the existence of B Corps, and progressive firms like 3M, Patagonia, Eileen Fisher and Kao, that companies *can* do the right thing if left to their own devices. On the other hand, it is worth noting that the vast majority of large corporations are too busy meeting quarterly shareholder expectations to commit to serious change.

This is especially true if that change comes at the expense of a core product or service, and thus threatens the survival of the corporation. It is for these reasons that, in 2022, we still have companies manufacturing and marketing cigarettes, fossil fuels, synthetic pesticides and automatic weapons.

Companies provide a reliable vehicle for maintaining and transmitting power, and thus act as conservators of the status quo. Yes, some companies fail, and new companies come along and shake things up. But, very quickly those new upstarts, through the power of investment, become the very thing they sought to dethrone.

Keep in mind that Google, almost from its inception, proclaimed the novel corporate value of "Don't be evil"[281]. Assumed to be partly tongue-in-cheek, this declaration was nonetheless a reminder that companies do bad things, and a heads-up that plucky upstart Google would not be like that. 20 years on, and Google is as big as they get, having gained mightily from the steady decimation of consumer privacy. They work for the US Defence Department[282], they've ignored claims of sexual harassment[283] and they've pandered to Chinese censorship[284]. Clearly, being good whilst being massive is not easy.

None of this is to say that Google is inherently "bad". Likewise for many of the other tech giants that have sprung up in the last twenty years. They've mostly stayed within the law whilst aiming to profit their shareholders, as companies are generally expected to do. They've given us a wealth of novel and sometimes useful services that we clearly enjoy using.

Rather, it serves to highlight the fact that we should not expect any company to turn their back on profit for the betterment of their consumers, or society as a whole. We might wish them to, and it is nice when some do, but we cannot expect it. This is, per the previous chapter, why we require strong regulation, so that it is clear to companies what we find acceptable, and where we draw the line.

---

[281] Don't Be Evil, Wikipedia (https://bit.ly/3sYiFAh)

[282] Google's cloud division lands deal with the Department of Defense, Lauren Feiner, CNBC (https://cnb.cx/3ste9JM)

[283] Google Execs Ignored Reports of Sexual Harassment: Lawsuit, Robert Handa, CNBC (https://bit.ly/3gDGlH8)

[284] Google Plans to Launch Censored Search Engine in China, Leaked Documents Reveal, Ryan Gallagher, The Intercept (https://bit.ly/3VY4GaK)

The only influence we can exert over corporations is through our individual consumption of their products. This is partly why I no longer use Facebook, Twitter and a host of other services. If enough of us vote with our fingers, change might yet happen. But, with more than eight billion potential customers to draw upon, I'm not holding my breath for my individual protest to register: this is something we all need to do together.

CONCLUSION

Hopefully, in reaching this point, you will have experienced a cognitive journey along the arc of a clear and compelling narrative. You need not have agreed with each and every point, and surely will not have found the book exhaustive. However, you have ideally arrived here with a more refined understanding of the ways in which we need to serve our children better when it comes to screens.

Of course, this is not just a childhood issue: it affects all of us. However, childhood is where the problems described here are felt most keenly, and where the damage seems the most cruel, the most permanent and the least defensible. We must not forget that, for better or worse, today's children will become tomorrow's adults.

In terms of structure, the book aims to document and explore the nature of childhood. In doing so it draws on a range of theories and viewpoints to detail how childhood has changed. It focuses on recent, rapid shifts in culture, and how these have shocked our lives. It considers what children need, what is missing from modern childhood, and how this has opened the door for screens to become ubiquitous.

With the scene set, consideration is given to the various

phenomena we associate with the word "technology", and how our experience of reality is inseparable from our tools. A range of different lenses are applied to the question of whether screens really are bad for us, with the aim of dispelling any sense that concern over screens is just a moral panic or a modern Luddite movement. There is no doubt that screens, and the software they run, can be hugely beneficial. However, the current economic paradigm, which positions the user as the product, not the customer, means that our screens are weaponised against us. They are, in fact, not our own tools: rather, they belong to the companies that seek to mine our data and plunder our attention.

Hopefully, as an adult capable of honest self-reflection, you have come to see how the growth of screens has negatively impacted your own life, and the many ways in which your own wellbeing is compromised by such devices.

In order to understand the situation we are in, it is important to understand where we have been, and so we have recapped the route by which we arrived in this predicament. The book explores, in ways which were opaque at the time, the many individual intellectual and technical innovations that led from massive and expensive computational machines to the cheap, powerful and ubiquitous screens we own today. It links the absurd cultural power of screens to the 7.2 trillion factor improvement in price/performance seen over the past 74 years, which today allows a computer to routinely simulate and mediate so many facets of our lives. Long embedded within a lush, fantastical and inviting narrative, screens have failed to live up to their liberating and democratising promise. They have not made us better informed, nor more caring, yet we still believe the storytellers who promised that they would. Our old narratives have become threadbare, scarcely credible and incapable of holding water. It is time for a change of scene.

The book closes with a small selection of the many options available to us, the ways in which we might proceed from here. With a focus first on the individual as the smallest unit of action, the circle is then expanded to consider the family, the school, the government and the corporation. At each of these levels we have access to different avenues through which we can shift our culture towards the positive. Every decision we make is risky, as is every action we undertake. But, far more perilous is the decision to do nothing. The levers and dials may be small, and poorly marked, but they exist, and we must use them.

And so, here we are, at the end, with but a few words to sum up.

Human beings have, since the dawn of our species, been defined by the creation, application and improvement of technology. Devoid of most physical and instinctual means of survival, we have had to depend on our ample brains, and our ability to cooperate in order to carve out a place in this chaotic world. What started in an ecological niche has grown to encompass the entire planet. In living out this story some of us have been lucky enough to appreciate keenly the centrality of technology to our lives. We depend on it, it animates us, and we worship it. Technology keeps the darkness from the cave: without it we are naked weaklings, desperately clinging to an unpredictable and uncaring planet, hurtling through mind-numbingly vast space.

It is no wonder that to question technology, to suggest that we have progressed enough, is to invite scorn, to be ridiculed, to be called naive and to be seen as out of touch.

But this is, in closing, exactly what I would like to suggest. *The time has come for us to accept that further technological development is fundamentally incompatible with human flourishing and sustainability.* Technology has given us so much, but it is also the root cause of all of the issues facing us today. There are many who believe that better technology, more technology, will solve the issues created by our previous technologies. This argument is akin to believing that during a wildfire, more fire will solve the problems being caused by the existing fire. True, some fire might be used to create a break, but in general, more fire will lead only to more fire.

In growing up, in facing the next step of the human story, we need to learn to put technology in its place. Exempting a narrow band of developments that focus on improving energy efficiency, I believe that we need to turn off the engine of technological development in order to save ourselves. We need to see clearly that indefinite growth on a finite planet is a recipe for disaster. We need to draw down and scale back our technological appendages, and recover some of our earlier practices and ways of being.

Such a change would represent a pivotal moment for a species whose very identity is defined by technological progress. It would represent a paradigm shift, the end of an era, a defiance of so much accumulated wisdom. This is no short order. And yet, no matter how difficult it might prove to be, it will certainly be more palatable than the alternative: the annihilation of ourselves and the many creatures and plants with whom we share our home.

Succeeding in this endeavour represents a chance to prove that we are indeed the wise, wise ape, *homo sapiens sapiens*[285], the name that we have, without evident merit, chosen to give ourselves.

---

[285] Homo sapiens sapiens, Encyclopædia Britannica (https://bit.ly/3ZxqmfV)

Screens That Eat Children

Only one question really remains to be answered: *are we wise enough?*

EPILOGUE - AN AUTOBIOGRAPHICAL SKETCH

Although knowing the creator of text is not a prerequisite for enjoying it, I find that learning where an author comes from can help contextualise their work in meaningful ways. With that in mind, this final part of the book offers a short autobiographical sketch, shared as a way to understand how I came to hold the views that I do.

Born in Vienna, my mum was a post-war latch key kid. Her parents, an orphan and a refugee, worked shifts in order to support their small family. Her father was a train captain, and her mother worked in various factories. Aged twenty one and speaking only German, she escaped the stifling confines of Viennese life and set off for the promised land...England.

Born in the industrial north of that country, my father's parents moved south in search of a better life. This they found in the form of a sprawling manor estate, on which my grandfather spent his life gardening, whilst my grandmother kept house, raised their children, ran a B&B and worked in the nearby tourist office. Their tied cottage was close enough to the local golf course for my father to pick up the game, and he eventually left school at fifteen to become a trainee pro.

For reasons that we might charitably call virtuous, my father took to helping foreign girls learn English, and it was in undertaking this noble work that he met my mother. An apparently stormy early relationship survived the post-war challenges of introducing an Austrian partner into an English family, and to the surprise of many, they were married.

By 1974, with my dad having earned his Professional Golf Association qualification, my parents determined that a lifetime spent teaching golf on an open practice hole in the rain would not suffice, and so they started to look for sunnier climes. An initial interest in moving to Germany led, somewhat unexpectedly, to an interview, conducted in a pub in London, for a job at the Royal Hong Kong Golf Club. And so it came to be that my parents sold all their possessions, said farewell to their friends and family, and took four consecutive flights to the very edge of Britain's declining empire.

Situated in Hong Kong's north, near the market town of Fanling, "The Royal" sits close to the border with China. This part of Hong Kong, the New Territories, was a relatively late addition to the colony, and still surprisingly lawless even in the 1970s. Police officers working the area were instructed to flee at the first sign of serious trouble, preferring not to take on the fiercely independent indigenous villagers, many of whom lived in highly defensible walled villages. Tigers roamed the jungle into the 1940s[286], and even today four-meter long Burmese python hunt for civet cat, deer and wild boar. Only eight years before their arrival, using the Hong Kong riots of 1967 as a

---

[286] Hong Kong has more skyscrapers than nearly any city. But 60 years ago, tigers were still seen in the wild, Jenni Marsh, CNN (https://cnn.it/3FC5tZn)

pretence, a group of adventurous Red Guards had crossed the border up the road from Fanling, engaging in a gun battle which left five police dead[287].

Hot, incredibly humid, and buzzing with Cantonese language and industry, it must have been a different world.

My father was stationed at Deep Water Bay, the golf club's city-side course: with Fanling a three-hour drive away, this short nine-hole course gave city dwelling members a chance to play during the week. Nestled in the hills, it remains today a sleepy reminder of Hong Kong's colonial history, and of the city's great inequality. Hard working caddies walk the course, visible in their broad-brimmed and black-clothed hats, carrying the clubs and cleaning the balls of Hong Kong's wealthiest residents.

Living one headland over, in Repulse Bay, my father still vividly remembers the shock of having arrived in such a very different and wonderful place. The photo below shows Deep Water Bay's clubhouse and ninth hole, as well as the adjacent beach.

---

[287] Hong Kong (Border Incidents), UK Parliament (https://bit.ly/3Nw7KXP)

Screens That Eat Children

Image E.1 - Deep Water Bay 1961 (Doug Brentlinger via Gwulo)

My parents spent weekdays at home in Repulse Bay, before loading up their white VW Beetle to make the long drive to Fanling for the weekend. There they would stay with the family of my father's boss, Joe Hardwick. My father would give lessons by day and in the evenings they would socialise on the club's veranda. By all accounts it was a warmly generous, and rather glamorous, way of life. In 1977 my sister arrived, followed three years later by myself, conceived after much trying, in the house beside the first tee of Fanling's Old Course.

In 1981 my father became Head Pro at the new and audacious Clear Water Bay Golf & Country Club, which perches on a formerly mountainous peninsula in the east of the New Territories. The course's designers had had to blast away the top of the mountain range in order to squeeze in a golf course[288], something the founders had conceived of

---

[288] My father on the 14th hole at CWB, early 1980s

from the deck of their yacht. Clearly not environmentalists, they certainly did not lack a certain kind of vision. Overnight we left the safe and somewhat staid confines of old Hong Kong society and ventured into the brash world of Hong Kong's new money.

Aged one and a half, I scarcely noticed.

Image E.2 - Clearwater Water Bay, 14th Hole, 1982 (Parker Family)

In many ways this new life would treat me very well. Our family was loving, and my parents kind, conscientious and very hard working. Although certainly never rich, we were definitely privileged: enough of the immense wealth that surrounded us trickled our way, affording us a life of comfort and enjoyment. In retrospect these years appear as a bright parade of Chinese festivals, family celebrations, days out hiking, junk[289] trips, swimming and sunshine. Constantly surrounded by the din of activity, there were fireworks, cymbals, lion dances, lucky red packets and roast

---

[289] A traditional Chinese fishing boat, converted to a pleasure craft

suckling pigs galore. Incense was always on the heavy, humid air, to this day the only kind that really makes me feel at home. Although people came and went, I was lucky in early childhood to be surrounded by a small number of very close friends[290], the kind whose formative impact lasts a lifetime. Summers were generally spent in England and Austria, learning to be a little more English, and improving our German.

In material and familial terms, all was well.

Image E.3 - Christmas 1984 (Parker Family)

And yet I was also a "sickly child", constantly ill with fever and sinus infections. I vividly recall days spent bed bound, my mother patiently nursing me through the delirium. I'd stagger through stifling fever dreams in which nothing was ever quite right. In one, which returned often, my grandmother and I fell upon hard times after accidentally purchasing inordinate quantities of lumber. All of this left me prone to worrying, which sat uneasily with bouts of youthful hyperactivity. As a child I can't have been easy to bear, and adolescence only made it worse. Beyond my close

---

[290] Benedict Gray, Trent Barrett and Nick O'Neill chief amongst them

friends I found companionship difficult, with thick glasses and a nerdy disposition making me easy to pick on. I often felt myself sticking out, trying too hard to fit in, never at home, often a stranger. In adolescence I found succour in alcohol, adrenaline and foolish behaviour. By day I worked hard at school, and golf was a constant source of distraction and ambition. Mostly, however, I failed to meaningfully deal with steadily accumulating feelings of anger, loneliness, anxiety and despair.

And here is where this personal story connects most obviously with the broader themes of this book, for without me realising, my own childhood was simply one of many boats being tossed by the waves of cultural upheaval.

As a child of the newly emerging meritocracy, I was primed to succeed. Well educated, well connected, internationally oriented and in the heart of the action, anything seemed possible. And yet, beyond earning a living by winning golf tournaments, to which I strived but never quite achieved, life seemed completely devoid of structure and meaning. I would, it was expected, finish my education, get a job, earn money, consume material resources, have a family...and eventually perish. Each of these milestones seemed impossibly remote, entirely unachievable and interminably dull.

Despite this, I faithfully followed the rules, got good grades at school, completed my undergraduate studies in England, returned to Hong Kong and got a "great job" in a bank. I then promptly fell into a deep rut of anxiety, depression and despair.

It all took me completely by surprise, but in retrospect, it was rather predictable. Lacking access to a suitable and sustainable hero system, I lived awash in an assortment of capitalist sub-cultures, each of which would ultimately prove inimical to my own wellbeing. My life, which seemed to have offered endless options, had led me down a steadily narrowing path, in which conspicuous consumption seemed to be the only way to prove that I mattered.

Just as it all became entirely unbearable, the wheels fell off and I was forced, through an extended period of convalescence, to take stock. In the process of starting to put some of the pieces of myself back together, I was fortunate enough to spend time volunteering with some wonderful people, learning to help others, and beginning to work with children. And whilst my mental health remains a work in progress, these struggles have come to help me appreciate, through the lens of my own experience and the writings of others, what we might need to offer our own children.

Studying Computer Science at university helped me to discover that computers offered the safety and predictability that seemed so elusive when in the company of other humans. Computers followed rules, did what you told them to, and never made fun of you. They were rational to the extreme, and in the process of making them do my bidding I managed to find meaning within the world.

Over time, computers led me to work in schools, and I began to see that hiding behind a screen, although comfortable, was not allowing me to become the person I wanted to be. In training to become a teacher I found ways to balance my interests and skills, whilst developing myself in new ways. I found that I understood those for whom computing was a safe haven, whilst also being able to help timid newcomers to become more confident and capable.

Worryingly, over time, I've come to find ever growing numbers of people hiding behind screens, missing out on some of the best experiences that life has to offer, or viewing them through a distorting lens. I have a profound sense of sympathy for these individuals, for whom social interactions can feel painfully awkward, yet am deeply distrustful of the big tech leaders who themselves hide behind screens, and who wish to reshape the world in their own image. Recently I encountered an advert for "the first AI that can flirt"[291], and listening to it was deeply unsettling for these very reasons. What does it tell us when people want to make computers that can act like humans? What feelings are they supposed to evoke? In what ways are they intended to bring us comfort?

Today, I am a husband and father to a loving family, and a teacher who gets to do work that I find incredibly meaningful and interesting. I have a supportive web of family and friends, and work with tremendous colleagues, students and collaborators. I've come to realise that life is not about happiness and success, it is about the daily ups and downs, about being there for people who in turn are there for you. The real heroes, it turns out, are not the sports stars, the CEOs, the Hollywood stars or the YouTubers: they are the mums and dads, the coworkers, the people working the market stall, the bus driver and the lady serving you wonton. Heroic living is in the mundane details, an insight that contemporary society is rather keen to keep out of sight, and out of mind.

---

[291] What's Her Secret, Sonantic (https://bit.ly/3h6OFzo)

APPENDIX 1
ICHK IT POLICY FULL TEXT

1. Introduction & Context

1.1 Digital technology (e.g. IT) represents a subset of all technologies: that vast array of tools, scripts, habits of mind and beliefs which sustain human life. As with any technology, IT is best viewed as just one more response to the challenges raised by our evolutionary need to survive. Rather than being taken as a given, technologies, in all their forms, ought to be constantly and critically appraised, for they infer changeable costs and benefits.

1.2 From its genesis in the mid-nineteenth century, IT has been offered to us within a narrative of enhanced productivity, freedom, voice and purpose. These claims contain elements of truth, but as with any complex phenomenon, there is always space for alternative expressions of latent potential: over recent years, commercial pressure has changed the IT landscape considerably, bringing us addictive design, behavioural modification and rapid, unexpected cultural shifts.

1.3 The latest generation of IT platforms have been intentionally engineered to establish repetitious and compulsive behaviours in users, in order to compete for the largest possible share of consumer attention. This can be seen in the growing number of people for whom a mobile phone is a constant companion and, in this guise, serves as a compelling source of distraction, rather than a tool that promotes focused attention or less superficial engagement with life's possibilities. Even, and perhaps especially, those in the technology industry are coming to understand the negative potential of these devices, and to regret the ways in which business models have placed a premium on their most destructive tendencies.

1.4 So it is, we are no longer the customer, but rather a product, positioned and manipulated by social media algorithms, data-mined, categorised and packaged for sale to advertisers.

1.5 Our students, aged 10-18, find themselves operating within these shifting conditions, buffeted by conditions beyond their understanding and control, at a time in social history where we lack many traditional signposts on the journey to becoming a productive[292] human being. The adolescent years are, as Erik Erikson makes clear, a time of identity work and vital self-production, where children become adults. Yet, these are the same years where executive function (and thus long range planning and impulse control) are still being developed.

1.6 In the light of the above, **ICHK accepts its responsibility to be forward looking in the ways we frame IT use for the students in our care**.

2. General Principles

2.1 This policy aims to reclaim some of the individual and social spaces that our students have lost to IT over the past decade. The focus is on promoting learning, creating freedom from distraction and fostering positive IT skills and habits within the wider profile of productive human development. As such, our vision is that at ICHK:

The use of IT furthers school-centered learning

2.2 The following sections outline how this plays out in practice.

---

[292] Productive in the Aristotelian sense of producing one's self i.e. making manifest the latent potentialities within.

3. Mobile Phones

3.1 Guidance for Years 7-11:

- Mobile phones should not be used or carried in school, other than when directed by staff for learning purposes.
    - As a school, our advice to parents is to avoid giving smartphones to children under the age of 13. Such devices, in our experience, carry with them a strong tendency of causing avoidable social and learning issues for children.
    - With this in mind, teachers are asked to avoid putting students in situations where they feel should have such a phone. Generally speaking, this means that mobile phones and apps should be avoided, but that they might selectively be used, provided they appear on our pre-approved list (see 7.2). However, in such cases, group work or school device-friendly (e.g. MacOS or ChromeOS) alternatives should be used to enable stress-free access for students without phones.
- ICHK endorses and seeks to support a culture in which we protect ourselves from the distractions designed into these devices.
- Each student is issued with a transparent phone locker in their form tutor room, with the expectation that their phone (should they bring one to school) is set to silent and docked for the entire day other than when expressly required, on the instructions of staff, for learning purposes.
- Students can choose to access their phone under exceptional circumstances, but ICHK cultural norms dictate that this is discouraged and not

standard practice.

3.2 Guidance for Years 12 & 13:

- Students may choose to dock their phone in their tutor room, or carry it discreetly on their person.
- Students may use their phones around school, but are expected to be good role models to younger students.
- Students failing to meet these guidelines may be asked to restrict their phone use.

Parents needing to contact students during the school day can do so by calling Reception, who will then relay a message to the student in question.

4. School Device

4.1 Each student has a sanctioned school device (Mac or Chromebook laptop in Years 7 to 11, student choice in Years 12 and 13), which is their sole IT learning technology.

4.2 Each student is placed within a Technology Stream, initially through self-selection, and subsequently by the decisions that they make:

- **Green Stream** - students sign up to this policy with the expectation that they will reliably abide by it, as part of their Approaches to Learning.
- **Amber Stream** - students sign up to this policy knowing that they require support in order to manage their IT use.
- **Red Stream** - students resist this policy or consistently struggle to manage their IT use. Red stream students may require a personalised suite of software and settings to assist in developing self

control. In extreme cases, a moratorium on computer use, and restrictions to various digital facilities, may be mandated.

4.3 Student devices display a prominent sticker, identifying their stream, and advertising to teachers the kind of support and controls they may require. Student devices must also display the ICHK inventory sticker.

4.4 Students are expected to observe the following protocols around device use:

- Devices are to remain out of sight at all times, until a teacher requests they be used.
- Devices are to be used only for school-centered learning, including at break time.
- Devices may be used during break, for school-centered learning, only in C108 and the Library.
    o This is extended to include C106, for Year 10 & 11 students, during Break 2.
- Students should never touch or access another person's device or accounts without prior and express permission from the person to whom the device or account belongs.

4.5 Teachers are expected to aim for a healthy mix of learning experiences, balancing screen time against a range of other learning activities, in keeping with the school's vision. In general, IT use should be in keeping with ICHK's 5+1 Model: teachers should focus on romantic learning experiences in the Lower School, before gradually developing towards the philosophic, as students move into and through the Senior School. As a rough guide this means that, in Years 7 to 9, IT use will tend towards the expressive, the creative, the emotionally engaging, the sensational, while, beyond that, gradually, it will come too to incorporate more of a move towards rounded research, use of organisational software, compiling and amending of complicated documents, abstraction and presentation of data.

4.6 ICHK offers a device purchase service, should families wish to use it. Families using this service benefit from the full educational discount offered by our vendors.

4.7 Notwithstanding their being privately owned, student devices will remain under the aegis of the IT department and subject to the IT policies at ICHK. The school will implement the following two settings on student machines, which students will not amend:

- ICHK Administrator account – allowing access to and repair of student computers by ICHK staff
- Computer Name – allowing for computers to be recognized on the school network

5. Gaming

5.1 Teachers may invite students to play video games as part of learning in school.

5.2 Beyond this, video game playing is not permitted within school. This encompasses all video games, including those played on mobile phones, console devices, laptops and tablets.

5.3 During break, students are encouraged to be active and social outdoors, or to use classrooms for socialising, reading or playing board games (to be provided by the school).

6. Digital Accessories

6.1 In general, digital accessories (e.g. smart watches,

wireless ear pods, etc) are not to be worn in school. However:

- Non-distracting, limited-function fitness trackers can be worn.
- Smart watches can be worn if switched to airplane mode with notifications turned off.
- Earphones can be used during lesson time, at the teacher's discretion

7. Working Online

7.1 ICHK will provide students with access to a suite of online facilities, overseen and controlled by the school, including Gibbon, Google Apps and ICHK Sites.

- ICHK Sites is intended as a public exhibition space for students to publish work of which they are proud and which represents them as learners and practitioners in a wide variety of settings.
- Students will receive explicit tuition regarding sharing publicly on the web. This is an important opportunity for students to become familiar with issues around sharing and exhibiting online.

7.2 In addition, teachers may request students to set up an account, or install an app, with a free online service outside of school control. In this case, teachers will ensure that:

- the account is age appropriate and that, where the service is age restricted, students are of the required age to join.
- students understand the terms of their enrolment (e.g. that their work may be made public; that they are contributing to a research project; that their work is open to comment).

- students register using their ICHK email address, appreciate that these accounts are now associated with their school identity, and use them only on that basis.
- they have checked with the Director of Technology (using [this pre-approved list](#)) to make sure the account or app in question is appropriate for student use.

8. Ongoing Education

8.1 In order to help develop and maintain positive norms around this policy, the following ongoing education will be implemented:

- New students joining ICHK at the beginning of each school year will be introduced to the policy via a set of simulations and presentations.
- Existing students, and those joining during the year, will experience annual simulations and presentations regarding elements of the policy.
- The policy will be built into the schools IT Free Learning map.
- All students will be asked to sign an IT Agreement, which will be used by teachers to help students reflect on their use of IT.
- A summary poster will be displayed in each classroom for ongoing reference.

9. Privacy

9.1 ICHK supports the rights of parents and students to determine the level of digital privacy that suits them. Students will, through Human Technologies and Free Learning, be encouraged to consider privacy as a concept that impacts their lives, and will receive on-going pastoral guidance on this matter, as and when required.

9.2 Parents will be offered a range of optional privacy settings, via Gibbon's Application Form and Data Updater, which they can use to inform the school of any restrictions they wish to apply to the use of their child's likeness. The school will do its best to honour these wishes in all cases, with the exception of the two cases noted below:

1. For school media that includes a broad cross-section of the student body, such as promotional videos, where checking the privacy settings of each and every student is impractical, the school will:
    a. Release the media initially to parents only, using an unlisted link.
    b. Offer parents a period of 3 weeks, during which they can identify their children and request their removal if required.
    c. Remove any students, as per parental requests.
    d. Release the media to a wider audience
2. All students will be included in the annual ICHK yearbook, which is published for internal use.

10. Digital Signatures

10.1 ICHK Secondary has moved from paper permission slips to digital signatures, offered via Gibbon.

10.2 In signing the IT Agreement associated with this policy, parents will be asked to indicate that they agree to give consent for school trips via an encrypted digital link provided by Gibbon. By signing, they agree to use the clicking of this link as an equivalent to their physical signature.

11. Parental Concerns

11.1 We appreciate that different parents will have a range of views concerning both use of the Internet and what is appropriate for young people to do or have exposure to online. If parents' views conflict with aspects of this policy or if they feel that its terms are not being observed by members of the ICHK community, they are invited to contact the Technology Director (ict@ichk.edu.hk).

12. Observations, Concerns and Provisos

12.1 The following are ideas that have come up during the process of crafting this policy, and are offered as an insight into the process:

- There is no gap between our commitment to adult-adult transactions and a policy that mandates the removal of student choice in regard to mobile phones, provided that our message and, by extension, the intentions that inform it, is communicated patiently and comprehensively.
- Student discomfort at being separated from their mobile phones should be taken seriously, discussed, explored and examined as a symptom of precisely the condition that this policy seeks to address.
- As staff, with additional and other responsibilities, mobile phones remain a critical part of our daily technological repertoire. This will be explained to students, so that the potential for misunderstanding is minimized. In order to support the legitimacy of this argument, staff should be mindful of the ways in which they use their own phones in the presence of students.
- It is anticipated that resistant students will develop new 'work-arounds' for the practices that the policy

prohibits, such as in-class chat with laptops or carrying a second, secreted phone. Dealing with this phenomenon should remain always proportional but firm - we should not elevate the misuse of digital technology to an unwarranted level of anxiety, but we must maintain the school's protocols.
- There are likely to be occasions of a forgetful student leaving their phone at school and who having reason to contact parents on the way home.
- This will be addressed by physical reminders at school and on the school buses. All parties concerned will be reminded of the possibility.
- Buses will leave no earlier than 3:35pm (i.e. five minutes after the end of school) in order to provide an opportunity for students to collect their phones
- Should students be leaving school early, they will need to politely and discreetly collect their phone from their tutor room.
- Phones should be turned off before being docked each day. A student whose phone disrupts class as a consequence of this condition not being met risks losing IT privileges e.g. bringing a phone into school at all and/or enjoying green or amber status.
- Teachers will need to be effective models of positive phone use for students.

13. Evidence & Resources

13.1 The following resources have been influential in the crafting of this policy, and in some cases are linked from within the policy text.

- Technopoly: The Surrender of Culture to Technology by Neil Postman
- The Internet Is Not the Answer by Andrew Keen

Screens That Eat Children

- Irresistible by Adam Alter
  - "...now you can shop online and connect to your workplace any time of day...all you need are wi-fi and a web browser. Life is more convenient than ever, but convenience has also weaponised temptation" - p.19
- A Dark Consensus About Screens and Kids Begins to Emerge in Silicon Valley via The New York Times
  - "We thought we could control it...And this is beyond our power to control. This is going straight to the pleasure centers of the developing brain. This is beyond our capacity as regular parents to understand."
- Ten Arguments for Deleting Your Social Media Accounts Right Now by Jaron Lanier
- Why every social media site is a dumpster fire via Vox
- 5+1 Model by ICHK
- The Adolescent Brain: Why Executive Functioning in Teens Is a Challenge by By Dr. Mireya Nadal-Vicens and Dr. Gene Beresin
- France to ban mobile phones in schools from September via The Guardian
- This is not a new problem, e.g. The Isolator via LaughingSquid
- Gaming and sleep, e.g. Learning, Parenting and Living with the Brain in Mind via John Joseph 1:46:30)
- How Technology is Changing the Way Children Think and Focus via Psychology Today
- Steve Jobs Was a Low-Tech Parent via New York Times
- Five days at outdoor education camp without screens improves preteen skills with nonverbal emotion cues via Science Direct
- Why Our Screens Make Us Less Happy via TED

(great analogy at the end)
- [Why Apple's Tim Cook doesn't want his nephew to use social networks](#) via **MarketWatch**
- [Brain Drain: The Mere Presence of One's Own Smartphone Reduces Available Cognitive Capacity](#) via **University of Chicago Press Journals**
  - "Results from two experiments indicate that even when people are successful at maintaining sustained attention—as when avoiding the temptation to check their phones—the mere presence of these devices reduces available cognitive capacity. Moreover, these cognitive costs are highest for those highest in smartphone dependence."
- [Digital Technology Is Gambling With Children's Minds](#) via **Education Week**
- [Middle School Misfortunes Then and Now, One Teacher's Take](#) via **Wait Until 8th**
- [We spent 1,643 years watching this video](#) via **The Day**
- [Health apps threaten to overwhelm NHS](#) via **The Day**
- [Disabled receive 'horrific' online abuse](#) via **The Day**
- [Fears social media is fuelling teen suicides](#) via **The Day**
- [How to escape the 'hyperactive hivemind' of modern work](#) via **BBC**
- [The workspace that takes away your phone](#) via **BBC**

14. Licence & Credits

14.1 Licence

- This document is © [ICHK](#), 2018
- This document is shared under a Creative Commons BY-NC-SA license

14.2 Credits

- Seesaw icon by Prosymbols from Flaticon, licensed under CC 3.0 BY
- Smartphone icon by Smashicons from Flaticon, licensed under CC 3.0 BY

APPENDIX 2
ICHK IT POLICY AGREEMENT

Introduction

The use of information technology (IT) at ICHK furthers school-centered learning. Each student will have access to IT tools essential to fulfilling learning objectives and assignments. This access will be balanced against the need to be protected from distraction, to be safe and to lead a balanced life.

Access to technology at ICHK is a privilege and not a right, and its use is governed by this policy (see full text at bit.ly/2YhkE1y). Violation of this policy is liable to result in disciplinary action, including activity monitoring and the suspension or removal of technology use privileges. All students are required to observe the terms of this policy, and access is granted only upon receipt of a signed copy of this document.

Definitions, Terms & Conditions

Information Technology (IT) - The school network and electronic equipment, as well as all electronic devices brought on campus: computers, mobile phones, tablets, cameras, storage devices, etc.

User Responsibility - In signing this document, you accept that you are solely responsible for your actions, or the actions of others when undertaken or attempted with your consent, while using your user profile or any device, even if only temporarily under your control. Your responsibility is to use IT acceptably and appropriately, given our context as a place of education for young people. The network is for the purpose of school-centered learning and should be used with due consideration for the rest of the community. The school network is monitored and action will be taken against anyone misusing IT.

Mobile Phones

- As a school, our advice to parents is to avoid giving smartphones to children under the age of 13. Such devices, in our experience, carry with them a strong tendency of causing avoidable social and learning issues for children.
- Mobile phones should not be used or carried in school, other than when directed by staff for learning purposes. Any phones brought into school must be docked in the phone locker in a student's form room.
- When phones are used for learning purposes, teachers will keep in mind that not all students have phones, and will avoid putting students in situations where they feel they should have such a phone.
- Students can choose to access their phone under exceptional circumstances, but ICHK cultural norms dictate that this is discouraged and not standard practice.
- Years 12 & 13 students may choose to dock their phone in their tutor room, or carry it discreetly on their person. These students may use their phones around school, but are expected to be good role models to younger students.

School Device

- Each student has a sanctioned school device (Mac or Chromebook laptop in Years 7 to 11, student choice in Years 12 and 13), which is their sole IT learning technology.
- Each student is placed within a Technology Stream,

initially through self-selection, and subsequently by the decisions that they make:
- o **Green Stream** - students sign up to this policy with the expectation that they will reliably abide by it, as part of their Approaches to Learning.
- o **Amber Stream** - students sign up to this policy knowing that they require support in order to manage their IT use.
- o **Red Stream** - students resist this policy or consistently struggle to manage their IT use, requiring restrictions to be applied to device and/or network usage.

- Student devices display a prominent sticker, identifying their stream, as well as the ICHK inventory sticker.
- Students are expected to observe the following protocols around device use:
  - o Devices are to remain out of sight at all times, until a teacher requests they be used.
  - o Devices are to be used only for school-centered learning, including at break time.
  - o Devices may be used during break, for school-centered learning, only in C108 and the Library.
    - This is extended to include C106, for Year 10 & 11 students, during Break 2.
  - o Students should never touch or access another person's device or accounts without prior and express permission from the person to whom the device or account belongs.
- Student devices will remain under the aegis of the IT department and subject to the IT policies at ICHK. The school will implement the following two settings on student machines, which students

will not amend: ICHK Administrator account; Computer Name.

Gaming
- Teachers may invite students to play video games as part of learning in school.
- Beyond this, video game playing is not permitted within school. This encompasses all video games, including those played on mobile phones, console devices, laptops and tablets.

Digital Accessories
- In general, digital accessories (e.g. smart watches, wireless ear pods, etc) are not to be worn in school. However:
    - Non-distracting, limited-function fitness trackers can be worn.
    - Smart watches can be worn if switched to airplane mode with notifications turned off.
    - Earphones can be used during lesson time, at the teacher's discretion

Working Online

- Students will use a suite of online tools provided by the school, as well as additional tools requested by their teachers, drawn from a pre-approved list (see bit.ly/3aHYuwR) vetted by the Director of Technology.

Student Agreement

I have read and understood this policy. By signing this policy I agree to its conditions and accept my responsibility as a user, as well as possible consequences of misuse.

Name of Student _____

Tutor Group _____   *Stream* ☐ **Green**
                                                      ☐ **Amber**
                                                      ☐ **Red**

Student Signature _____
Date _____

Parent/Guardian Agreement

As the parent or legal guardian of the above student, I have read this policy and, having understood its Terms & Conditions, grant permission for my child to use IT as described. I understand that network access is intended for educational purposes. I also understand that reasonable precautions have been taken by the school to provide for online safety but that the school cannot be held responsible should students act in breach of the IT Policy. I further understand that willful violation of the IT Agreement is liable to result in disciplinary action.

I understand that parents of students are responsible for willful or negligent damage or loss caused by their child to devices belonging to school or to another student. In addition, I acknowledge that ICHK uses electronic signatures (in the form of encrypted electronic links sent to my email address), that when I click such links it is the equivalent to my physical signature.

I have read and understood this policy. By signing this policy I agree to its conditions.

Name of Parent/Guardian _____

Parent/Guardian Signature _____

Date _____

APPENDIX 3
ICHK IT POLICY FULL VISUAL OVERVIEW

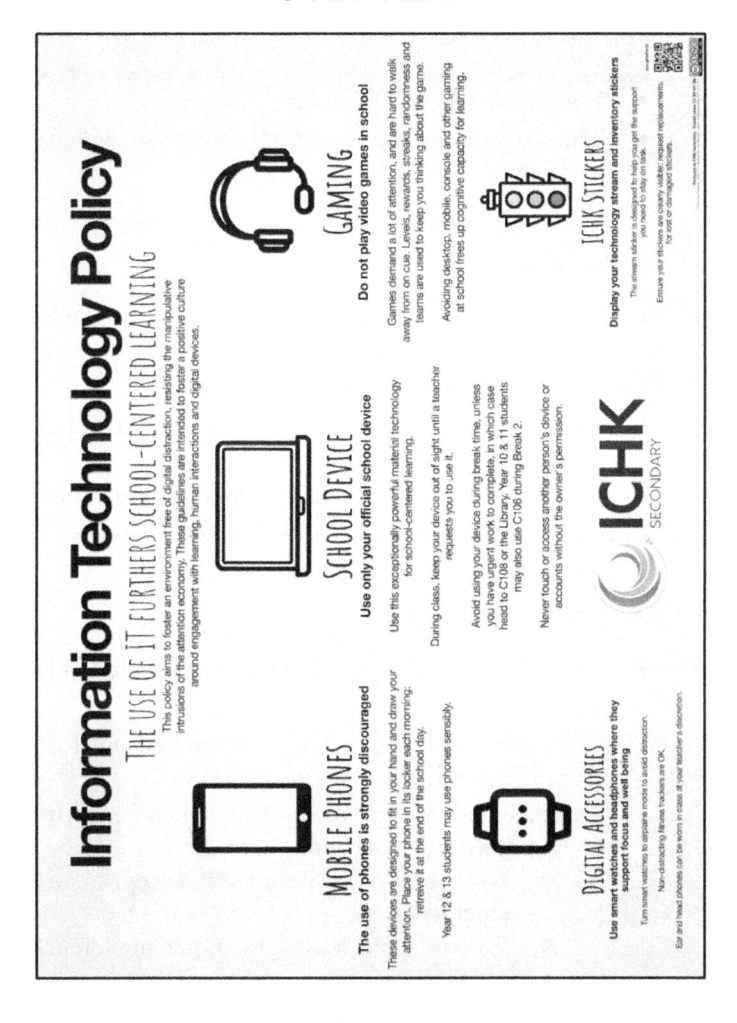

https://bit.ly/3WsKJtb

APPENDIX 4
EXAMPLE DEVICE USE CONTRACT

Rules

- Follow the schools' IT Policy.
- The machine belongs to [child], but exists within our family's rules.

Time & Place

- The computer is to be used at the dining room or the desk in the study.
- The computer is to be charged in the study.
- On weekdays computer-based homework is to be finished in 45 minutes.
- On the weekend, or on special occasions, the laptop can be used instead of iPad time.

Accounts & Passwords

- The computer has a standard account for school use (e.g. no personal email, chat games).
- The computer has a second standard account for free time (we decide together what is OK).
- We might ask for you to show us the contents of your computer and accounts.
    - We won't look without you, except in an emergency.
    - We do have access to a parent admin account.
- Passwords are your private business: make them strong, and don't share them.
    - Do not learn your friends' passwords.

Miscellaneous

- Use your school Gmail chat/Hangouts for school-work only: keep school and personal accounts separate.
- Tell us immediately if laptop is lost/broken/stole, or if anything happens that worries you.
- Be nice online (and offline), talk to mum or dad if others are being unkind.
- Be an upstander, not a bystander.

Screens That Eat Children

WORKING WITH ROSS

Ross presenting his What The Tech? keynote at 21CLHK, Hong Kong, 2024

Thanks for investing the time to make it this far. If you feel awakened to the problems posed by technology, and would like further input, then please feel free to get in touch with Ross via info@screensthateatchildren.com.

With over 20 years' experience in public speaking, technology and education, Ross is well positioned to help individuals, families and schools live more effectively, sustainably and positively with technology.

Ross is available to provide the following services, each of which can be customised to suit your needs:

- Individual & family consulting
- School consulting
    - Strategic planning
    - Policy writing
    - Professional development
    - Parent workshops
    - Student presentations
- Conference keynotes, presentations and workshops
- Analysis and on-screen work for media organisations

Made in United States
North Haven, CT
02 May 2024